THE KING
OF STING

THE KING OF STING

THE AMAZING TRUE STORY OF
A MODERN AMERICAN OUTLAW

CRAIG GLAZER

with Sal Manna

SKYHORSE PUBLISHING

Skyhorse Publishing books may be purchased in bulk at special discounts for sales promotion, corporate gifts, fund-raising, or educational purposes. Special editions can also be created to specifications. For details, contact the Special Sales Department, Skyhorse Publishing, 555 Eighth Avenue, Suite 903, New York, NY 10018 or info@skyhorsepublishing.com.

www.skyhorsepublishing.com

10 9 8 7 6 5 4 3 2 1

Paperback ISBN: 978-1-60239-978-5

Library of Congress Cataloging-in-Publication Data

Glazer, Craig.
The king of sting : the amazing true story of a modern American outlaw / Craig Glazer with Sal Manna.
p. cm.

ISBN 978-1-60239-249-6 (alk. paper)
1. Glazer, Craig. 2. Swindlers and swindling—United States—Biography.
3. Undercover operations—United States. I. Manna, Sal. II. Title.
HV6692.G53A3 2008
364.16'3092—dc22
[B]
2008008707

Printed in the United States of America

TO MY MOTHER Rita, my grandpa Bennie, my father Stan, and Don Woodbeck: the people who helped make me who I am, for good and bad. And also to my nephews Jake and Alex, in the hope that reading my story they will make better choices in their lives than I made in mine.

Contents

CONTENTS

Authors' Note

SOME NAMES IN this book have been changed to protect the privacy and/or safety of individuals. Where dialogue or an account of events was not available from public records or press reports, it has been reconstructed from memory. The sequence of certain events has also been altered for the sake of clarity. But, as incredible as it may seem, this is a true story.

THE KING
OF STING

1

Higher Education

"Arizona was a crazy, crazy place," remembers Otis Thrasher, one of Arizona's first narcotics agents. "Every kid who had a nickel could go down to Mexico and be a drug dealer."

— *The Kansas City Times*, February 12, 1983

THE CHICANO WITH the pockmarked face jabbed me hard with the butt of his gun, and I doubled over. The follow-up, his knee to my chest, put me on the floor gasping for air. Nearby, I could see the blood from Bob's split nose dripping steadily on the carpet of the Tempe apartment. This was supposed to be just a bunch of college kids throwing their money together to buy some weed, but somehow, we wound up in a room with three nasty-looking bad guys with a shotgun and a couple of .38s who were taking our money and kicking our asses.

I was in Sin City, Tempe's ghetto of student apartments—every one of them with a beanbag chair, an *Easy Rider* or *Clockwork Orange* poster on the wall, and a package of Zig-Zag rolling papers in a drawer. All the kids in this particular room, about ten of them, were older than me and clean-cut—chinos, Bass loafers, button-down Pendleton shirts—hardly the image of the doper in anti-drug commercials. I was a little rougher, more of the leather jacket rocker type, but none of us were tie-dyed hippies.

It was 1971 and the streets were full of kids like me, long-haired eighteen-year-olds who could vote for the first time and were protesting the war in Vietnam. We didn't simply question authority, we denied its existence. We wanted to be free to do what we wanted—and what we wanted was sex, drugs, and rock 'n' roll. I was just an upper-middle-class Jewish boy from Kansas, taking part in a cultural revolution.

I had no idea that getting ripped off that night would change my life forever.

Just fifteen minutes earlier, I had heard a knock on the front door and Bob, the gangly, awkward kid who lived in the apartment, answered with an easy smile. A big man with a red beard stood in the doorway, a Chicano on each side of him—one older with a scarred face, the other younger and smaller but just as tough-looking.

"Do you have the cash?" asked the big man.

Bob pointed to the table in the middle of the room. Stacked neatly were separate piles of bills, held together by rubber bands. My $300 was the smallest contribution to the pool of $10,000. My fellow student, Steve Asher, who brought me to the apartment, had the biggest pile. The big man, who looked like a cross between Ernest Borgnine of *McHale's Navy* and a red-bearded Viking, seemed pleased. He nodded to the scarred Chicano, who returned to the van they drove up in. In a few seconds, he came back lugging a burlap gunnysack that reeked of weed.

"Can we check the shit out first?" Bob asked.

The big man entered the room, followed by the Chicanos. Bob closed the door behind them.

"You want a sample?" asked the big man. "You don't trust me?"

"Hey man, be cool. We've never done this with you before. Just to show it's good shit."

The big man slowly looked at everyone in the room.

"Okay," he told his compadres. The scarred Chicano opened the burlap sack and pulled out a shotgun, which he pointed at each of our faces. We were all too stunned to move. Almost simultaneously, the big man and the younger Chicano had both pulled out handguns.

I looked at my $300 on the table. My last $300. Damn.

. . .

MY SIN CITY apartment was costing $175 a month. I was working as a salesman in a clothing store and a floor sweeper in a pizza parlor, but at $1.85 an hour, I wasn't making nearly enough money. I had asked my father for a loan but he said, "That's your problem to solve." He reminded me that tuition for out-of-state students was expensive and that it was my "stupid decision" to go to Arizona State University, so I had to live with it. "It's time you proved yourself," he said.

I had met Asher at a campus party. He graduated a couple years earlier from my high school, Shawnee Mission East in Overland Park, Kansas. Asher took me under his wing because he knew I needed money and he knew how I could make some. He called it "investing," which meant I was buying weed wholesale and selling it retail. My father was a businessman, so I understood the concept.

Asher didn't need the money. He had it all, and he knew it. He was blond, David Cassidy handsome, and living in the Lemon Terrace Club, the most expensive apartment complex in Sin City. The son of a wealthy electronics company owner, he had the best-looking girl-friends, credit cards from his parents, and drove a cherry red Trans Am. I was tooling around in the yellow Ford Galaxie Grandpa Bennie gave me as a going-away present.

Asher liked having a sidekick. He could tell me what to do and that made him feel better about himself. For me, at least it was better than being alone. Besides, one of his girlfriends was a high school senior with long brown hair named Karen Curtis. She reminded me of a Kewpie doll, a small body with big eyes. She was so perfectly pretty that every-where she went, heads turned. I was a rocker and she was a little more straightlaced but I hoped that someday we might get together.

"If you need money, you can invest," Asher had said.

"This is cool?"

"As cool as an Eskimo's toilet."

. . .

NOW I WAS about to lose it all.

"Okay kids, playtime's over," said the big man with the red beard. "Turn around and up against the wall."

We did what he said. The younger Chicano searched us, taking out our wallets and stuffing the cash in his pocket. He found a lot in Asher's wallet, but mine was empty. He threw it at the back of my head.

Meanwhile, the big man scooped up the pile of money from the table and shoveled the bills into the gunnysack. After he finished, he crossed the room and grabbed Bob by the shoulder, pushing him flat against the wall.

"You're a real smart-ass, ain't ya?" he asked, his face close to Bob's. He pulled a long bowie knife from his belt and continued berating Bob. "No sonuvabitch pussy like you asks me to do shit." He placed the knife tip under Bob's nose. "Someone oughta teach you some manners," he said. Bob's face was red with fear. The big man pressed the shiny blade upward and Bob tried to stand on his tiptoes so it wouldn't cut him.

"Don't hurt me," he whimpered.

The big man pushed the knife into Bob's skin. Bob would have been lifted off the floor except that the blade split his nose open first. He put his hands over his face, trying to stop the flow of blood and tears streaming down his cheeks as he crumpled to the floor.

I'm no saint, that's for sure, but no matter what I did later, and what anyone might think of me after reading about the life I've lived, I never hurt an innocent person and I hated it when other people did. Bob was just a naïve kid. The big man and his friends had their money. They could have just left it at that.

I turned from facing the wall and took a step towards Bob. It was just an instinct, and I didn't really have a plan in mind. It was that move that made the Chicano put me on the floor. "Chingo, you stupid, eh?" he asked as he looked down on me.

Yeah, it was a pretty stupid move. I was at the mercy of these assholes. Being helpless, unable to fight back, is the worst feeling in the world.

The three of them walked backward to the door and left. Nobody moved until we heard their van speed away. There was a rush of air as everyone let loose a sigh of relief at the same time. Bob ran into the bathroom. I pulled myself up, wincing with pain.

"We have to call the police," someone said.

"What the hell are we going to tell them?" answered Asher. "'Well, Officer, we were making a pot deal and these bad guys came in and took our money. Do you think you can get it back for us?'"

End of discussion. Rip-offs happened all the time. They were never reported.

As I got into Asher's Trans Am outside the apartment, I asked if he knew the robbers.

"Forget about them."

"They took my last $300."

"What? You want to go after them? We're lucky we're alive. They've killed kids before, that's what I've heard—even when they get the money."

"So you do know them."

"Heard of them. They're called Prairie Pirates. Welcome to the real Wild West."

Nothing was going right. Asher could go back to his nice apartment and, after a beer, a bong, and a babe, shrug it off. But I had none of that waiting at home for me. I was a nobody—and now I was broke too.

I went to my shabby little apartment and sulked as I watched movies late into the night on my tiny black-and-white TV. I could always lose myself in the movies. Ever since I was little, I would imagine myself as the hero. Lots of kids do that. But I believed it.

Just days after getting ripped off, a movie came on that had me glued to the screen: *The St. Valentine's Day Massacre*, a gangster flick by Roger Corman that came out a few years earlier, in 1967. A true story, it was about a hit squad from Al Capone's South Side Chicago Italian Mob gunning down seven of George "Bugs" Moran's North Side Irish hoods; except this bloodbath wasn't one of those stand-up shoot-outs or a black sedan driving past a restaurant and spraying it with bullets.

It was February 14, 1929, and Moran's gang was holed up in a small garage at 2122 North Clark Street. Shortly after 11 a.m., they were surprised by two men in police uniforms, accompanied by two men who seemed to be undercover cops. Moran's men outnumbered them and outgunned them, but they gave up without a struggle, since taking down cops was not a good thing, not even for gangsters. Besides, the Chicago Police Department was there to be bought, so the hoods thought they had nothing to fear. They figured that someone must have made a mistake somewhere, that maybe these cops were rookies and didn't know what was what. Moran's men even felt lucky, because if their captors were Capone's men, surely they'd be dead already.

So when the seven were instructed to put their hands on the brick wall inside the garage, they did as they were told without any resistance. When they turned their backs, the two men in street clothes ripped open their long coats. Moran's men never saw the two tommy guns. It took just a couple of minutes to riddle their bodies with 140 bullets. With only four men, and in broad daylight, Capone's men mowed down the opposition without a fight.

It was the badges that got them, not the guns.

I had a crazy idea.

. . .

ASHER AND KAREN came by to take me to Fridays & Saturdays on Scottsdale Road, Phoenix's main strip. With pitchers of beer running ninety-five cents apiece, the bar was a college student's favorite hang-out. Being underage didn't stop me or anyone else from drinking. Vermont issued ID cards to all residents over seventeen, and these could be easily copied and altered. Surprisingly, considering that it's such a small state, on any given night there were an awful lot of people in Phoenix who claimed to be residents of Vermont.

Rather than go downstairs where a band was playing and watch Asher and Karen dance, searching Karen's eyes for anything that said I'd be a better partner, I walked upstairs to the bar and ordered a beer.

"One of the boys up front trips a mine and it takes out him and the two guys behind him. Their guts get blown on top of my helmet."

The blond man playing pool had captivated the dozen college kids around him. His audience was dead silent. The only sound you could hear was the squeaking as he chalked the tip of his stick. Vietnam was scary and serious, especially to college kids with student deferments that would expire upon graduation. To me, that was too far away to even worry about. To me, Vietnam was a war movie set in a jungle.

"I'm a Navy guy, a squid with these jarheads, and now we're run-nin' back the way we came. I was the tail, now I'm the lead, and now there's a bunch of slopes waitin' for us. They open fire."

Tall, tanned, and looking much older than his twenty-three years, he coolly dropped a combination into a side pocket.

"Woulda thought I was a dead man except there was no time to think. I jump off the trail with two of the Marines behind me. I'm hit in the leg. They get it in their backs. I'm draggin' one of 'em by his belt and he's bleedin' so much my hand keeps slippin' off. I'm hopping on one leg and the gooks are closing in."

I was mesmerized. Here was a guy who had really fought "bad guys." He took his time sinking another ball. I wanted to yell, "GO ON!"

"Pop! Pop! Pop! One by one, the Charlie motherfuckers go down." He surveyed the situation on the table. "Three in the corner." The ball goes in.

"What happened?" one of the college kids asked.

The man raised his cue and pointed it at a wiry, seedy-looking guy seated on a bar stool a few feet away. He reminded me of Jim Morrison from the Doors, with those same small snake eyes. "Milwaukee Jim was sitting in a sniper's nest. He blew them away. Pop! Pop! Pop! Saved my sorry ass."

Milwaukee Jim, aka James Wojt, former forward observer, second lieutenant, United States Marine Corps, snapped off a salute.

"Got me a Purple Heart and," the tall blond man said, pausing long enough to sink the eight ball for the win, "a Bronze Star."

"What'd you get, Jim?" another kid asked.

He spoke slowly, as if he were fighting a speech impediment. "Didn't ... get ... shit."

The tall blond man sounded tougher than anyone I'd ever seen this side of Charles Bronson.

I found Asher and Karen at the downstairs bar and asked who he was.

"Don Woodbeck," Asher said. "Says he was in Nam. Now he's a smuggler. Goes back and forth across the border."

"Does he know the guys who ripped us off?"

"Probably. Why?"

"Can you introduce me?"

"I don't really know him and I don't want to."

"Maybe he can help get our money back."

"Are you nuts? That's over. It never happened."

Asher took Karen by the arm and led her away. I went back upstairs to the pool table, where Don waited for a new player to rack the balls for the next game.

I nervously approached him.

"Don Woodbeck?"

"And you are?"

"Craig Glazer. I have a business proposition for you. Can we talk in private?"

Don looked around and waved his hand. "Can't you see this is my office?"

Everybody laughed. I was being embarrassed and I didn't like it. I grabbed a cocktail napkin, wrote down my phone number and dropped it on the pool table.

"When you're through with your games and want to make some real money, call me." I walked away.

• • •

"SO, TELL ME how you're going to make me rich," Don said over the phone.

I was glad he called. As things eventually turned out, maybe it wasn't so fortunate for Don. Or maybe we ended up exactly where we were supposed to.

"Some college kids and I got ripped off a few days ago," I told him.

"Live and learn."

"I want to get my money back. Maybe you can make some money too."

"Don't see how so far."

"Thought maybe you'd know something about a big guy with a red beard."

Don was silent.

"Hello? You still there?"

"You're too young to be a cop," he said. "And you're too stupid to be a dealer, at least for long."

"Which means?"

"I'll be at the Eight Ball Apartments in Mesa. Bungalow 6."

I drove over and knocked on the door. Don and Milwaukee Jim were waiting inside the converted motel room. I learned later that Jim didn't come out of the war as well as Don. Shot in the back, he had suffered through numerous operations in Army hospitals. Doses of morphine relieved the pain but he walked and talked noticeably slower than most people. He was quiet but deadly. He was also fiercely loyal to Don, whom he looked up to as the leader of the pack, and because Jim had saved his life, Don would do anything for him in return.

"So you know the man with the red beard?" I asked.

"Oh yeah. J.D."

He told me that the last time he saw him, J.D. had a gun pointed at the head of a pollo, what locals called an uneducated Mexican who spoke little or no English. He had forced the pollo to kneel down next to Don on the desert sand in a remote area outside Gila Bend, Arizona. Then a bullet from J.D.'s gun buried itself in the skull of the Mexican.

"Why was he going to kill you?"

"Shit happens," said Don. Jim nodded.

I wasn't sure I believed anything Don said, including his Nam story, but it didn't matter. Don had the same kind of power and the same kind of presence as Charles Bronson. They say some guys have a swagger about them, but I never met anyone who actually had a swagger until I met Don—and I haven't met any since either.

"Ever see *The St. Valentine's Day Massacre*?" I asked.

"I don't go to movies."

I told him the story.

"Kid, you're in fantasy land."

"But it happened. I mean, it was in a movie but it really happened."

Don shook his head. I kept talking.

"J.D. won't remember me. I set up a deal. We use other people he wouldn't know. While it's going down, you come in, say you're the law, show badges. I turn around and do the same thing, like I was undercover. We arrest J.D. and everybody else!"

"We'll have to read them their Miranda rights." He was making fun of me again. I plowed ahead.

"They don't fight back because we're cops. They even think you're a cop now. They think there are dozens of other cops all over the place. They figure they'll just go through the system. We take their guns, their money and their grass. And then we just leave them."

"What a great idea," Don said with a smirk. "You're going to pose as a cop. How old are you?"

"Eighteen."

"You're going to get a big boom-boom gun and you're going to stick these guys up and tell them you're a cop? They'll fall for that. Sure, I can see that."

He turned to Milwaukee Jim and laughed. "The kid ain't left yet?"

"We'll be a team," I said.

"I don't know you, kid."

"I don't know you either," I said stubbornly.

Don looked me over. He must have thought I had some major balls to talk to him like that.

"Ever shot at a human being?" he asked.

"Went hunting once with my father. But no, not a person."

"Then let's go shooting," Don said.

The three of us drove to the desert outside Mesa. As we pulled onto a dirt road next to an Indian reservation, I wondered if maybe I had made a mistake. I had doubts about Woodbeck, about how safe I'd be around him. On the other hand, the excitement of doing something different, something right out of the movies, was irresistible. There are some things you just don't turn down. At least I don't.

Milwaukee Jim opened the trunk of Don's car. Inside was a stock-pile of weapons—rifles, shotguns, handguns. "Pick one," Woodbeck said. I grabbed a .45-caliber Browning automatic.

"You're a big talker, kid, but you don't know shit about the world." He picked up a Smith & Wesson Airweight five-shot .38 and loaded the chambers.

Holding it with both hands, he aimed the gun between my eyes.

"What the fuck?!"

"You can see the bullets in the cylinders, can't you?" he said calmly.

"Yes!" Maybe getting involved with this crazy mother was a bad idea, a very bad idea.

"You know this is the real deal, don't you? That I can blow your head off right now. You know that, don't you, college boy?"

"Hey, listen …" I was getting ready to try to talk my way out of this.

Don lowered the gun. "You were scared, weren't you?"

Not that I would admit to him.

"If we try your idea …" he began.

"If?"

"If. Then we'll use these guns because with these, the guys on the other end of the barrel can see the bullets in the chambers. They'll know how serious we are."

I smiled. "We? So we're doing this?"

Don ignored me. "The Browning's too big anyway. The Smith can fit in a smaller holster. And automatics jam. Can't have that in a gunfight."

"Hold on, there's not going to be any gunfight," I said. "The whole point is that nobody gets hurt."

Milwaukee Jim laughed.

"All I care about is that I'm not the one getting hurt," Don said. He loaded another Smith & Wesson and jammed it into my belt on my right side. "Set 'em up."

Milwaukee Jim slapped silhouette targets on the thorns of a huge cactus about twenty-five feet away and on a cactus next to me. Don walked to the far one.

"When Jim says 'go,' draw your weapon as fast as you can and hit the target next to me. Empty the gun. I'll do the same and hit the target next to you."

"Why do we have to stand next to them?"

"I sure as hell ain't going to do nothing with you if I can't count on you with a gun in your hands facing another human being."

"What if I miss and shoot you?"

"Then Jim will kill you. Ain't that right, Milwaukee?"

"That's … right."

This was nuts.

Suddenly another possibility occurred to me. "What if you hit me?" I asked Don.

"Then you'll be dead and we won't have to go through with this stupid-ass idea of yours. Win-win."

Woodbeck would say something like that and you figured he didn't mean it—but you wouldn't swear your life on it either. He reminded me of gunslingers in Westerns who strut around town with a "you must respect me" attitude, and the townfolk just hope he's the new sheriff instead of the outlaw he once was.

"Ready?" Don asked.

"Um, no, not really."

"One … two … three …" Milwaukee Jim counted so slow I could feel the drops of sweat forming and drifting down my face.

"GO!"

Woodbeck and I both drew and fired immediately. I aimed at the far side of the target and prayed I wouldn't hit him. I was pretty sure he wouldn't hit me. Pretty sure.

When the smoke cleared and my ears stopped ringing, I was still standing. There is no better feeling than being that close to gunshots and realizing none of them hit you. Seriously. It's better than sex.

Don was still standing too. All five of my shots hit the target, though they were scattered everywhere. All five of his were within a few inches of the bull's-eye.

"Not bad for a big talker," Don said.

I was proud of myself. "Let's do it again. If we're going to pull this off, it has to feel natural."

Don looked at me. "All right, *we*."

He was the toughest sonuvabitch around. He was the partner I needed.

2

A Portrait of the
Con Artist as a Young Man

How did a middle-class youth with plenty of money and obvious talents get himself into such a mess?

—*The Kansas City Star*, June 28, 1979

I ALWAYS HAD the gift of gab. I inherited that from my father. Stan was a playboy right out of Central Casting, a cross between Dean Martin and Cesar Romero. He was tall, handsome, funny, creative, a big-time storyteller, and the offspring of a family of hustlers. He was also a horrible father.

When I was five years old, I had this habit of smelling my food before I ate it, which annoyed Stan. One night at dinner I bent over to smell my mashed potatoes and gravy, and he couldn't take it anymore. He put his hand on the back of my neck and shoved my head in the bowl. I ran from the table screaming.

When I was eight, he forced me to fight my best friend. "You think you can beat Craig in a fight?" he goaded Johnny. "Go ahead. Sock him in the jaw."

Johnny didn't want to, but with Stan egging him on, he eventually did. Three times. I never threw a punch back. Johnny said he was sorry and Stan let me know I was a disappointment. "Why didn't you fight him?" he asked, but I was crying too hard to answer.

Then when I was ten, he took me into the backyard to throw a baseball around. But I have no idyllic father-son memories of playing catch with Stan. He threw me fastballs as hard as he could. Finally, when I couldn't get my glove up quick enough, the ball smacked me in the face, and I started bleeding. My eye swelled up. My dad said: "Get up, big baby. You should have caught it."

He thought I was lazy. His not-so-affectionate nickname for me was Larry Lardbutt. When I wouldn't do my homework, he'd take a jockey whip and raise welts on my body. I didn't say anything to the other kids in school because I thought every child was hit like that. But I knew I didn't like it.

He always seemed to be mad at me. I was his firstborn, so maybe he was trying to make me macho like him. Maybe he wanted to get me ready to go out into a hard world. He'd get pissed off whenever I wasn't up to his standards, which was often.

My brother Jeff, two years younger than me, was his favorite. He was better at everything—an A student and a natural at any sport. I was the kind of student whom teachers say has potential but "just doesn't apply himself." Jeff was quieter, more patient, and with his tall, angular good looks, it was easy to see he was Stan's son. I had to wear cowboy boots to catch up to his couple of extra inches in height.

After Jeff and I, there wasn't much left for Jack, who was born a year later. Poor Jack. When it came to attention, he received less than zero. When Jeff followed me to Shawnee Mission East, he inherited my popularity. By the time Jack arrived, he could only inherit my bad reputation.

I can't explain how or why my mother, Rita, wound up with Stan, other than to say that opposites attract. Stan had charisma to burn and probably sweet-talked her right off her feet. She was a prize, no doubt about that—blonde, with green eyes and very good-looking. Maybe she was just naïve. She came from a family of grocers. Family rumor has it that her father may have been an Italian, not Jewish at all. After he died, her mother married Bennie Studna.

A PORTRAIT OF THE CON ARTIST AS A YOUNG MAN

My Grandpa Bennie was a tough character with a heart of gold. He was five foot two, in-your-face, and took no shit. He reminded me of Popeye, except instead of wearing a sailor suit, he had his own uniform—brown fedora, brown pants pulled up to his chest by suspenders, white shirt, and always puffing on a cigar.

He used to buy horses out of Mexico and then sell them to the U.S. Army, back in the days when it still had a cavalry. He ran public horse auctions for a while, until he noticed that buyers were bidding on the biggest horses instead of the best ones. He discovered that they were buying them by the pound—for dog food and for meat in Europe. He loved horses, so he quit the business that day and went into selling used cars.

Grandpa Bennie always stood by me. Maybe he forgave me for all the trouble I got into because he knew about getting into trouble himself. He had a rap sheet for rolling back odometers on his used cars.

Grandpa Bennie never liked Stan. He called everyone "pardner" except for Stan, whom he referred to as a "counterfeit sonuvabitch." When Bennie found out my parents were getting divorced, he confronted Stan with a gun. "You big sonuvabitch," he said, "I'm gonna put a bullet between your eyes." Stan talked him out of it.

Years later, when Grandpa Bennie was in his eighties and my father wouldn't pay him back $25,000 he borrowed, the old man went to Stan's office brandishing a pitchfork and threatened to run him through with it. "You're gonna pay me and I don't mean maybe!" he demanded.

"Get the fuck out of here," said Stan.

What Bennie didn't know was that Stan always kept a gun under his desktop. The old man lunged forward with the pitchfork and just missed skewering my father. Thankfully, Stan never pulled the gun on him.

Bennie eventually did get his money back in full, but it wasn't from Stan. He never knew that Jeff and I took a couple hundred dollars every week out of our paychecks and sent him a check under Stan's name.

Besides not shooting Grandpa Bennie, Stan had other good qualities, such as his ability to entertain. When I was four or five years old, I'd sit on the stairs overlooking cocktail parties at home and marvel as he rattled off jokes that would have the adults laughing the entire night. He was hysterically funny and he could command a room. He had a bit of a modeling career in the '60s and early '70s and had even hung out in Hollywood.

People looking at them from the outside might have thought Stan and Rita were the John and Jackie Kennedy of Kansas City—except Jewish and without the money. It's not so great being a Jew in the Midwest if you don't have money, because then you're just a Jew. Stan represented, to some people, everything bad about rich people without having the advantage of actually being rich.

He did come up with some great ideas though. A few were pretty off-the-wall, but some were brilliant. Kansas City had been the home of the country's first true shopping center, Country Club Plaza, back in the '20s. In 1961, Stan helped create one of the first single-building shopping centers, with different retail departments all within view of the customers, not unlike Wal-Mart, which was founded the following year. The place was called Sav-On, and Stan was president of the company.

Before the Sav-On success, when my classmates' parents would ask, "How's your dad?" it was meant as kind of a joke. They knew he was always up to something shady, some scheme that would fail. Miraculously, Sav-On was an immediate hit.

The grand opening was like a movie premiere and I was so excited. The best part was, my father's store had a toy department. I took a shopping cart and filled it with a Rifleman gun, a Bat Masterson gun set, a Roy Rogers cowboy outfit, and everything else an eight-year-old boy could want.

"What are you doing?" said my father.

"It's our store. I can get what I want."

He slapped my face. "Goddamn you! You don't steal! This is not *our* store. This is *my* store." I threw a tantrum, but he would only let me keep the Rifleman gun. We were never able to celebrate as a family anything good that happened, and our success never lasted either.

Stan was forced out of Sav-On. Soon after that, he told us at a family meeting that we were being evicted from our house with a pool, Stan's status symbol. Two weeks later, the house was robbed—convenient timing for Stan to file an insurance claim. Not so convenient for me: the cops arrived to fill out their police reports at my tenth birthday party.

People didn't trust Stan. They would laugh at his jokes, admire his chutzpah, and enjoy the money he made them, but they sensed he would never be a loyal friend. For some, it was more than a sense. My dad, married or not, was a ladies' man. Many of his business acquaintances figured he had either already screwed their wives or that it was only a matter of time before he did, so the first chance they had, they would cut him out of their business deals.

Once, when I was ten years old and my mother was about to go out of town, he took me to lunch at Winstead's, the landmark Kansas City drive-in burger joint. "Men are different than women," he said. "Daddies sometimes want other women as friends. Sometimes they bring a friend home and she stays the night. We're just friends so you don't have to tell Mommy about her. You want another milkshake?"

Nice father-son talk.

Stan was admired because every man wanted to be him. He was hated because they weren't him. He was an arrogant putdown artist everyone laughed with until they had a chance to put *him* down. Then the "successful businessman" became the "show-off." Suddenly Stan "the smart guy" became Stan "the conniving kike." We were not country club material. We were not welcome in the homes of society. Even other Jews kept us at a distance. When it came to social get-togethers, not many of his "friends" wanted Stan anywhere near their wives.

My classmates said their parents warned them not to hang out with me because I would grow up to be nothing more than a shyster like my father. On the rare occasion a school friend would invite me to dinner, that family would sit around the table and belittle my family.

I guess they didn't think I understood what they were saying. It hurt, but I can't say I blame them now. After all, my dad had probably fucked my friend's mother.

I stopped laughing at Stan's cocktail party jokes when I opened a living room cabinet and found his stash of comedy albums—Jonathan Winters, Lenny Bruce, Shelley Berman, Bob Newhart. I listened to them all, and discovered that his jokes were their jokes.

At a time when I didn't know who I was, I was angry that my father wasn't who he said he was.

I learned from Stan that you could get away with almost anything if you were clever enough. He'd run stop signs all the time, but when a cop would pull him over, he'd "badge" him—Stan was an honorary deputy sheriff—and get out of the ticket.

When we'd go to Kansas City Chiefs games, he'd badge us in. He'd flash it at the gate guard and say we were kids from the orphanage. Because of that, we never had actual seats. We'd sit on the concrete steps in the aisles.

Apparently using phony badges to get ahead in the world was a family trait I inherited.

• • •

I WENT TO Hebrew school from the time I was seven years old. If my parents' idea was to give me an education in religion, it sure didn't work. Hebrew school just kept me out of the house and busy after regular school hours. They put me in the Boy Scouts for the same reason.

To get rid of me on weekends, they would send me to my grandmother's house or give me a quarter to go to the movies. I was just as happy to sit in front of the television. I loved Westerns or anything with guns and action, and I would escape into series like *The Legend of Jesse James*, *The Life and Legend of Wyatt Earp*, and *Bat Masterson*. I knew they were all real people. They were also hometown heroes: the James Gang was from Missouri, as was the Dalton Gang, and Earp and Masterson were lawmen in Dodge City, Kansas.

There were also B-movie Westerns rerun on the tube, including my favorite, *Johnny Concho* with Frank Sinatra. There was something about a hero who was, at best, on the edge of the law, if not an outright outlaw, that attracted me.

I became addicted to those characters. On Saturdays I'd watch TV from 5:30 in the morning until the middle of the afternoon—taking in the punk attitude of the Bowery Boys and the exotic adventures of the ultimate outsider, Tarzan.

I'd create my own stories too, filled with good guys and bad guys. I'd be James Bond, 007. I'd wear a little suit and put a cap gun in my shoulder holster, or I'd dress up in my Army uniform and play soldier. Most kids understood that it was just make-believe. But for me it was serious.

When the other kids would want to go outside to play, I'd still want to be Davy Crockett in the story I was telling.

"Let's play baseball," they'd say.

"You can't go now," I'd answer. "The movie isn't over yet." The movie wasn't on TV, it was running in my imagination. When they would finally leave, I'd just play all the parts. I was in a movie that hadn't been made yet.

I wanted to be somebody, which apparently my father didn't think I was. I wanted to be famous. I wanted to be the good guy, like Errol Flynn, great with a sword and with women, but still a scoundrel.

Another good guy I loved was Jack Lord in *Stoney Burke*, a TV series about a rodeo rider, and so I wore a black cowboy hat and black shirt just like him. I wore the same outfit for a Junior Rodeo I competed in when I was about thirteen. While I was riding, the horse suddenly reared up, throwing me out of the saddle. My hands got tangled up in the reins, and the horse dragged me on the dusty ground all over the arena.

I was getting knocked around and scratched up pretty good until Grandpa Bennie jumped over the fence, ran out with his cane and beat the horse until it stopped. That he would beat a horse, an animal he loved, showed how much he cared about me.

His only criticism? "You look like a drugstore cowboy," he scolded. "No real cowboy wears a black shirt. I'll get you a white one."

As I grew older, I only allowed my grandmother to see my acted-out dramas. That same year I was thirteen, I was at her house, dressed up like a soldier—green camouflage pants and shirt, helmet and toy gun—and a bunch of slightly older teenage girls came by and saw me. These were girls I had just started to want to go out with. They laughed, and I was crushed.

I went to my first day of junior high school dressed in a business suit, complete with white socks, and carrying a briefcase. Everyone laughed then too. But that's how grown-ups dressed and I was pretending to be a grown-up, which I figured followed junior high. I wasn't embarrassed because I was too old to be playing dress-up. I was embarrassed because I still believed in my pretend life.

The next summer, at Boy Scout camp in Missouri—with all-Jewish Troop 61—I was handed a letter from my mother saying that she and my father were getting divorced. I was too young to think about it then but Stan had probably, finally, slept with one too many of her friends.

There was a letter from my father too. He didn't want to hurt me, of course. "I'll always be your dad," he wrote, "and maybe your mom and I will get back together one day. And, no matter what, I'll still take you to Chiefs games." Great.

• • •

ANDY THOMAS WAS the drummer in a rock band and the coolest guy in high school. I met him because he was teaching Jack how to play. He was a bad boy with a bad reputation—and there's nothing cooler than that.

He was blond and Christian. I was dark and Jewish. We both looked older than we were. I was no longer playing at 007, army soldier, or Wild West legend. I became "the bad kid."

"I bet if you and I went out on the town," he said, "we'd kill!"

We wore leather jackets, we cursed, we smoked weed, and we caused trouble.

The second concert I ever saw was Jimi Hendrix. I was fifteen years old and went with Andy and my friend Marc Mackie, whom I had known since we were twelve years old and in Hebrew school together. I smoked my first dope in Marc's garage before the concert. We had a corncob pipe and we put in a whole gram of hash that had cost us eight dollars. We passed it around.

"You feel anything?"

"No."

"Maybe we're supposed to hold it longer."

"They say you can see colors change."

But nothing was happening. We had no idea we were supposed to inhale! We had practiced by using cigarettes, holding the smoke in our cheeks and blowing it out. By the time we figured it out, there wasn't any hash left.

We tried again before a Led Zeppelin show, this time rolling a joint.

"Feel anything?"

"No."

We couldn't figure out what we were doing wrong this time, so we smoked another one. I remember the Moody Blues' "Nights in White Satin" was playing—and we started laughing uncontrollably. The next day we woke up wearing the same clothes as the night before. We had smoked so much that we passed out and missed the concert.

Oh yeah, we were *bad*.

I caused trouble at Boy Scout camp too. Fireworks were not allowed but I bought twenty M-80s for a dime apiece and sold them for a dollar each. Then a few of the older Scouts, including me, took three M-80s and laid them on some rocks. I set them up with a timed fuse using a cigarette, like Andy had shown me, and we went far away to play Frisbee.

The explosion startled everyone at Camp Osceola. I just laughed.

The next thing I knew I was called to the Scoutmaster's office.

"You set off those firecrackers."

"How could I? I wasn't anywhere near them."

"I don't know how they went off but you bought them and showed the other kids how to light them."

The other Scouts had ratted me out.

"Craig, admit you did it. You'll have to clean the shitter today but we'll let it go at that."

I agreed and we shook hands on the deal.

Then, at the ceremony to advance to the next level, to become a Brave, in front of fifty of the kids I'd been in Scouts with for years, and all their parents—except mine, of course—my name was not called.

They had lied to me.

That night, with my tentmate Archie, the biggest guy in the troop, I dragged each of the snitches out of their tents and tied them to trees. I smeared shoe polish on their faces and filled their underwear with shaving cream.

And I left them there.

It was a typical hazing ritual for the Tenderfoots, but for me it was filled with vengeance. The next morning, the Scoutmaster again called me to his office.

"Did you do this?"

"Absolutely."

"Why?"

"They told on me and you lied to me."

"You can go home."

That was fine with me.

When I was old enough to drive, Andy, Marc, and I would go to the University of Missouri at Columbia or even as far as the University of Texas at Austin and rush the fraternities. No one guessed we were still in high school. I'd come up with some harebrained story about being a transfer student from Topeka Junior College and the frat bros would fix me up with sorority girls as an incentive to pledge.

The danger of being found out made it even more exciting. But I never was caught. Not even by the University of Texas fraternity that went so far as to accept me! I graciously declined the invitation because, I told them, a Greek had raped my mother and she would never speak to me again if I joined a frat. They believed me.

. . .

ANDY WOULD SAY, "Get into a fight. Girls love that." He was right. Picking fights and picking up girls worked hand in hand. Besides, I loved the biblical story of Samson. He was a Jew who beat the shit out of people. I convinced myself that, by taking no shit, I was standing up for Jews.

Most of the time, all I had to do was yell "I'll fuck you up!" and the fight would never happen. I was all lightning and fury, and they'd get scared enough to find a way not to throw that first punch.

If there was going to be a fight, though, I wanted to be the guy landing the first punch. That was a lesson I learned early and one that would come in handy later. I'd scream bloody murder— "Motherfucker! Cocksucker!"—and the other guy would be so flustered that it gave me a chance to hit him first.

That tactic didn't always work.

Andy and I were going to a Sly and the Family Stone concert. As usual, I had a switchblade in my boot. I had never used it but it was cool to have. Before the show, we cruised Alan's, a well-known drive-in hamburger place at Country Club Plaza. There were three kids from Southwest High School sitting on the hood of a car and, for some reason, they shouted something at us. There had always been a fierce rivalry between our two schools. I, of course, flipped them off.

As we parked, they started to come toward us. I wasn't worried. I figured I could scare them off pretty easy. Then I saw that there were three or four more students behind them. Andy slinked away. They surrounded me. I swung the first punch but missed. Immediately they had me on the ground, my arms pinned.

They hit me a dozen or more times, cracking my nose. I screamed for help. I thought they might kill me. I tried to pull out my switchblade but couldn't reach it. I'm glad. I think if I had shown it to them, they would have taken it and cut me up bad.

By the time the police arrived, scattering the guys hitting me, I was a bloody mess.

But I was still alive. I mean, it didn't hurt so much that I couldn't recover. From that moment on, I wasn't afraid of getting into a fight or getting hit. I figured as long as they didn't kill me, so what?

I was mad at Andy for not coming to my defense though. He apologized. "I'll help you get them back," he said. Revenge has always been a surefire motive for me. We drove around trying to find the kids. But we never did.

I didn't have to win a fight, to win a fight. I lost more than I won, but the story of what happened would often come out different, leaving me as the kid brave enough to take on anyone. My reputation grew. I loved it when kids said, "Don't fuck with Glazer." Some of them were afraid of me. But at least they knew my name.

Stan noticed that I was hanging out with the cool kids. "Let me give you a tip," he said. "You might want to be nice to the not-so-popular kids. They'll be running this town someday, not your friends. Your friends will be the bag boys and used car salesmen."

"Oh yeah? How do you know?"

"Because when I was growing up, all the kids who couldn't get laid are now the bankers and lawyers." I didn't know whether that was a lesson he had learned or suffered. But he was right, for once, and I took his advice to heart.

In the school cafeteria I'd sit with the unpopular kids, the geeks, the way uncool. It wasn't just because of what Stan said though. Part of it was because to them I was a hero, and I needed and wanted that hero worship. Another part of it was because I knew deep inside that I was just like them—someone who had been hurt and was feeling helpless. What made us different was that I chose to fight back.

I even threatened to kick Rabbi Margolies's ass.

Morris Margolies was in his early thirties and stocky. He said he had been a minor league pitcher, "just like the Dodgers' Sandy Koufax," he liked to say. When my parents were still together, he'd come over to our house and play catch with Jeff and I. We had a new friend, a rare adult we thought we could count on.

When my parents started the divorce process, we expected him to come over and help save their marriage. Parents are supposed to stay together no matter what, right? That's what he tried to do for other couples in trouble in his congregation. That was part of his job. But he never did it for us. I wondered if maybe it was because once Stan had been forced out of Sav-On we could no longer donate to his Beth Shalom synagogue like the other families. I had already learned that money gave you respect.

One night when I was fifteen, I was in his Hebrew class at Beth Shalom. I was telling jokes and disrupting the class and he finally got fed up. He told me to step out into the hall.

"What's with the bad attitude?" he asked. "Do you want to grow up to be a gangster?"

"It's better than being a phony."

"You think I'm a phony?"

"Sure do. All you care about is money."

"If you continue to act like a delinquent, I will not sign your confirmation letter and you will not go to Israel with everyone else next year."

"Big fuckin' deal," I said. "I don't want to go to Israel! I want to go to Hawaii, asshole."

"You're a Jew," he said calmly.

"But I don't believe in God."

His face turned red. "Get out of this synagogue right now."

"I'll meet you outside." I was ready to fight my rabbi.

When I saw that he wasn't going to mix it up with me, I detonated the atom bomb.

"It's people like you who make people not like Jews!"

I stormed out.

The following Monday, after a Boy Scout meeting at Beth Shalom, all of the kids were waiting for our parents to pick us up. We were at a creek, finding smooth stones and trying to skip them across the water. I picked up a rock and threw it as high as I could so that it would make a bigger splash. I missed the creek.

Crack! The rock smashed the windshield of a car. The rabbi's car.

I never went back to Hebrew School or Boy Scouts.

· · ·

MY MOTHER DIDN'T have much luck with Oliver, her second husband, either.

It was Christmastime and so I put up a Christmas tree. Forget the religious part. For lots of Jews, Christmas is just a nice holiday. But Oliver was Christian and he took offense. "You're a Jew," he said, drunk as usual. "Take it down."

"No."

"Then get out of my house."

"This isn't your house! And I don't like the way you treat my mother!"

Before I knew it, he punched me in the face. Instead of hitting him back, I ran down to the basement to find my baseball bat because I was going to kill him. By the time I retrieved the bat, the police had already arrived.

"He's a hippie, he's on drugs," Oliver told them, "and I want him out of here."

Andy was living with his grandmother in North Kansas City, the Italian neighborhood. They had an extra room and I moved in. Andy wasn't going to college. The summer after high school graduation, I guess we sensed that our lives were about to change forever. We loved pinball so we went downtown to play at an arcade, knowing that this was going to be one of our last excursions together.

We were driving back home through a bad part of town when we stopped at a red light and saw a drunk standing along the side of the road screaming. We also heard the yelps of a dog. We looked closer and saw that the man was kicking a dog having puppies.

"Hey motherfucker!" I yelled, pissed off. "Stop that, you asshole!"

He pulled out a gun and shot at us. Fortunately he was so drunk he missed. After Andy hit the gas and we sped away, I looked back and saw that he was still kicking the poor dog.

"Stop the car! We're going back."

"You nuts? No way," said Andy.

He was probably right. We might have been killed if we went back. Sometimes good intentions can have bad consequences. I'd learn that soon enough.

That trip with Andy was the first time I had been shot at. It wouldn't be the last.

I was completing my application to ASU in the basement of my father's house. He looked over my shoulder. Where it asked for a projected major, I wrote "TV-Radio."

"Only five people in a million ever make it in the movie business, you fuckin' idiot," he said. "Put down 'Business Law.'"

I didn't move. He slapped me across the back of the head, crossed out "TV-Radio" and wrote in "Business Law."

I couldn't wait to get to college.

3

Flash for the Cash

"This is crazy," said Charles D. Sherman, special agent in charge of the Kansas City district office of the federal Drug Enforcement Administration. "People end up dead doing stuff like this."

—*The Kansas City Star*, May 17, 1981

IF MY PLAN worked, it would be the perfect crime, just like you hear about in the movies. In my head, we were the good guys, the movie heroes. I imagined it playing out like this: since we would hit a big-time dealer, the cops wouldn't mind. They would think of us as vigilantes in the nasty, dirty, underground world of drugs, so they'd turn their heads. And once they looked away, we'd get the weed, the money, and our revenge on J.D. We'd get away with it all. I might wear a black cowboy hat but I would still be a good guy, because only good guys rip off the bad guys.

It was easy to sit around and plan how we were going to stick guns in the faces of J.D. and his gang, announce we were the police, tell them to put their hands up, pretend to arrest them, take their cash and stash, and then get the hell out of there. It was another thing to actually pull our plan off, especially since we had never done anything like this before. Especially since we weren't cops.

"I just want to get J.D. and my money back," I told Don.

"We will. But we need a trial run."

For me, this was a one-shot deal, not a career, but Don was figuring that if this worked, he could pull it off again and again. Even though I was wary, I could see that he was right about doing a trial run. So many things could go wrong, the biggest being that we could get killed.

Woodbeck had been a deliveryman for a goodfella, Charlie Costa, helping ship grass from Mexico to Costa's home base in Chicago using rental cars. He knew that cops would rarely stop a rental and calculated that he could stuff 600 pounds into the trunk of a mid-size Ford. With Milwaukee Jim driving one and Don another—and by keeping to the speed limit—they delivered more than half a ton every run.

Costa was not a "made man," an official member of the Mafia, even though his father, "Contract" Costa, was a soldier for the Gambinos, one of the most powerful Mob families in America. Costa was only in his late twenties and a perfect specimen of an Italian man: tall, dark, and handsome. Like everyone else who grew up in the '60s, he had different ideas from those of the older generation, particularly the generation born in Sicily. He wanted all the trappings that came with being rich—he lived in an expensive Chicagoland estate, wore the finest clothes, and drove an Excalibur—but he didn't want to get dirty. He wanted to be accepted into society; his predecessors could care less. They had their own society, the Mafia, their family.

Costa wanted to go legit. He also desperately craved the spotlight, which was not a good thing in his family business. So he decided to follow in the footsteps of his hero, Bob Guccione, who had made his fortune with *Penthouse*. There would always be room for another jizz rag, he figured. Before starting his own magazine, Costa gained experience by coordinating photo shoots for, he said, *Penthouse*.

Somehow, though, he kept getting dragged back into the gutter. A dope deal in St. Louis had gone wrong, and at the end of it, one of his associates was gunned down in a phone booth, his own brother Tommy had been wounded, and the Mob had been ripped off to the tune of $70,000.

Soon after, he was assigned to set up a feature to include girls from Arizona State. Naturally, he called Woodbeck for assistance. Don, of course, called me. My job was to recruit girls on campus who would take their clothes off for the camera. But I struck out. Every single girl I talked to said there was no way that she'd show up for the test photo session.

Nevertheless, Charlie and Tommy, wearing a plaster cast on his leg, arrived at the Phoenix airport. Each of them escorted a Playboy Jet Bunny, women from Hugh Hefner's personal stock who were assigned to accompany him and his guests on the Playboy Jet. Costa was now traveling among the elite in sex magazine circles. As for me, I was eighteen years old. I had only seen women who looked like that in centerfolds.

Don and I met them at the terminal. Costa shook hands with Don but not with me.

"How ya doin', ya ole horse thief?" Don said.

"Who's the lobster?" Costa asked Don.

I found out later that "lobster" meant someone who was new to their activities, a "fish out of water."

"He's Craig. He's a bright guy. We're working together."

I felt proud to hear Don say that. But Costa still didn't shake my hand. He led Don and Tommy to one limousine while the women and myself took another following behind. En route to the hotel, the Costa brothers told Don about the trouble in St. Louis. "I took one in the leg," said Tommy. "Joey wasn't so lucky."

Charlie set his jaw. "We're going to have to do something about this."

"You know, maybe we can help you out," Don said. "My partner has an idea. We can get the money back and the cops will never know anything happened."

Costa wasn't so sure that was possible. "I want to talk to this guy."

He ordered our procession to stop by the side of the road and his driver brought me to his limo. I got in next to Don. As we continued to the hotel, I told Charlie my idea about phony busts. Costa looked at Don. "You think you can pull this off?"

"Absolutely."

Charlie turned to me but spoke to Don. "You think the lobster's up to it?"

I stared hard back at him.

Don nodded. "Kid's got balls."

Costa shrugged. "Okay. The asshole's name is Big Bruce. He's out of Boston, actually Cambridge. He puts deals together. He did the one in St. Louis. I'll connect you with someone who can reach him. I'll give you backup. I want you to teach him a lesson. I don't care so much about the money. It's the principle. But I want half of what you get."

We went to the photo shoot. Every girl I had tried to talk into coming to pose nude, every one that said she "would never ever do that," showed up.

As Sly Stone sang, "Everybody wants to be a star."

· · ·

FOR OUR BADGES, we made a stop at the local hockshop, called The Jewel Box, which had a ready supply. Retired cops would sell their shields for a few bucks for the gold or silver in them. Sometimes, though, the pawnshop would keep the badges and, even though it was illegal, sell them.

None of them, however, actually said "Boston Police." But it didn't matter. They looked real enough. When someone flashes a badge at you from five feet away in the middle of a bust, no one's reading the words on it.

We also needed weed to show the potential buyers. Don bought twenty pounds in Bisbee, where his buddy and fellow Nam vet "Digger" Dave Doolittle lived. Digger got his nickname because his father owned a funeral chapel and Dave would often dig the graves.

Don bought the grass wholesale, for about thirty dollars a pound. The Mexicans across the border used trash compactors to form the bricks, wrapped them in butcher paper, and then wrapped them again in red, blue, or yellow cellophane. On the street, the weed was worth about eighty dollars a pound. With the prices today, that same weed would go for as much as $2,000 a pound. Times were different, and in the days before airport metal detectors and security checks, you could go cross-country with the weed in your suitcase and not worry too much about getting caught. You could even bring guns in your baggage.

We did both. We sprinkled the bricks with baby powder to counteract any smell that escaped the other wrappings, placed them in a black trash bag, and laid them in a suitcase. We put our guns on top, with our badges strapped to them. If by chance someone did open our luggage, they might think we were cops and just let it go through. If not, well, we'd think of something.

I would miss a few classes at Arizona State but I had a good excuse. That doesn't mean I was going to give any of my professors a note that said, "I'm flying to Boston with a pretty bad dude and we're going to rip off a drug dealer. I should be back in time for the midterm," but it was still a pretty good excuse.

I wanted to get the sting over with as soon as possible but Don said we might as well stop in Chicago to see Costa on our way to Boston. "Come on, Craig, Charlie is gonna take us to another photo shoot. We're gonna see more naked girls!" I had never been to Chicago. In fact, I had never flown anywhere except to Miami on a family vacation. He didn't have to twist my arm too hard.

Costa's estate in the suburbs was sprawling and impressive, but what intrigued me most was what he had in his living room. Not the enormous black leather chair that looked more like a throne, but what was in front of it—a drop floor concealing a small but handy incinerator. Just in case any unwanted company with a warrant happened by, anything illegal could be instantly turned into ash.

After Chicago, we continued to Boston and drove to Cambridge to meet our contact. Dr. Marino's office was half of a huge, colonial building with white pillars; the other half was his home, where the dentist lived with his wife and three kids. We were escorted into his

office, which smelled like Listerine and was filled with the sounds of
Mantovani Muzak. Both made me want to hurl.

"You come highly recommended," said the thin, pasty, middle-aged
Marino, shaking hands with us. "Charlie tells me you've done this
many times."

"Yeah, that's why we're here," I said. I wasn't bluffing; I was acting. I
was the grizzled outlaw, the part I'd been playing since I was five years
old. My audience might be a lot older but there was the same pleasure
in pretending.

"I hope this isn't like pulling teeth." Marino's thin black moustache
quivered with a laugh. "Dentist humor." I didn't know how Marino
knew Costa but this dentist seemed too straight to do us any good.

"So," Marino said matter-of-factly, "anyone interested in a little
nitrous?"

Well, maybe he wasn't as straight as I thought.

We passed on the laughing gas and he pointed us down the hallway.
"Take a left and that's the front door to my home. My wife will show
you to your rooms. Grab a shower and we'll have dinner at six. My
wife is a great cook. Hope you like chicken cacciatore."

Marino and his wife came to dinner dressed like they were going
out for the evening. Don and I felt like country bumpkins in our
denim shirts and jeans. They proudly introduced us to their three
perfect children, ages ten, eight, and six, and we sat down to eat. "So
what's the plan?" Marino asked.

"We can talk about it later," Don said, tilting his head toward the
wife and kids.

"Oh, it's okay. Isn't that right, honey?"

"Of course."

I hesitated at first but went ahead. "You introduce us as the sellers.
We set up the deal. When it goes down, we turn the tables on the
buyers and supposedly arrest them. Our backup comes in…"

"Backup?" Marino asked.

"Yeah, guys dressed as cops so it looks all official."

"You mean me," said Marino.

"No, guys, guys Costa has here." I assumed there would be half a dozen Gambino goons as backup.

"Sorry, I'm your only 'guy.'"

I looked at Don. This could be trouble. "Doc, you're married, you have kids," I said. "You live here. These guys aren't going to be too happy. They could come after your ass."

"I'm all you've got."

Don and I looked at each other. "Well, then, I guess you come with us," said Don.

Marino was so excited he jumped up and gave Don a soul shake.

"Honey, if I'm playing an undercover detective, what color shirt do you think I should wear?"

His wife thought about it for a second. "Blue, a light blue. That's what I would think."

And I thought *my* family was weird.

"Want me to get one out for you?"

"Thank you, dear."

Hell yeah, we were in big trouble. We had to come up with something that might scare a drug buyer into not doing something stupid, like pulling a gun and shooting us all. I had an idea, as usual.

I asked Marino for a *TV Guide* and a reel-to-reel tape recorder. After dinner, I set up the tape recorder in front of the television in Marino's living room and tuned in the cop show *Adam-12*. Officers Pete Malloy and Jim Reed and the rest of the Los Angeles Police Department would be our backup.

When I finished taping segments of the show, Marino walked us back to our rooms.

"Hey, if you guys need some help getting to sleep." He took a jar of white pills out of his pocket. Quaaludes. He shook a few into each of our hands.

Definitely not as straight as he looked.

Marino arranged for me and Don to meet Big Bruce for lunch at a sports bar in downtown Boston. Posters of Beantown baseball stars Ted Williams and Carl Yastrzemski looked down on us in our corner booth. Big Bruce was about twenty-eight years old, six feet tall, and muscular in a longshoreman's kind of way. His large hooked nose made his face look like the front end of a '54 Pontiac.

"So where you from?" he asked.

"Phoenix," I answered. Don gave me a "What the hell are you telling him that for?" look.

"Know Keith Whittington? Runs a bar down there, a strip joint."

Don jumped in. "Never met him." Don wouldn't say he had if Keith were his own brother. The less information the better. I may have been the guy with all the ideas but I still had a lot to learn. "Hey, how 'bout some beers here?" Don shouted to a waitress. He pulled out a formidable roll of hundred-dollar bills and peeled off the top one in full view of Big Bruce, whose eyes widened. He didn't know that below the two hundred-dollar bills on top, the rest was singles.

Big Bruce got down to business. "You can get two hundred pounds?"

"Just say when and where," I told him.

"How much?"

"A hundred fifty per pound," I said.

"Too high."

"Too bad," I snapped back.

Big Bruce started to get up from the booth. Don put his hand firmly on his arm. "Now come on, fellas. We're here to get this done. Craig, do you think we can lower the price for our new friend here?"

The hardball negotiating tasted and smelled like the real thing, just like we planned. I hesitated appropriately before saying, "One forty."

Big Bruce rose to start to leave again.

"Damn it, Craig," said Don, "you're such a little Jew sometimes."

I glared at Don. The Jew comment was good, but it wasn't in the script. "One twenty-five," I said. "That's it."

I stared at Big Bruce.

"Well then," he said, pleased with his wheeling and dealing, "let's go outside and try a sample."

We walked Big Bruce to our rental car in the parking lot and opened the trunk. We showed him the twenty pounds, now unwrapped in the suitcase, and took one of the joints we had already rolled and placed on top. We got in the car and he lit up the fat doobie. "Smells good," he said as he took a toke, "and tastes great." He inhaled deep and waited.

"No kick. Mexican dirt weed."

"What?" Great, we get a marijuana connoisseur.

"I'm not going to have my buyer put his money down for this crap."

We came all this way for nothing? I sure didn't want to go back to Costa without the cash he expected us to get for him. I tried to save the deal.

"How about we drop the price? Ninety bucks."

"I don't know. Let me think about it."

I reached into my pocket and absent-mindedly took out a couple of the quaaludes the dentist had given us. I was rolling them around in my hand when Big Bruce grabbed my wrist.

"Rorer 714s," he said authoritatively, examining them. "Pharmaceutical, not bathtub."

I nodded, not knowing where he was going.

"Can you get more?"

"Well, uh…"

"Absolutely," said Don. "How many are you talking about?"

"I don't want you jammin' me on the price."

"How much you been payin'?" Don asked.

"Fifteen cents a pop but that's in quantity."

"What quantity?" I inquired.

"Can you handle half a million?"

Hell, we couldn't handle more than a jar from a Cambridge dentist.

"Half a million? Sure," Don said.

"For how much?"

"How about ten cents?" I offered. We came in looking at maybe leaving with about $25,000. At ten cents a pill, we now had a chance at twice that much.

Big Bruce stuck out his meaty hand and we shook.

"Tonight," said Big Bruce. "Same place we planned."

. . .

AT MARINO'S HOUSE, Don and I each took a pair of handcuffs and loaded our .38s. Don had taught me to keep the first chamber empty. "If the weapon falls, you don't want it to discharge and blow your foot off," he said. Second chamber, a scatter shot. You don't even need to aim under pressure. You can wound three or four with just one shot. The remaining three rounds were hollow points. "They can penetrate a car door," Don said. "That's for the kill. If you have to."

Don had cut up a pair of shoulder holsters so we could wear them upside down and wedged under our left armpits. That way there was no telltale bulge beneath our black leather jackets. We would have to draw left-handed, but it was one smooth motion and we didn't have to reach across our chests.

The word "sample" would be the cue to draw our guns.

It was late October, dreary, cold, and about to rain. I'd be lying if I didn't say I was scared what might happen. Don drove our rental car within a couple blocks of the address we were given. We had already scoped it out a couple of hours earlier, to make sure we knew the layout. Marino, dressed in a suit, of course, got out carrying the tape recorder.

"Give us time to get into the room before you come up," I told him.

"In that stairwell, this stuff is going to sound like every cop in the city has arrived."

"We're counting on that, Doc," Don said.

We drove to the four-story brick building and parked on the street in front. Big Bruce, waiting for us, walked to the car. "Let's see it," he said.

We went to the trunk. Inside were two suitcases stacked on top of each other. Inside they were filled with books and newspapers, giving them weight, covered by a black plastic sheet and a few 'ludes scattered on top. I opened the first suitcase to show Big Bruce. As I leaned over to turn it towards him, my handcuffs fell out of my jacket pocket and onto the cobblestone street.

They probably sounded like a tinny "clank" but to me, they were church bells announcing a funeral. Mine. I felt the .38 weigh heavily in my shoulder holster.

"What the hell is that?" asked Bruce.

Don took charge. "Can you believe this kid? Look at these." He picked up the cuffs. "He wants to be a magician so he goes to a magic store and buys these trick handcuffs."

"Really."

"Yeah. Let me show you how they work."

I figured where Don was going. "Aw, come on. I want to show him," I said.

Don looked at Big Bruce and shrugged, like a mother saying, "He's a good boy. If he wants to go out and play, why not?"

I started to place the handcuffs around Big Bruce's thick wrists. "You know, these are like the ones Houdini used."

"Get them the fuck off me! We don't have time for magic tricks."

I looked disappointed. Big Bruce thought he had hurt my feelings. "Show them to me later," he said by way of apology. I was relieved. Yep, maybe I would show them to him later.

Don closed the suitcase and carried it up the walkway. He had his keys on a leather strap hanging from his jeans pocket and slapped it against his leg out of habit.

"Oh, by the way," Big Bruce said as casually as he could, "there are a few more guys up there than I told you." He pointed to the second-floor window.

"What the hell do you mean?" Don's usual slight Southwestern drawl was sharp.

"They wouldn't front me all of the money. It's a lot of dough. They want to see you face to face."

"What if we don't want to see them?" Don shot back.

"It's take it or leave it," said Big Bruce.

"How many guys are in there?" I asked.

"'Bout a dozen."

My heart sank. I was geared up for maybe five guys. What if they didn't believe we were cops? A dozen! What if they all went for us? People might get shot. One of them might be me. Crap. What did I get myself into?

"Everything's cool, man," Big Bruce went on. "You got nothing to worry about. They're all my friends." For a guy who didn't know who the hell we were, he was mighty sure the people in the apartment were his friends.

It was thirty-five degrees and I was drenched in sweat. I could feel the index card in my shirt pocket, the one on which I written the Miranda warning, being soaked through.

"I don't know about this," I said to Don. Big Bruce walked toward the building ahead of us while we held back a bit and talked out of his earshot. "What if there's a shootout?"

"What's the matter? You expected this to be perfect—like in your head?"

"No, but..."

"Five, ten, a dozen, who cares? We can take them all."

"We don't have enough bullets." I did the math—two guns, four loaded rounds each. Way less than a dozen.

"We're not going to shoot anybody, dumbfuck," Don said. "I thought your brilliant idea was we would talk them into getting arrested. Remember, we're the police. There are twenty cops backing us up."

No, there was only a dentist. Suddenly my brilliant idea from the movies didn't seem that great to me in reality. "We're in this together, brother, or we're not in it at all. You want to bail, Craig, that's fine. But I had better not ever see you again." Don turned his back and walked up to Big Bruce entering the building.

There are moments in life when you have to either step back or jump into the unknown and take your chances. I thought about what

I would step back to—school, a boring job. There wasn't any movie in that. I wanted more.

I went to Don. "Well?" he asked.

"I guess I'm as ready as I'll ever be," I answered.

Don slowly smiled. "Hell yes. This is going to be like popcorn."

We went up the stairwell to the second floor apartment. We could hear a lot of noise coming from inside. My heart was pumping—hard. Don had been in these sorts of situations before. Not me. All I knew was that I had to go through with this. I had to prove to myself that I could do it.

Big Bruce knocked and the door opened. I looked around carefully as Don and I entered behind him. A dozen men were sitting or standing in groups of two or three, drinking out of paper cups. Most of them were in their twenties. One redheaded kid was playing air drums to Led Zeppelin's "Communication Breakdown." There was a pair of older men too, who looked around forty-five or fifty. While the others wore jeans, T-shirts, and maybe a string of beads around their neck, they wore slacks and Ban-lon shirts. They were from my father's generation and I didn't trust them.

They were in the business of buying dope and pills. They didn't understand the words to our music, didn't know if it was a long-haired boy or a girl walking down the street, and they didn't understand why kids would burn the flag. To them, the world had gone crazy. But making a buck was making a buck, so if the kids wanted dope and pills, they sold dope and pills.

Across the room was the radiator. On top of the piece of plywood that rested on it, where usually there was a pan of water to soak up the humidity when the heat was on, were piles of cash. Just like in Tempe when I was ripped off. Each packet of twenties and fifties had a name written on a scrap of paper slipped beneath its rubber band. Each wanted his share of the 'ludes and there would be no mistaking who was supposed to get how much for his money.

"Where's the shit?" asked one of the older men.

Don laid the suitcase down on a chair next to him. I took the dentist's jar of pills from a coat pocket and shook it. Every eye was on that jar.

"Give 'em a SAMPLE!" said Don.

I opened the jar and tossed the pills into the middle of the room. Everybody but the two older men dropped to the floor scrambling after the 'ludes. In that same instant, Don and I drew our guns. Our right hands flashed our police badges. I yelled, "BOSTON POLICE! NOBODY MOVE!"

But the older men did. Don roared. "BOSTON NARCOTICS! YOU'RE UNDER ARREST!"

One of the older men moved a hand toward the back of his pants. Don jumped over a coffeetable, went airborne, and slammed him to the ground.

"FREEZE, MOTHERFUCKER!" He pointed his gun at the man's head.

"I'm froze, I'm froze." His hands went up. Don felt around his belt, found a pistol, and put it in his own belt.

Big Bruce looked at me. "What the fuck?"

"Everybody against the wall," I ordered. "Hands up where we can see them." I pointed my gun at Big Bruce. "You too."

"Uh, man, listen, like I live down the hall," said the redheaded kid. "I was just down here listening to some tunes. I got nothing to do with any of this shit."

"SHUT UP!" I growled. "You're under arrest. We can talk about this when we get downtown."

I found my card with the Miranda warning—but all that was left was a smear of blue ink. Woodbeck continued pushing the men against the wall, and took three more guns. There were so many guys that they had to squeeze tightly next to each other. I wondered where the hell Marino was.

"Their rights, Officer," Don prodded, wondering if something had gone wrong. "Read them their rights."

I guess my rehearsing paid off because I was able to recite it from memory.

"You have the right to remain silent. Anything you say can and will be used against you in a court of law." With everyone facing the wall, I saw Don quickly rip out the telephone cord. "If you do not have or cannot afford an attorney, one will be appointed for you by the Commonwealth of Massachusetts. Do you understand your rights as I have read them?" No one answered. "DO YOU UNDERSTAND YOUR RIGHTS?" I screamed, and this time there was a smattering of yeses.

"Does anyone have anything to say?" Nothing. I liked playing a cop. I would make a good one, I thought. Don began frisking each of them, starting at the far end of the line.

"One Adam-twelve, one Adam-twelve, we have a ten-thirty in progress. All units respond immediately."

Finally, the recording came on, just loud enough and garbled enough for it to sound as though the entire Boston Police Department had come out in force for this bust. I thanked Reed and Malloy for the sound effects.

Marino entered moments later. "Lieutenant," he said to me, "We have everything secure in the building."

"The money's over there, Detective," I told him. Marino stepped quickly to the radiator, emptied our suitcase and shoveled in the $50,000.

Big Bruce got my attention. "You're a cop? What am I supposed to do?"

One of the men in Ban-lon shot him a glance that could kill and probably had. "Fucker," he said viciously. "You set us up."

Big Bruce's face went snow white. He was going to have some explaining to do after this was over. That would make Costa very happy. As Don continued a professional job of frisking from the other end of the lineup, I went to Big Bruce and took his wallet. There was $4,000 in it. I showed it to him and then put it in my pocket.

A police siren wailed. A walkie-talkie scratched out, "This is code six-seven-three dash Zebra ... We have Officer Remkin and Officer Brown upstairs ... will proceed to the Seventeenth Division station house ... Roger that."

Don patted down a young man with a five-day growth of beard but who otherwise fit right in with the others. He took out his wallet. What Don found inside startled him—a Boston Police badge. He gave Don a wink. "Who are you guys?" asked the man under his breath. "Why didn't I know about this?" Don took the badge—and showed it to me. He smiled, as if to say, "Look, got a real one!" Don shoved the badge into his own pocket. He then twisted the man's arm and jerked it behind him. He slapped a pair of handcuffs on one wrist and then the other.

"Sir, I suggest you cooperate."

A strange look came over the undercover cop's face. "Oh my God," he said in a whisper. He knew we were not cops, and knew he couldn't do anything about it.

Another man spoke up. "I ain't going to prison," he said.

"That's not for us to decide, sir," I told him.

Our victims were getting restless. There were only three of us holding them. It was time to get out of there. "Let's bring the paddy wagon around," I told Don, talking over the background banter playing on the tape recorder. "The uniforms are behind us and they'll escort the prisoners downstairs two at a time. Gentlemen, please remain as you are until you are instructed to move."

We silently backed out the door. On the landing, we stomped our feet to make it sound like dozens of men running up the stairs.

"The uniforms are here," Don yelled loud enough for the men in the apartment to hear.

"Take over, Sergeant."

As we sped down the stairs we could hear...

"You'll wonder where the yellow went, when you brush your teeth with Pepsodent..." I had accidentally recorded one of the TV commercials.

Marino had already started the car when I jumped in the back and Don flew into the passenger seat. The dentist floored the accelerator. It was more than a half hour before anyone spoke.

"Hell yes," said Don finally. "I do believe we made Bullet Bob Hayes look slow getting out of there."

I busted out laughing. We were as giddy as little kids. The tension flooded out of me. I felt like a wide receiver catching the winning touchdown pass on the final play of the game in front of 80,000 fans. I guess I was good at something after all. And the toughest sonuvabitch I knew thought I was pretty good too. Don offered his hand over the front seat and we soul shook. "Popcorn. Just like I said." Yep, we had done it.

When we arrived at Logan International, Don threw the briefcase filled with cash onto the airline ticket counter. "Yes, may I help you?" asked the middle-aged female reservations clerk.

"Two tickets to Phoenix," I said.

"Make that three," said Marino.

Don shook his head. "You're not coming with us."

"I am too," the dentist insisted. "At least for a few days. I want to enjoy this before I have to come back."

"Why not?" I asked Don.

The ticket agent interrupted. "Um, I'm sorry, sir, but the last flight to Phoenix is on the runway. There is one taking off in the morning though. Would you like me to book you gentlemen on that one?" We had to get out of town right away.

"Kansas City?" I suggested. We'd be good and safe at home.

She looked at her flight schedule monitor. "Sorry, last one left at 9:45."

"How about we take the next plane smokin'," Don said. "Where's that one goin'?"

"Well, the next flight available leaves for New York."

"Hell yes, New York. That's where we're goin'."

Would the cops be after us? We didn't think so, but just to be on the safe side, we hid in the restroom until the flight was due to board. But we had gotten away clean—just like in the movies.

We heard later that it took a few minutes before Big Bruce and the others realized the "cops" were gone and not coming back. When they found the tape recorder, they put two and two together. Some were pissed, some just shook their heads. Everybody got out of the apartment as quickly as they could, especially Big Bruce. To save his neck, he later tried to spin a somewhat different story about the rip-off.

"Swear to God, there were at least seven of them. Had AKs too. Sheeeeiiitttt. Mean mothers, these guys. We didn't have a friggin' chance."

"We heard there were only three of them."

"They said they were cops! What was I supposed to do?"

"But you didn't get arrested."

"They disappeared, man. Just left. I don't know. Maybe they were vice squad guys going independent."

Big Bruce and the others never knew who stung them.

They do now.

4

A Life of Crime

"Obviously in my 20s I was an outlaw," (Glazer) says of his wild and woolly days of robbing drug dealers … "I don't deny it."
—*The Kansas City Star*, February 25, 2000

THE BEST PART was that what I had done was straight out of the movies—but better than any movie because it was real. The high was tremendous, and I wanted it again. I still wanted to get my revenge on J.D., but I also wanted to do another sting, and another and another. My career as the King of Sting had begun.

After a day of celebrating in Manhattan, the dentist returned to Boston. I never saw him again, but he sure had one helluva colorful story to tell his wife and kids—and they were probably proud of him too.

Heading back to Phoenix, Don and I stopped in Chicago to deliver Charlie his share. He pitched us on buying stock in the magazine he was about to launch. Hustlers never rest. We passed on the skin mag, but we did give him $3,000 to buy his used limo. Wouldn't that look cool, an eighteen-year-old college kid tooling around in a limousine? Now that would be a babe magnet. Charlie said the limo would be in Phoenix in a week, but just like the backup he promised for Boston, it never arrived.

I knew that if I was going to survive a life of crime, I needed Don, but I thought also that maybe he needed me. Hanging with him in Boston and New York, in hotel rooms and on planes, I had my first chance to learn more about him.

We looked so different—he was light-skinned and I was darker, he was six foot three and I was about five foot ten. Don was from a lower-middle-class family, one that never aspired to education or tasted money or success. I was more sophisticated, more educated. But, like me, he was from the Midwest and was the oldest brother. In his case, he was born in Cincinnati and had three younger brothers. Like me, he was rowdy and rebellious, and struggled against any authority figure.

Our biggest difference was that I used the movies to escape my everyday life. I guess they gave me hope that my life could mean something more. For Don, life was what it was. When his conservative, God-fearing parents couldn't handle him anymore, they shipped him off to a military school in North Carolina to "make a man out of him."

But Don was the kind of guy who would tear down any fence built around him—and eat the barbed wire too. Set him on a straight path and he'd have to wander off onto a dirt road going who-knows-where "to find a little action, just for the hell of it." So, in 1965, when he was seventeen, he bolted from the school and from home and joined the Navy. He didn't see the world but he did see Vietnam. And what he saw there, he didn't like at all.

At one point, he told me, his ship docked in Australia and the sailors went on R&R. When they returned, he didn't. According to Don, he got a job as a disc jockey, a perfect gig for someone who could bullshit as well as he could. He was gone ninety days before they found him and brought him back. Fortunately, his captain liked him and didn't charge him with any offense. Don was that kind of guy, like Yul Brynner in *The Magnificent Seven*. Black hat and hard as nails, but likeable.

But Don did have to pay a price. The captain assigned him to shore duty with the Marines. Along with guarding supplies shuttled into the port of Da Nang, he was sent out on patrols into the jungle. The result of one of those patrols was the blood-and-guts story he told around the pool table when I first met him.

Don also told me about being in a Saigon movie theater when a bomb blew it all to hell. Maybe that's why he didn't much like going to the movies. He joked that all he got out of the Navy was two Bronze Stars, two Purple Hearts, and two tattoos—an anchor on his left bicep and a small, red devil on his right buttock.

Woodbeck returned to the U.S. in the latter half of 1967 and was discharged early the following year. But the country he had left had changed. Elvis and leather jackets were out, and Jane Fonda and long hair were in. People were divided into hawks and doves. The country had been turned upside down and inside out, and he didn't fit in anywhere.

He was just twenty years old but he looked, talked, and even walked like a much older Lee Marvin, with already thinning blond hair. He was good with his fists and even better with a gun. He was fearless too. And "he could sell you a dime for a quarter," according to his brother Tom. He had all the credentials for a life of crime.

He told me that after getting out of the Navy, he teamed up with a fifty-year-old veteran con artist named Augie Hunter in California. Together, they raided a large department store's jewelry display. They split up and a getaway driver spirited Don straight to the airport, where he flew to New York City. His girlfriend was already packed for their flight to Geneva, Switzerland.

A knock on the door canceled his plans. The FBI came calling after the driver confessed to the heist. Hunter, who had taken the $100,000 in precious gems, was never heard from again. At least that's what he told me. I was never sure how much of that was true. What was true was that his parents moved to Arizona while he was in Nam. "Trying to lose me," he said with a laugh. So after Don served his jail time in California, he relocated to Arizona too. He enrolled in Mesa Community College but, as you might expect, didn't stay for long. He wasn't the kind of guy looking for a degree or a steady job. He wasn't the kind of guy who hoped or figured he'd reach retirement.

I don't think many of us in our generation did. We just wanted to "do our own thing." Our movie was *Easy Rider*. When Billy, Dennis Hopper's character, says, "All we represent to them, man, is somebody who needs a haircut," Jack Nicholson's George character answers, "Oh, no. What you represent to them is freedom." Billy answers back, "What the hell is wrong with freedom? That's what it's all about."

"Freedom" was my generation's buzzword. We wanted freedom to grow our hair long, freedom to not wear bras, freedom to turn up the music, freedom to get high. I suppose that if the previous generation did all of those things, then our "freedom" would have been to shave our heads, put on bras, turn down the volume, and say no to drugs, which is exactly what the generation that came after us did.

A big part of that freedom was smoking grass. We all did, even future presidents. It was no big deal. We knew grass didn't make you crazy, like it said in those ridiculous movies they played in high school. We figured it probably didn't give you cancer like cigarettes either. Smoking cigarettes was the older generation's sign of rebellion against society. Nobody was cooler than Humphrey Bogart in *Casablanca*, right? Now it was our turn. Grass was our generation's rebellion.

The fact that possessing grass was illegal only made smoking it more attractive. Of course, "holding" also made us criminals. It was probably the first truly illegal thing we did in our lives. For some people, when they crossed that line with grass even a little, going farther—such as dealing—was an easy step to take. If you bought, you sold, even if it was just to friends. Don said he didn't smoke weed until he was twenty-one, after Nam. That seemed hard to believe, but that's what he said. Maybe he changed because of the war. A lot of guys changed after Vietnam. By the time I met him he was doing more than smoking weed. Don shot heroin—and he made me try it too.

He had a gram of China White and had already shot up. We were going out that night and he wanted me to be right there with him. But I was scared of needles. So he grabbed my arm and jammed the needle in. It was a "skin shot," missing the vein, but when he did it again, he connected. Then he gave me an apple to eat, because the vitamin A was supposed to help soothe my stomach. It didn't, and I threw up.

Still, I know why people get addicted to heroin. It's a weird feeling, like your entire body is itchy. I had the greatest rush.

"What do you want to do?" Don asked.

"Let's go to the movies!" I said.

We strapped on our guns. We almost never went out without being armed: a .38 Smith & Wesson revolver holstered or strapped to the ankle or a nine-shot Colt .25s in a jacket or even a jean pocket. Sometimes we carried both. I remember we saw a double feature: *Billy Jack*, about a counterculture outsider who gets revenge through violence, and *Super Fly*, a movie not given enough credit for making cocaine hip for white people. Nobody was cooler than the character Priest.

The next time I did horse, I was by myself, and shot myself up. This time I couldn't sleep. It was almost like I had the flu, my nose stuffy and sniffling. And my dick started bleeding. I'm pretty confident that it is never a good thing if your dick is bleeding.

Heroin is labeled a "controlled substance." Like hell. It's an uncontrolled substance. You can't control what it does to you. You're at its mercy. I have never been comfortable being a victim of anyone or anything. The rush was like getting to the top of a roller coaster and enjoying the fear of falling. Only with heroin, you really might crash at the bottom. Now here I was experiencing a "baby jones," a need for more, even with my dick bleeding. I was scared big time.

I never did heroin again, at least of my own free will. I opened the small safe in Don's apartment, took out the rest of the heroin he had, and flushed it down the toilet. I wanted to save not only myself but him too.

"We don't need to become junkies," I told Don.

He was pissed that I had thrown so much money away. Though he would still do heroin on occasion, it wasn't a lot and he didn't become an addict, and he never let it interfere with our stings. We didn't even smoke dope before a sting. That was business, a deadly business. Weed made me physically lethargic and also slowed down my thought processes. I knew I needed to have all my wits about me, be as sharp and quick-thinking as I could. It probably helped that many times our victims had been smoking. You bet it impaired their ability to react. We counted on that. For me, I sure didn't want to get killed because of a joint.

. . .

WHEN DON MOVED to Arizona, he fell in with a group of other vets who, finding they had no skills other than those of war, smuggled stolen goods across the border. Using trucks and planes, they transported cars, guns, TVs, Levis, refrigerators, anything, south to a Mexican syndicate. On the return trip—waste not, want not—the Mexicans would send marijuana, often up to a ton and a half every couple of weeks.

Don flew one of the planes, even though he didn't have a license and had never taken an official flying lesson, and Milwaukee Jim rode in the plane with him. They trusted each other with their lives and flying together was just another risky adventure for them. Digger Dave was on the ground, driving the trucks.

Paid $300 on a weekly basis—never a cut of the action—Don was also a guard for the shipments once they had landed and for the money that was collected for the weed at a Scottsdale massage parlor. With so many law enforcement officials on the syndicate's payroll, there was little fear of getting caught by them.

J.D. was the enforcer and boss of the Prairie Pirates north of the border. He was the connection between the cartel families who grew the weed in Mexico and the Anglos who brought it up to the U.S., such as Costa. He organized and led the Anglos, Chicanos, and Mexican nationals who roamed the vast, open spaces of the Southwest during those early days of the drug wars. Before I ever heard the phrase "Mexican Mafia," J.D. was one of its captains. Occasionally, they'd invade the cities, like a gang of outlaws riding into Tombstone. They'd blow into town and rip off new, unsuspecting weed dealers, while also stealing cash from those who wanted to buy. That's what they were doing when I ran into J.D. in the student apartment in Sin City.

The problems between J.D. and Don started when Don discovered that the shipments he protected included heroin. For Don, there was a big difference between smuggling weed and heroin. It had to do with prison, not morality. Simply, if you were caught smuggling weed, you might go to prison for a couple of years; but if you were caught smuggling heroin, you could go to federal prison for twenty years or more. Heroin was high risk—and Don wasn't getting paid near enough to take that chance.

"We've been haulin' balloons, right?" Don asked J.D. at the massage parlor. Heroin was transported in balloons to keep the moisture out.

"So?"

"I don't like it."

J.D. sneered. "Don't matter what you like or don't like."

"You got it wrong there. I want out."

"You can't do that."

Don started to leave.

J.D. stopped him. "Listen, Don, don't be such a pussy."

"Pussy?" Don would've punched anyone else who called him that, but he didn't want to tangle with J.D., at least not then. "Naw, I'm just not being stupid. It's too damn dangerous smuggling that stuff."

J.D. pondered that for a moment. "Okay, you don't have to anymore … after the next run. You're already scheduled and I need you."

"I'll do weed. That's okay."

"I said just one more."

"Just one."

"That's what I said." J.D. wasn't happy.

Don landed the Cessna in the middle of the night at a nondescript landing area a dozen miles west of Gila Bend. Waiting were
two Mexicans and an Indian, laborers they regularly used on these
runs, and a large white van that provided the only lights for the dusty
runway with its headlamps. Just as Don and Milwaukee Jim stepped
out of the plane ...

BANG!

A gunshot echoed in the darkness.

BANG!

Another one whistled over their heads.

Don reached for his .38. As he touched the handle, he felt the cold
pressure of a pistol against his ear.

"Leave it."

Don turned slightly and asked, "What's goin' on, J.D.?" J.D., the
pistol in his hand, spit onto the desert floor.

"The shipment's here," Don said. "What's the problem?"

"You. You said this was your last run. It is."

"I don't know why I fuckin' trusted you."

J.D. laughed. "Me neither."

Half a dozen of J.D.'s armed men surrounded Don, Milwaukee
Jim, and the three others. They had arrived in a pickup truck that had
been camouflaged so that Don could not spot it from the air. Now
the pickup drove closer, its headlights lending more illumination. But
there were still large areas of blackness.

"First you say 'no' to this and then tomorrow you'll say 'no' to
something else," explained J.D. "I can't have that."

"You don't have to do this," Don told him. "Not to Jim. Not to them."

Milwaukee was stoic. He knew about death, about the killers
and the killed. The two Mexicans and the Indian did not and were
frightened out of their minds. Anyone in that situation would be
scared, and Don was too, but he knew that if he wanted to survive,
he couldn't panic. So Don played it cool.

"Bring them over here," J.D. yelled to his men. "Out in the open. Line them up." Don whispered to Milwaukee Jim, "Get in the middle."

"Shut up and kneel down!" J.D. shouted. His men shoved them to their knees. Don and Jim were in the middle with the others on both sides of them.

Under his breath, Don told Milwaukee, "On the first shot."

J.D. walked to the Mexican next to Don and leveled his gun between his eyes. The Mexican opened his mouth to scream...

BANG!

Don and Jim scrambled to their feet and ran in opposite directions, as did the other Mexican and the Indian. J.D. and his men were surprised for a split second before they fired blindly into the dark areas where Don and the others were running.

Don sprinted as strong and hard as he could for as long as he could. After a while, he heard a truck engine, first close and then moving away. He rested among the cactus in one of the numerous rocky outcroppings that dotted the otherwise lifeless desert. He looked back and saw the truck's headlights grow smaller in the distance. Then he ran some more.

He never thought he'd cross paths with J.D. again, but he would—and I'd be there too.

· · ·

WHEN I RETURNED from the Boston sting, Karen was waiting at the Phoenix airport. She had broken up with Steve before I went off to Boston.

"Glad to see me?" she asked with a smile. You bet I was. Didn't the movie hero always get the girl too?

I wanted to tell her about Boston. I wanted to tell my dad. I was about to burst wanting to tell someone. But I knew that I couldn't. I felt like the Warren Beatty character in *McCabe and Mrs. Miller*, which had just come out. Everyone thinks he's a harmless nebbish, but in truth, he's a gunslinger. I had my own secret from the everyday world and I got a kick knowing that I was very different from what people expected. I had done something dangerous and exciting, something most people would only see in a movie. I couldn't help but smile every time I thought about the Boston sting.

A few days later, Karen and I were supposed to go to a Who concert. I put on my best Nik-Nik, one of those silky body-hugging shirts with the colorful Rorschach inkblot designs on them, very '70s disco, and she met me at my apartment.

"I've never slept on a waterbed," she said, sitting down on the edge. If there was ever a line said by a girl in the '70s that meant she wanted to sleep with you, that was the one. She shifted her weight, which slid the material of her dress higher up her thighs, and I could see she wasn't wearing underwear.

We never made it to the Who concert.

Another good thing about my father, Stan—he helped me sleep with my first real girlfriend. I was fifteen and so was the blonde who worked at the community pool. He went up to her and said, "Mary, can you teach my son to swim?"

Not long after, we screwed on my father's bed, with the Mediterranean-design headboard and dark red décor. The Who's "Magic Bus" was playing on the stereo.

I was crazy about Mary. We were together for more than a year. Then she went to Italy on an educational year abroad program. I was heartbroken. I wrote her letters just about every day. Within a month, I was no longer getting letters back. By the time she returned, Andy had befriended me and I was a bad boy. By the time she returned, Mary was smoking cigarettes and dating around. I don't think I ever forgave her. I'm not sure any of us forgive our first heartbreaker.

A couple of weeks after Karen and I slept together, she introduced me to her parents. To them, I was just some college kid, probably too screwed up for their daughter, who was a senior in high school. We met at the Phoenix Country Club for lunch. They were country club people, and I certainly was not.

"You have never been here?" asked prim and proper Mrs. Curtis.

"Well, no." I might as well have admitted to having a contagious disease.

"You do golf though?" asked the square-jawed Mr. Curtis.

"Absolutely," I lied.

"You're out of town this weekend, Daddy, why not have Craig play as your guest?"

Mr. Curtis stared stone-faced at her. Through clenched teeth, he finally said, "But you'll be taking the college boards."

"Craig can still come. He can invite a couple of his friends," Karen pleaded. Mr. Curtis couldn't say no to his precious baby girl.

When I asked Don to play, he said, "Sure, I golf. Shit, I do everything." He had moved to a new apartment. He also bought a spider monkey; anyone with a spider monkey is probably not the country club type either.

Don, Milwaukee Jim, Digger Dave, and I—the foursome from hell—descended on the exclusive golf club. Forget the golf pants and shirts. We wore jeans, tennis shoes, and football jerseys.

"Are we going to get those little golf carts?" Don asked, wide-eyed.

I went to the pro shop, rented clubs and two electric carts, and signed for them with Karen's name, just as she said I could. We drove to the first tee and Don jumped out, wielding an iron that he swung hard at the ball. It jumped to the right about sixty yards. "You don't know how to play, do you?" I asked.

"Not unless there's a windmill and a clown's face," he boomed.

None of them knew how to play. I tried the best I could but I wasn't any better. It was half an hour before we finished the first hole. Golfers behind us were not pleased. When I suggested that they play through, Don stopped me. "They can wait. They have the time. They're not going to work anywhere."

By the second hole, Don was bored. He snapped his fingers. "Let's play golf hockey!"

Don heaved a ball as far as he could onto the fairway. "Yeeee-haaaa!" he screamed and took off in his golf cart with Milwaukee Jim, who was letting loose war whoops alongside him. They chugged towards the ball and swung wildly with their clubs.

I looked at Digger. "We can't let them score, now, can we?" We jumped into our cart and chased Don and Jim down the fairway. Golf hockey quickly turned into demolition derby, and pretty soon, there was a cart with a flashing red light on its canopy headed for us.

"It's the cops!" Don yelled.

"We can't escape from a golf course," I told him. "They know who we are."

"Bullshit," he answered. "They know who you are." The three hopped into Don's Grand Prix and rode off into the sunset. I waited for the security guards.

"Are you out of your minds?" they asked. "What are you doing?"

I shrugged. "Golf hockey."

When Karen heard about the incident, she didn't think it was so funny.

"That Woodbeck is crude and if he's your friend you'll never be accepted."

"Accepted? By who?"

"He's a bad influence on you."

"Don't sound like my parents."

"Somebody should."

Imagine how she would have reacted if she had known what we had done in Boston.

• • •

WHEN YOU'RE HOOKED, anything makes sense as long as you get high in the end, and I was hooked on the movie cops-and-robbers adventure and danger of stings just as bad as any drug. At the beginning, we didn't use the word "sting." We called it a "mission." *The Sting* with Robert Redford and Paul Newman came out in 1973, two years later, and that's when the word became popular and when we started to call them stings. Even then, I believe we were the first to use the word for illegal operations involving people pretending to be law enforcement.

One of our earliest and easiest stings was perhaps our best acting job.

I stood at the passenger arrival gate at Phoenix Sky Harbor holding up a sign reading "GREENBLATT." Wearing a dark sport coat, I could have been a limousine driver, which was good, since that's the part I was playing. That's who Ed Greenblatt and his brother Sam thought I was when they got off the flight from New York.

"You must be our man," said Ed.

"I'll take your briefcase."

"Sorry," said Sam, "I'll hold onto it."

"Very well, sir. Follow me."

Woodbeck, similarly and awkwardly outfitted in a dark sport coat, waited at the town car we had rented. We ushered Ed and Sam into the back and took our seats up front, with Don driving.

"Will J.D. be at the hotel?" Ed asked.

"He's waiting for you, sir," I said, as we pulled into traffic. Ed and Sam were J.D.'s accountants and they would occasionally fly in to deliver funds that were off the books. Knowing their schedule, we cut them off at the pass.

"Please, call me Ed, and this is my brother, Sam. Damn, why is it always this hot down here?"

"Can't tell you … Ed," I answered. "J.D. did ask me, however, to count the money before we get to the hotel. He does not like surprises."

Sam sounded suspicious. "We've been making this run for three years. He's never questioned us before."

"I know, but we're new on the job," Woodbeck chimed in, "and my partner here wants to make sure we do things on the up-and-up."

"That's what J.D. told us and that's what I'm going to do," I said to the brothers, before adding angrily to Don, "Is that all right with you?"

Sam opened his briefcase and handed me a pair of heavy bank deposit bags. I opened one. "There's twenty-five grand in each," said Ed. "Hundred dollar bills, random numbers, untraceable."

"Guess J.D. doesn't pay taxes on any of this, huh?" I said with a smile.

"Not as long as we're his accountants," said Sam with a laugh.

I dropped my smile. "Then you must know that not paying taxes is a federal crime." Ed and Sam cocked their heads slightly, like dogs trying to figure out what the guy holding the food bowl was saying.

"We're with the Internal Revenue Service, gentlemen, and you are under arrest."

"Are you kidding me?" Ed asked.

I flashed a Treasury Department badge, while Don pulled the town car to the side of the road. We each took out one of the Greenblatts, cuffed them, read them their rights, deposited them back in the car, and headed downtown to "headquarters."

I extracted a radio hand mike from the glove compartment. I looked at Don for a moment, long enough for the Greenblatts to notice my hesitation, then spoke into it. "Agents Brown and Schwartz, we're still waiting for our targets, over." Don shot a glance in my direction that was so sudden Ed and Sam couldn't have missed it.

From the radio speaker, a voice answered, "Ten-four. We're standing by. Over and out." It was Milwaukee Jim, who was following us in his pickup, equipped as we were with a CB radio.

"What are you doing?" Don asked.

"We have fifty grand here."

"So?"

"Nobody knows we have these guys. Nobody knows how much there is but us and them." I nodded my head toward the Greenblatts.

"I hope you're not saying what I think you're saying."

"Listen, you're not getting any younger and they passed you over for that promotion."

Ed saw the opening and plunged in. "You can keep the money," he said. "It's not that important to us." Not important enough to go to prison for, he was thinking.

Woodbeck's face reddened and he turned to me. "What kind of agent do you think I am? When this is over, I want a new partner."

Ed plowed ahead. "If you just let us go, we won't say anything about it."

"Shut up, Ed!" Woodbeck barked.

"Yes, sir."

"I was just thinking about your wife," I said to Don. "If you don't want to think about yourself, that's fine. But what about her? The insurance isn't going to cover..."

"Leave her out of this."

I pushed. "She needs the operation. You should do it for Carol."

"Don't say my wife's name when we're undercover, okay?"

"It's only money," Ed suggested. "How's that compare to someone's life? It doesn't."

"Doctors are expensive," added Sam.

Woodbeck began to tear up. I couldn't believe it, but he did. Without another word, he stopped the car on the side of the road. He nodded slightly and I jumped out, unlocked the rear doors and pulled Ed and Sam out.

"You'll never see us again," said Ed.

"Just the cost of doing business," said his brother.

I started to unlock their handcuffs but they couldn't wait. They took off running.

I yelled after them. "Hey, let me get those off!"

But they were booking it down the road. I turned just in time to see a police car drive past us.

"Let's go, let's go, let's go!" Don shouted.

He turned the car around and we headed in the opposite direction. From the side mirror I could see the police pull up next to these two guys in suits running down the road with their hands cuffed behind their backs. They had some explaining to do—but nowhere in their story would there be anything about dirty IRS agents Brown and Schwartz.

. . .

A STING WHERE the victim walked away thanking you for taking their money, like with the Greenblatts, we called a "soft" sting. A sting where we had to pull guns we called a "hard" sting. Some were harder than others.

Preparation for a sting was like rehearsing scenes in a movie. We would gather at Don's apartment and lay out the script. This was no two-man show either. Milwaukee Jim and Digger Dave, a barrel-chested redneck with a high-pitched voice, were regulars. Milwaukee Jim didn't like my influence on Don. I was the young guy but I had replaced him as Don's right-hand man. He didn't dig that "the punk kid" was running things. Jim wore moccasins and smelled of incense but he was the pit bull of our crew. Fortunately, Don held the leash.

The rest of our crew was a cast of characters we could call on depending on the mission. Rod Wilkerson, nickname Big Red, was a Vietnam vet with red hair, a red beard, a wife, and kids. Richard Lewis was more Elliott Gould Jewish and from Boston. He was a friend of Marino's and the dentist put us together. Lewis was a tough street kid, an expert on drugs who carried around a medical drug-testing kit. He was a heroin addict and always high on something. He also wrote bad poetry, and I could never figure out which was a worse character flaw. His poetry bored the shit out of me.

Jack the Ripper was a friend of Lewis's. I never knew Jack's real name. A small Irish guy, he was the oldest in our crew, in his late thirties, another Vietnam vet, and our most deadly crew member other than Milwaukee Jim. I never wanted to hang out with him because I wasn't sure of his loyalties other than to Lewis.

From Minnesota was Jim Partridge, a long-haired but well-dressed Robert Plant type. He wasn't a particularly tough guy but he liked to be where the action was. Apparently that extended to his girlfriends, one of whom was also dating Reggie Jackson at the time.

Bucky Walsh looked like a cross between Moe from the Three Stooges and a Chicago bouncer. In fact, his dad was a Chicago cop. He was ripped, a serious weightlifter, the most muscular member of the crew. Once we were at an off-campus party and someone said something they shouldn't have to Bucky. The guy was backed up by three of his friends. I was ready to come to Bucky's aid.

"Don't need your help," he said.

He took all of them out on his own. He even "curbed" one of them: beat him up, laid him on his stomach, opened his mouth onto a concrete curb and kicked him in the head, knocking out his teeth. It was nice knowing Bucky was around—and on our side.

We even had two women, Janet and Joanna, our hippie chicks. Janet was tall with long brown hair; Joanna was small with curly brown hair. Both were about nineteen, smelled like patchouli oil, and loved to get stoned. Janet and Joanna saw Don and I as counterculture heroes, rebels in the drug world who ripped off the nasty dealers and spread weed among the people. Right on, brothers and sisters! I didn't think we were exactly hippie Robin Hoods but if other people did, that was cool.

Other than the phony cover of being cops, surprise was our greatest asset and that was why we had Joanna and Janet in the group. "They don't expect a girl to rip them off," I told them.

"Woman," said Joanna sharply.

"Yeah, right. Women's lib," Woodbeck sneered.

There was also my lifelong friend Marc, who looked like he could be my brother, but taller and with curly hair. He had followed me out to Arizona State and was a theater major. He was truly a "lobster" and never felt comfortable with the stings. He was just doing whatever his best friend did. But I hoped his acting skills would help him get over on our targets.

I was the writer and director of each sting, each movie I imagined in my head. I would always think about where the camera would be, what would be seen on the screen, what was happening behind the scenes.

Don was the producer, providing the material and the encouragement. Whenever I doubted I had the courage to do something, he would push me. "Don't worry, you can do it," he'd say. My own father never did that.

We even had a little Hollywood glitz. Each of us wore around our neck a symbol of our gang—a small gold fist on a chain. It wasn't quite like Hollywood, though, since we didn't have any stuntmen taking our places for the action scenes. My first sting where shots were fired was life or death.

5

Bullets and Bikers

Glazer told ... a story that has struck some listeners as more bizarre than many that make it to the silver screen.

—*Los Angeles Times*, May 6, 1984

DON KNEW EVERY dealer and delinquent around, every nook and cranny in the underworld. He had been a deliveryman or middleman for drug deals throughout the sunny Southwest and beyond. One of the major weed dealers in the Phoenix area was a fast-talking know-it-all New York transplant named Hondo, whose long, curly hair reminded me of Tommy Chong. Hondo lived in Sin City, a perfect location for an entrepreneur selling to college students, a regular neighborhood weed bank. He was in a perfect place for us too. We needed enough "show weed" to impress prospective victims. We sure weren't going to buy any, like we did for the Boston sting, if we could take it.

Since Hondo would recognize Don, I would be the buyer along with Marc. This was his first sting and, though he wasn't a tough guy and had never done anything like this before, I hoped his acting skills would pull him through. If it wasn't for Bucky stationed as the lookout, Lewis handling communications on a CB, and Don and Jim poised to bust in as phony cops with guns drawn, this would be your average everyday weed deal.

Hondo opened a closet in his apartment. Stacked to the ceiling were hundreds of bricks of weed in red plastic wrappers.

"I have Mexican. I have Acapulco Gold. I have Jamaican," he said proudly, displaying his array of product like a model unveiling the prizes on a game show.

"Come on, I want you to try them," said the super salesman. Also in the apartment were two black guys in their late twenties. Even though it was just six in the afternoon, one of them was sleeping in the back bedroom. I had my .38 in a holster under my left armpit and my .25 in a pocket. Marc had a .32, a silver-barreled, pearl-handled Saturday Night Special he bought at The Jewel Box.

"Marc's the tester," I told Hondo, an excuse to avoid smoking on the job. Besides, I already knew what Hondo's "Mexican, Acapulco Gold, Jamaican" really was—Mexican, Mexican, Mexican. It was "powder weed." For the good stuff, the growers poured Coke onto the bricks to get the air out and make the grass stick together better. They didn't do that for the cheap crap like Hondo had. When you broke open one of those bricks, the marijuana dust would fly all over the place.

It didn't matter. Marc was getting high.

"It's the best," Hondo lied. "Knew you'd like it. Now ..."

He wanted to see our money for the buy. With my right hand I dug into my pocket and showed him a thick wad of our "flash cash."

With my left hand, I drew my .38.

"POLICE! DON'T MOVE! YOU'RE UNDER ARREST!"

Marc drew his gun too—and the barrel fell off.

Fortunately, at the same moment, Don and Milwaukee Jim rushed in the front door.

"Hey, the Duck's here," said a surprised Hondo. Woodbeck's nickname was Donald Duck. "You're a ...?"

"Shut the fuck up!" said Don.

He saw Marc trying to reattach the gun barrel.

"How cheap was that sonuvabitch?" Don asked him.

Marc was embarrassed. I ordered him to check out the guy in the back room and bring him to us. Meanwhile, Bucky joined us and began shoving the weed bricks into bushel baskets.

Marc came back a minute later.

"I can't …"

"Jesus H. Christ, you're a freakin' mosquito!" Don brushed past him.

In the bedroom, the black guy was hiding under the bed and wouldn't come out. Marc had threatened to shoot him if he didn't. But the guy just didn't believe Marc.

Don kicked the bed. "We're taking you to jail, cocksucker!"

He believed Don.

We finished the sting as usual, with the victims standing facing the wall and us backing out of the room with the booty, this time weed instead of cash. As part of his punishment, we made Marc carry the baskets of weed to the trunk of Don's car. He was also demoted from gun-carrying operative to handling communications. Our lives were in the hands of the guys we went into battle with. We couldn't trust someone who let his gun barrel fall off. It was the last sting Marc was a part of—at least with Don. Many years down the road, I would give him a role in a sting that had a very different ending.

I went back to my apartment with Marc and Lewis. I was feeling pretty good about things. After we ripped off a dealer, they would trash-talk us on the street but it just wasn't worth the trouble for them to do anything else. They never could be sure if we were undercover cops gone bad. If we were, they did not want to tangle with us. So they would just move on and hope to avoid us in the future.

A knock on the door.

Lewis cracked it open. A black guy asked, "Is Greg around?" I often used "Greg" as my alias. I also used "Ringo," in honor of Johnny Ringo, the TV cowboy.

"Greg who?" Lewis hadn't been seen by the men at Hondo's and didn't know the man.

"We traced him here. Hondo wants his weed back or the money. One or the other."

Lewis looked behind the man and spotted a sniper on the roof of the adjoining apartment building. And another gunman behind a tree.

Lewis slammed the door shut. "Guys with guns," he said.

I pulled back the curtain on the sliding glass door just enough to survey the area in front of the apartment. Hondo's men were everywhere.

"Shit."

They had us.

"You're not cops," yelled the black guy still at the door. "The weed or the cash!"

"Get away from the door or I'll put one through it," I warned, my .38 in hand.

"I knew I shouldn't have done this," said Marc. He was nervous. So was I. I called Don.

"I'm not giving them the weed," he said.

"Well, I'm not giving them the money."

"So take them out," he said calmly. "They're low-level punks. They won't do anything."

"Don, they just might try to kill us. Even if they don't, if there's a shootout, the cops will come and we'll be in deep shit. I don't see how we're going to get out of here."

There was silence for a moment.

"All right, just stall them. I got this." He hung up.

We took stock of our arsenal: I had a 9mm semiautomatic carbine with a banana clip, a fourteen-shot .45, and my .38. Marc had his defective .32 and a Walthers PPK. Lewis had a .357. We also had our "walking around" weapons, the Colt .25s.

"We should call the cops," Marc said. He was starting to panic.

Lewis took down the crossbow I had on the wall. Karen thought it was a ridiculous decoration but forgave me because "boys will be boys."

"Who do you think you are, one of the Three Musketeers?" I asked. "Put that away. We'll probably put an arrow through ourselves with that."

Marc was coming unglued. "I don't want to get killed."

We moved the couch beneath the window and turned the coffee table on its side behind it. We put the dining room table on its edge to cover the sliding glass door. We tore the apartment to pieces, using every piece of furniture there was to block entrances and give us some cover.

But this wasn't the movies. If there was going to be a gunfight, a couch and a coffee table weren't going to do us much good.

"What if they all start coming towards us?" Marc asked.

"Stay low," I told him.

"I shouldn't be in the middle of this."

I looked out the front window. In the courtyard, in plain sight in front of the apartment building, was Don Woodbeck, bare-chested, a sawed-off shotgun in one hand, a carbine in the other, two shotgun sashes across his chest, and two handguns tucked into his pants.

"I'm Donald Wood-dick!" he screamed. "I'll stick my cock up your ass and leave splinters!"

Amazingly, he had walked right through Hondo's men and was now facing them, his back to us. Like I said, he had that swagger.

"Jeezus, the guy's nuts," Marc said. "He's going to get himself killed."

"Come and get some!" yelled Don. "I'll kill all of you mother-fuckers!"

Silence. They wanted to shoot him, they sure did, but in that split second they had to decide, their own sense of self-preservation took over and they figured maybe that wasn't the best course of action.

Within seconds, we could no longer see any of Hondo's men. They vanished.

I opened the door and Don strode in. "How ya doin', ya ole horse thief?" he said. "Told ya they wouldn't do anything. The small, quiet ones are the ones you have to watch for. The ones with the big mouths never do shit."

"What about you?" I asked.

"Oh, I'd do something," he said with a smile. "All they had to do was shoot first." He had his code and he kept to it, just like in the westerns.

"They're going to come back," said Marc as he wiped the sweat from his forehead. "Can we stay at your place?"

"You and Glazer," he said. "This ain't no slumber party." Lewis would have to find his own sanctuary.

From his apartment, Don called Hondo.

"You don't live here any longer," he told him. "You're gone."

"What do you mean?"

"I'm buying you a plane ticket back east. You either leave or you're dead."

"But I can't..."

Don drove to Hondo's apartment, found his car, and put a couple hundred dollars under the windshield wiper.

Don wouldn't have shot him dead in cold blood. But Hondo couldn't be so sure of that. We never heard from Hondo again.

. . .

BECAUSE HE HAD been one of the deliverymen, Don knew what J.D.'s smuggling trucks looked like and the place where they crossed the border, far from any government checkpoint. My idea was for us to pretend to be U.S. Border Patrol agents and intercept them. Just in case anything went wrong, I figured it'd be easier to pull off the sting a couple miles south of the border, near Yuma.

I looked forward to putting another hurt on J.D.

We weren't able to find Border Patrol insignias for our two vehicles, but we did obtain Yuma Sheriff's Department decals. Digger Dave's Chevy Impala and my yellow Ford Galaxie with the green interior looked enough like cop cars to have the desired effect on pollos driving trucks full of weed.

For the uniforms we went to a Yuma "One-Hour Martinizing" dry cleaners. Cops get an allowance to have their uniforms dry-cleaned, so there were always racks of them. Don and I went in and I asked if the attendant could look in back for my clothes, nonexistent of course. Don jumped over the counter and snatched several Yuma Police uniforms. We were out of there before the attendant returned.

Don, Milwaukee Jim, Digger Dave, and I based ourselves in a horrible, roach-infested Mexican motel with no air conditioning that made Motel 6 look like a Vegas resort paradise. With all of our gear in the cars, we headed out for our first stakeout. Near the spot Don told us about, we slapped the decals on our cars and scanned the road with binoculars—and waited. And waited.

Oh, there were trucks that came by. But they were carrying tomatoes, oranges, and grapes, not grass.

Finally Don spotted a possible smuggler. We leaped into our cars and cut the truck off.

We opened the back. It was filled with furniture.

We went to the motel to sleep. The next morning we tried again.

And we waited. Lying flat on our stomachs for hours, we waited.

"Bingo." Don spotted two white panel trucks headed our way.

"Are you sure?" Digger Dave asked in frustration.

Don stared at him.

We hurried to the intercept point, pulled over both trucks and badged the Mexican drivers. We opened the rears of each truck—each was stacked with stereos, cheap stereos. "Sonuvabitch!" I was pissed. Two days in the desert and two nights in a stinkin' motel and we had nothing to show for our efforts.

"Hold on." Don crawled into the back of one of the trucks and pushed aside the stereo boxes like a swimmer against the current. He reached the back wall. Nothing. He looked around. Then he tapped the back wall. There was a hollow sound. Don found the edge of the wall at a corner and pulled. The wall came down.

Behind it were hundreds of bricks of weed, probably 1,500 pounds. A Great Wall of Weed. There was the same in the other truck. The

Mexican drivers stood there scared shitless. While we maneuvered them in front of the trucks, leaving only open desert before their eyes, we said we wanted the weed but we didn't want them.

At first they didn't understand what we were getting at. We repeated it. Then the light bulbs turned on over their heads. They took off running, just like the Greenblatts.

Milwaukee Jim and Don knew the out-of-sight trail across the border so they took the trucks. Digger Dave and I drove the cars back.

We had nailed J.D. hard in the pocketbook again. I wondered if he was going to hit back.

· · ·

MOST STINGS PLAYED out according to the script. "Count me out the money," Don told a buyer named O'Malley who wanted 400 pounds of the weed we got from J.D. for $50,000. O'Malley was new to the game, a pudgy, thirty-something truck driver type who wanted to make a score. We hoped his innocence—and his fear of getting caught—would work in our favor.

In the fading light of dusk, Don and O'Malley were inside the unit we rented at U-Stor-It. We kept the 1,500 pounds of grass there, right in the middle of an otherwise middle-class, residential neighborhood. Beyond the facility's chain-link fence was a dusty alley several feet wide before the backyards of the houses on the next block. All that weed and someone else guarded it for us. What a sweet deal.

O'Malley carefully wetted his fingers every now and then to make sure none of the twenty-dollar bills stuck together. Don quickly put his hand on his elbow, halting his counting.

"Did you hear something?" Don asked.

"No. What?"

"Thought I heard something. Never mind, keep going. You're sure you weren't followed?"

"No," O'Malley said, suddenly not quite so sure.

"You have a gun?" Don asked.

"No." O'Malley wiped the sweat from his forehead with his hand.

"Well, that's okay. I do," Don said reassuringly.

Suddenly the garage door lifted up. Two Phoenix Department of Public Safety cops stood at the entrance. Of course, they were Bucky and I, wearing DPS dark blue uniforms with yellow stripes down the sides of the pants. We rented them from a costume shop.

"POLICE! YOU'RE UNDER ARREST!" we shouted, our guns leveled at Don and O'Malley.

Up went their hands. O'Malley, who had never been busted before, was visibly shaking.

I moved Don and O'Malley against a wall, handcuffed and searched them, and read them their rights. O'Malley was so distraught his face turned red. I hoped he wasn't about to keel over from a heart attack.

"Officer Walsh, search the area," I ordered. "I'll call in the collar. We'll wait here for backup."

Bucky exited the storage unit and so did I, leaving Don and O'Malley handcuffed but alone. Bucky and I walked a couple dozen yards away.

"I don't believe this, brother," Don said to O'Malley. "All that weed I'm losin'."

"Holy shit, all my money," said O'Malley. "Holy shit!"

"They've got us pretty good."

"I don't want to go to jail, Don."

Don looked around. "Hey, no one's here."

"What?"

"They're way over there. They're not even watching."

"So?"

"I left the side door open. Why don't we get out of here?"

"I don't know…"

"You want to spend ten years behind bars?"

"Jeezus."

"They didn't take our IDs. They don't know who we are."

"Jeezus."

"We got to go and we got to go now, brother."

O'Malley wouldn't move!

So Don took off first, hoping he'd follow. Bucky and I turned around expecting both of them to be gone but O'Malley was still standing there. I had no choice. I took out my .38—and fired over his head.

Finally O'Malley started running, still cuffed behind his back. He ran through the alley and into a backyard and jerked his head around to see if we were following … and ran smack into a swing set, one of the plastic seats hitting him right in the throat. He fell to the ground. It isn't easy to get up when you're handcuffed but he struggled to his feet, and then kept running.

The next day, O'Malley called Don to thank him for saving his ass. He was out $50,000. But he was grateful for avoiding an arrest and probably jail.

Don stroked his ego big time.

"Know what you were like yesterday, the way you were running?" he asked.

"What?"

"You were a gazelle, that's what you were, a gazelle."

"I guess I was, wasn't I?" O'Malley said proudly.

"You sure were."

Everyone walked away happy. In fact, O'Malley was so appreciative of what Don had done for him that he later agreed to another buy from Don.

We stung him again. That time he wasn't so happy.

∙ ∙ ∙

WHEN A STING strayed from the script that's when it became dangerous.

For most baby boomers who grew up in the '60s and '70s, patchouli oil reminds them of flower power and tie-dyed T-shirts. Patchouli oil reminds me of sitting next to Joanna in a van outside a motel in Phoenix getting ready to sting a bunch of biker badasses.

She made the connection, promising 5,000 hits of speed, pills delivered in what were called "pillows." The price was $50,000. I would usually play the inside but I knew the younger brother of one of the bikers and he knew me. Milwaukee Jim would have to go instead. He would bring in the show-bag. The bikers would have the $50,000. Once Jim saw the cash, he'd flash the curtain as the signal for us to supposedly bring in the rest of the speed. We'd come in and make the "bust."

"We'll give you seven minutes, that's all," I told Jim as we sat in our grossly orange van. Joanna was nervous, very nervous. "They're gonna have guns," she said.

"So do we, darlin'," said Don reassuringly. "We come in, flash badges, and we get out. Like popcorn."

"What if something goes wrong?"

"Get low and get outta my way," said Don.

"Showtime," I announced.

Don and I noted the time on our watches. Jim and Joanna stepped out of the van and walked to the door.

He knocked and the window curtain was pulled aside for a second. The door opened and we could hear the loud, hard thump of Black Sabbath. Jim and Joanna disappeared into the dimly lit room, the door closing behind them.

One minute…

I didn't like the idea of hitting bikers. They were too unpredictable, didn't play by the rules.

Two minutes…

When we hit them would they even give a fuck if we were cops? There was a knot in the pit of my stomach.

Three minutes…

Don looked out the van's side window at the motel room. I checked my .38. This time I put a bullet in the first chamber. I might not have time for a second shot.

Four minutes…

"Anything?"

Don shook his head.

Five minutes…

I could see Woodbeck getting nervous.

Six minutes…

He shook his head and said, "Let's go."

"But it's not time."

"Now, now, NOW!"

He ran to the motel door and busted it open.

"POLICE! FREEZE!"

I was right behind him, with my .38 leading. But the door was slammed on my hand and a shot went off.

I forced the door open again and one of the bikers was on me. Another had jumped Don, who wrapped the leather strap around his hand and hit the biker in the face with his ringful of keys. The man screamed.

Not long after Milwaukee Jim had entered the room, the bikers grew suspicious and attacked him. They were going to do worse to Joanna. If we had waited another minute, they would have been done for.

Our entrance gave Jim a chance to turn the tables and he went after a biker who was in the bathroom shooting up. The gang's leader was in a wheelchair, the result of a collision with a semi, and out of the action.

The biker who went after me was a small guy, the younger brother I knew, and he was kicking my ass as we rolled around on the floor. Finally I got him off me and put my gun to his head. I didn't realize that the head biker was sitting on his own weapon. Don did. When the disabled biker pulled his gun on me, Don kicked over his wheelchair and disarmed him.

We took control and rushed out of the room. But two armed security guards running to the scene spotted us.

"HEY!"

We jumped into the back of the van and Jim took the wheel.

"STOP!"

The guards fired several shots at us.

Don leveled his .38 at them.

"Don, don't shoot!" I didn't want us to be shooting cops, even if they were rent-a-cops.

"They're shooting at us!"

"We're getting away … NOW!"

We skidded out of the parking lot and only slowed down after a couple miles. So we wouldn't attract attention, we cruised down a residential street. But the cops wouldn't be far behind. After a few minutes, we reached a Sambo's restaurant with a crowd of people outside.

"Get in there and mix with them," I said. I handed Don my gun and badge. "I'll take the van."

"Know what you're doing, college boy?"

"I hope so."

"Me too. If you get caught, you don't know me, right?"

"Right."

Don, Jim, and Joanna hopped out. We would meet back at the apartment later. If we were lucky.

I slipped on my gold-and-red ASU sweatshirt, laid my student books on the passenger seat, put on my horn-rimmed glasses and jammed a Rolling Stones tape into the 8-track.

Within ten minutes, I heard a police siren behind me and a black-and-white pulled me over. In seconds, they were joined by several other squad cars surrounding my van. I took a deep breath.

"Where have you been tonight?" asked the sergeant.

"I pledged a fraternity and we're doing a scavenger hunt. I'm looking for horned toads."

"ASU?" he asked.

"Freshman."

"Have you been drinking?"

"No, sir."

"License please and step out of the vehicle."

He had me recite the alphabet backward. By this time the security guards arrived. They hurried up to the sergeant, who asked, "Is this kid one of them?"

"Don't know," said one guard. "But we fired at the van. Close range."

"Did you get the plate number?"

"No. Everything happened so fast that..."

"How many shots?" asked the frustrated sergeant.

"Four or five. I'm sure we hit it."

"Check it out," the sergeant ordered the uniforms.

I was fucked. It wouldn't just be about this sting either. There would be a domino effect involving the rest of the crew and many of the other stings. If they nailed me here, I might go to prison and never get out.

Their flashlights covered every inch of the outside of the van.

Any moment I expected to hear, "Found one!"

Instead, nothing.

"I know we hit it," said one of the guards. "We had to."

The sergeant was dubious of the ability of the rent-a-cops. "You couldn't have missed?" he sneered.

They were silent.

The sergeant turned to me. "I don't know what you've been up to tonight."

"Nothing, officer."

I think he knew I was involved. But he didn't have anything to go on if the dumb-as-a-board security guards couldn't ID the van or me.

"You could have been in serious trouble, son."

"I know, drinking and driving don't mix."

He handed me back my license. "Yeah, right."

"Thank you, officer."

Relieved, I drove away and turned up the 8-track, "Paint It Black" by the Stones.

Then, suddenly, a few miles down the street...

Chug ... chug ... chug...

The van sputtered and was about to come to a stop. I babied it to the next gas station. A stream of oil was leaking from underneath.

They *did* hit the van. The bullets had bounced off the ground and punctured the oil pan.

It was a close call. Too close.

. . .

WE RELIED ON being first and being worst. If the other guys were scared enough to back down, their brains telling them that was the best way to survive, then we had it made. But sometimes the other guys just didn't care.

I learned that lesson while riding in Don's Grand Prix one day. The music was up loud when we stopped at a light and a lowrider with a couple of gangbangers pulled up even with us. As we went down the highway, Don punched it and sped away. They hit the gas and again drew even with us. One of them gave us the finger. They ran up ahead. Don burned rubber and caught them.

"You don't know who you're messing with!" he yelled.

"Fuck you, asshole!" they shouted back.

They drove ahead a little and pulled onto the shoulder. We pulled up behind. The two of them got out of their car and started walking towards us.

Standing behind Don's car, we drew down on them.

"Phoenix police!"

They didn't have any weapons we could see, so we weren't going to shoot them.

But they kept coming.

"Freeze!" We flashed our badges.

They didn't give a flying fuck.

They would have walked right over us. But before they did, Don and I got back in his car and drove off.

"Do you believe that?" Don said. "There's just no respect for the law these days."

"Uh, Don," I said, "we're not really the law."

"They didn't know that!"

We laughed about the incident but it wouldn't have been so funny if we were in the middle of a sting and our victim didn't respect the badge. That's what would later happen in Ohio.

We had been hitting the local Mexican Mafia so often, getting out of town might not be a bad idea. Too many people, including the police, were getting to know about us. Just like Paladin in the Western TV series when I was a kid, we proudly proclaimed: "Have Gun, Will Travel." So Big Red asked us to do a mission in his neck of the woods, around Canton, Ohio.

It was winter and snow was on the ground. The set-up had Big Red making the connection and Milwaukee Jim and I as the "big time" distributors selling to a major local dealer named Brody, who operated out of an older house in a deteriorating section of town where a lot of hippies lived. We brought with us ten pounds of show weed, wrapped tight and baby powdered in our suitcase.

Inside the buyer's house, Big Red introduced Jim and I. Jim flashed the window blinds and Bucky and Don came through the door, pulled their guns, and "arrested" the buyer. I ripped out the telephone cords.

Everything went according to plan. The only other person in the house was the buyer's wife, a skinny woman named Helen who looked like Olive Oyl, but with glasses. Brody was in his late twenties, six foot two and husky, but he didn't fight being cuffed, which we did to his wife too.

Like popcorn.

Until we put Helen into a separate room, intending to lock it so we would have just a little more time to make our escape.

Brody went bananas. Apparently he thought we were going to do something to her.

"Leave my wife alone!" he screamed. Even though he was cuffed, he knocked Bucky—big, tough Bucky—into a wall. Then he put his head down like a bull and rammed into Don. All of us jumped on top of him trying to drag him to the floor.

"Sir, we are not going to do anything to your wife," I told him, trying to calm him down.

But he wouldn't stop. "You're a fuckin' snitch!" Brody spit at Big Red.

Bucky finally got the upper hand and started wailing on him. We had to drag him off before he killed the guy. The less damage to anybody or any thing during a sting, the less chance of a problem with the police.

While I poured a couple of bricks worth of grass all over the living room to discourage the buyer from calling the police too soon, Don tried to open his safe. Brody got up and slammed into Don again!

Don cocked his gun and put it to Brody's head. The lunatic said, "FUCK YOU!" I saw that Don was pretty tired of this guy. "Don, forget the safe. Let's go." Reluctantly, Don slipped his gun back into his holster.

As we got into our car, freaked out Brody, still handcuffed, bloody, no shirt, no shoes, ran out in the snow and torpedoed our car with his body! He was on the hood when I said, "Game over, man!" and hit the accelerator. Brody rolled off the car and onto the icy street. We left him in our rearview mirror.

But he wasn't finished, even when we returned to Arizona. He had Big Red arrested, the only person he knew among us, had him charged with kidnapping—for moving his wife into the other room with force—and extradited to Ohio. Big Red wouldn't give us up, thankfully, so we were safe. What saved Big Red was the weed. No matter what Brody and Helen said, with all that weed thrown around the house, obviously what had happened was a drug transaction gone wrong. No jury was going to convict one weed dealer on the word of another weed dealer. Big Red was freed.

• • •

FOR A STING in Las Vegas, we wanted to avoid pulling guns. There was just too much security and too many cameras in that Sin City. We would have to give our best performances.

Don was aware that a couple of money collectors would be gambling at the Riviera casino, a short break they usually enjoyed on their way to deliver the drug money to J.D. in Yuma. Don knew them but they had never spoken to him. After watching them play craps until midnight, Don, Digger Dave, and Milwaukee Jim, all dressed in suits—the first time I ever saw Don wear a suit—knocked on the door of their room.

"Sirs, we are agents of the United States Internal Revenue Service," said Don, loud and strong. "Please open the door."

When the Mexicans did so, Don flashed his Treasury Department badge. "We have information you may be carrying money from drug transactions. May we search your room?"

"No, no, no," said one of the surprised Mexicans. "We won money in casino tonight."

"We have been tracking your activities. You will need to explain the money you have in your possession." He could see a bit into the room and spotted a briefcase lying on the bed. Don figured J.D.'s loot was inside. "We would like to examine that briefcase."

The Mexicans were worried.

"You need a search warrant, yes?" one of them asked.

Don's expression said, "Don't piss me off, pal." His words said, "We can call for a search warrant right now."

The two Mexicans broke into a heated argument with each other in Spanish.

The Riviera's hotel manager, accompanied by a bellboy, interrupted them.

"Someone called saying there was a disturbance. It's late. Please keep your voices down for our guests trying to sleep." His hotel name tag read Dylan Kushner. "Is there something I can do to help?"

Don explained that they were IRS agents and they would get a search warrant for the entire room unless the Mexicans showed them what was in the briefcase.

Kushner thought for a moment.

"How about this," he suggested. "While you gentlemen obtain a search warrant, the hotel will put the briefcase in question in our safe. Then you don't have to go through the room of our guests here."

Don wasn't happy.

"You don't have a warrant at this moment," Kushner reiterated.

"You will have to answer for this later," Don said, "and you're responsible for anything that happens to that briefcase."

"Gentlemen, *por favor?*" said the manager. The Mexicans nodded in agreement.

"One of my men will be stationed outside this door," Don told them, pointing to Digger Dave. "No one is to leave this room." He turned to Kushner: "I will accompany you to the safe."

The Mexicans handed the hotel manager the briefcase.

"Thank you for your cooperation," said Kushner. "The Riviera would be pleased to comp your room for tonight."

"*Gracias.*"

"You know what, how about we give you tickets to the show tomorrow night too, and dinner is on us as well."

"*Gracias. Muchas gracias.*" They were grateful.

As soon as the door closed, they were on the phone to J.D.'s lawyer to figure out how to get out of this.

As soon as the door closed, Digger Dave left his post and met up with Don and Milwaukee Jim downstairs.

That's how we lifted $25,000 off J.D.

Jim Partridge played the bellhop. Hotel manager Dylan Kushner was one Craig Glazer.

. . .

CASH WAS MORE valuable to us than weed. Any weed we ripped off was more useful to pump prime a sting than to sell.

I convinced Karen to stash some of it at her condo—and she was not happy about that. Or about the fact that Don was trying to convince me to leave ASU. I was still going to college even as I was ripping off drug dealers and having gunfights. Don didn't see the point of me going to classes and eventually getting a diploma when we were already doing so well. But I figured that sometime soon I'd stop doing stings and go straight. I wasn't a lifelong criminal like Don. I wanted a career I could tell my mother about. I could quit the life anytime I wanted, right? Then maybe I could turn my adventures into a movie. Now wouldn't that be something!

"If you're going to go to classes," Don said, "then you need a bodyguard."

Through the underground we heard about threats on our lives from everyone from the Mexican Mafia to biker gangs. I didn't want to be shot and killed. So we were almost always armed. Don and I also tried not to go out in public alone. But he sure as hell wasn't going to class with me.

We paid Jack the Ripper fifty dollars a day to hang around with me on campus. He was clearly older and stuck out like a sore thumb but in classes with fifty or sixty students he was anonymous. My professors never asked about him.

One day, I was in humanities class. We were discussing philosophers such as Kierkegaard and Nietzsche. I liked Nietzsche, especially his belief that "what doesn't kill you only makes you stronger." I sure could relate to that.

Jack was falling asleep, as usual. I poked him to keep him awake. He shuddered and his .38 fell out of his shoulder holster underneath his denim jacket and onto the floor.

CLINK!

A girl near us heard the sound and looked around for what may have dropped.

"Oh, there's your... It's a gun!"

A male student jumped up: "GUN!"

All of the students moved away from us. "Someone please call security," said the professor, who was now looking at his seating chart.

Jack and I quickly walked out of the room. But a few days later I was given a note that I was to report to the assistant dean's office.

"Whose gun was it?" he asked.

"I don't know."

"I was told you didn't react. You just sat there?"

"I was daydreaming."

"You came to class with someone and left with him. Who was he?"

"Sorry, I don't know."

That was the last time I was on campus.

Just over a year after coming to Arizona to go to college, my life had completely changed. I had thought that someday I'd be a lawyer. Now I was on the other side of the law.

6

Kill or Be Killed

His life is somewhat of a fantasy world, fueled by reality. It's the game. It was like playing cowboys and Indians and cops and robbers. Craig, as a little boy, would say, "Bang. I'm dead" and close his eyes. When he was dead long enough he'd get up and say "I'm okay." (Now) it doesn't work like that.

—Stanford Glazer, *Los Angeles Times*, December 3, 1984

IT'S NOT GAMBLING if you know you'll still be rich after you leave the table. That's just entertainment. Excitement is all about putting up more money than you can afford to lose. That's the incredible feeling you get when you risk your life, whether you're a policeman, fireman, bungee jumper, or sting artist. The adrenaline pumps through you as much from fear as the possibility of victory. That feeling is why boxers keep on fighting past their prime. They can't get that sensation doing anything else.

But having success doing stings was like shooting heroin. I knew that if I wanted to avoid the crash that would surely come, I would have to give up the drug, but I just couldn't give up the stings. I wanted that high over and over again.

As much as I questioned whether I was truly going after J.D., as much as I noticed that members of the crew were getting a little sloppy in our preparation—they wouldn't show up for rehearsal or they'd leave early—I couldn't give it up. When it came to stings, I had a full-grown jones.

Success didn't make us filthy rich. The stings were expensive. Don and I paid each of the crew like employees: $300 to be the lookout, $500 if you carried a gun or were on the inside. We also paid all of the other costs—travel, hotels, cars, show weed and pills, etc.

But we did all right. With the assistance of our accountant, John Walters, we made down payments on several expensive condo townhouses in the Mummy Mountain area around Scottsdale and took out a lease option on the Badler Estate mansion in fancy Clearwater Hills, one of the first gated communities in Arizona back in the '50s.

Walters was a meek guy, the favorite accountant for the local country club crowd. We gave him our ill-gotten gains and he'd pool it with other real estate investments, essentially laundering the money, making it clean. When we would later sell the properties, we would be able to claim the profits as legit and keep the IRS off our backs. I knew that tax evasion, not murder or robbery, was how they put away Al Capone.

Don and I lived in one of the townhouses and used another as a storage facility where we could keep hundreds of pounds of weed to impress potential buyers. We had weed stashed all over town. Putting everything in one place might be a problem in case of trouble. We needed easy access. But we didn't buy flashy, outrageously expensive cars or live high on the hog. We kept a low profile.

I don't know what Don spent his extra money on, other than Tony Lama boots. He never seemed to have any cash on him. I saved as much as I could, thinking of the future. Don could never think past next week. For a while, we talked about opening a Phoenix branch of the San Francisco clothing store North Beach Leather. But, in the end, Don just didn't want to go straight.

After every sting, I wondered if there would be another.

Don would always say, "There'll be plenty."

Maybe I was hoping they would naturally dry up. Because if they didn't, I wasn't so sure I could ever step away.

. . .

KAREN STARTED WORK at Bobby McGee's, a hot new Scottsdale restaurant and nightclub created by Bob Sikora. Each of the waitresses dressed in a different costume; Karen was a Playboy Bunny. Back at her condo she kept some weed for us and about $10,000 in cash, in case there was an emergency, such as the need for a quick getaway out of town.

When her birthday came around, I drove to Bobby McGee's armed with a dozen roses to celebrate with her. She said she didn't feel like going out after work. My heart sank.

Something was wrong. We had been arguing a lot the last few weeks. More and more she wanted me to dump Woodbeck—and more and more Woodbeck was telling me to dump Karen.

"Hell yeah, you want to graduate college," Don said with a nasty voice. "You want to marry Karen. You'll have kids. You'll have a JOB! Then what?"

"Well…"

"I'll tell you what … the JOB will suck. But you stick it out. Years and years. Every day you go home after a hard day's work and have a few beers. On Saturdays you sit in your favorite chair and watch the Sun Devils on TV. You get a beer gut and promise to lose weight but never do. The kids grow up, move out, don't have time to visit pops. And Karen ain't looking like she used to either. You're bored, you're old, you're miserable. Know what happens then?"

"Well…"

"I'll tell you what happens then—you get sick and you die. The wifey collects the insurance because that's the only damn money you've got left. A few people show up at the funeral and say what a great guy you were. Blah, blah, blah. Then she marries some other asshole."

But I was in love, and love is deaf, dumb, and blind. The day after getting blown off for her birthday, I bought a $2,000 engagement ring from The Jewel Box pawnshop, of course, and asked her to come by. I was going to ask her to marry me.

She pulled up to my townhouse in a huge black Cadillac Eldorado. That was odd. Her car was a baby blue Mustang convertible. I walked out to meet her, the engagement ring in my hand.

"Whose car is that?" I asked.

"It's Bob's," she said. She handed me a brown paper bag. Inside was $10,000.

"You're too good to be involved with Woodbeck," she said. "He's going to get you in deep trouble."

"What are you talking about?"

"Bob says you're going to get me in trouble too."

"Maybe I'll pay Bob a visit," I said angrily.

"Leave him alone, Craig. I'm seeing him."

I felt like I had been hit in the stomach by a sledgehammer.

"But he's twice your age!"

"You were busy doing other things, busy with Woodbeck. Bob was here for me."

I slipped the ring into my pocket.

"I love you, Craig. You're the first man I ever slept with. But I can't be with you."

She got back in Sikora's Cadillac and drove away.

When I told Don about our breakup, he laughed.

"She said you were her first? Hard to believe that." Sometimes Don could be a totally insensitive asshole. "She did you a favor, man."

"Didn't you ever love a girl that much?"

He had been going out with a waitress at Coco's named Zana. I didn't think it was serious but Don's sudden silence made we wonder.

Still, maybe he was right. If I had stayed with Karen, what kind of movie would that make? They don't make movies about guys who get married and have kids and go home after a hard day's work and have a few beers. They make a movie about you if you do something extraordinary. Then they put you up on the screen ten feet high.

Then maybe your life means something.

Then maybe you don't ever really die.

. . .

WALTERS FLEW TO Florida and Don went with him to scout for more property to buy. While there, Don called me. He said a real estate broker in Phoenix who needed some fast cash wanted to get his hands on a quantity of weed so he could sell it. I refused to be a dealer but Don said this would be a quick and easy transaction because the guy lived not far from our stash condo. We weren't the ones doing the selling. It was just a matter of transportation.

"No muss, no fuss," said Don. "But be careful. Take Tom with you." Tom, one of Woodbeck's younger brothers, didn't like me much. That was understandable. I guess I had also become a brother to Don.

Tom and I loaded 200 pounds into his car and drove it a few blocks. I thought it was strange to see a handful of men in business suits walking around the neighborhood at 11 a.m. There also seemed to be an unusual number of telephone repair trucks, with workers high up on poles.

We parked a few hundred feet away from the buyer's address and walked to his place to show him a sample brick. He approved and Tom drove up to the house. The buyer and another man came out to meet us and do the unloading.

"I don't know about this," I told Tom. "Let's get out of here as soon as they're done." We watched from a little distance as the two men transferred the weed from the trunk into the house. As they brought in the last bricks, we hopped into Tom's car. Immediately, two cars came out of nowhere, headed right for us.

"HIT IT!" I yelled to Tom, who floored the accelerator.

The two undercover cop cars fishtailed just in time or they would have crashed into us. As Tom plowed across somebody's yard, I had my .25 in hand.

But we were trapped. Squad cars blocked any exit from the street and a police van blocked the alley in back. I threw my gun into the bushes before we stopped, raised our hands in the car, and surrendered.

One of the Department of Public Safety cops found my gun and, for some reason, thought it was Tom's. Maybe it was because I had cut my hair shorter, to look more like a cop, and Tom looked like a troublemaking hippie.

"Hollow points," he said. "Cop killers."

A couple of the uniformed cops grabbed Tom by his hair, pulled him from the car and beat the crap out of him. In the early '70s, cops beating up hippies was nearly an official sport in parts of America.

We were both sent to the Maricopa County jail. Meanwhile the police raided our condos and found 400 more pounds of weed at one of them. We were in jail for two days before Don was able to fly back from Florida and show up with a bail bondsman so we could get released. "Green is taking care of everything," Don said. We called Jordan Green our "fixer lawyer" because he had a knack for being able to fix anything. He had been a deputy Maricopa County attorney and an assistant Arizona attorney general. Green told us, "I'm handling it. You get one free pass. The charges will be dropped on a technicality."

They were. But the Feds, through the IRS, threatened us with a jeopardy tax assessment. They knew about our property and some $47,000 in a safe deposit box.

I tried to explain the cash by saying Grandpa Bennie had given me money and I had gambled and won. But it didn't work for J.D.'s money couriers in Vegas and it didn't pass muster here either. The agents told me that if I did not sign away the property and money in payment for the back taxes, they would continue to investigate the case. But if I cooperated then they would consider it closed.

I signed.

Good thing the woman in charge of the safe deposit boxes at our bank liked me. Before the IRS showed up, she let Don and Walters retrieve the $47,000. Don left behind in the otherwise empty box a paper wrap meant to hold $1,000. It was his way of needling the IRS, saying, "You didn't get everything."

. . .

BEING A CRIMINAL is a full-time job. You are constantly looking over your shoulder.

I went on a movie date with a girl from ASU. After the flick, *The Heartbreak Kid*, I noticed a couple of suspicious-looking Latinos following us. Then, as we got into my yellow Ford, I heard gunfire. I immediately pulled the .25 from my jean pocket.

"Get down!" I told her. "They're shooting at us!"

But when I looked around I realized they were nowhere to be seen. I had heard the backfire from a car.

"Why do you have a gun?" she asked.

"I'm training to be a police officer," I lied.

"I'm not that stupid."

She didn't say another word the entire trip home and I knew she would never return my phone call later.

. . .

DON AND I needed a vacation. By January 1973, we had earned it. We decided to go to Jamaica for the George Foreman–Joe Frazier heavy-weight championship fight set for Kingston and, on the way, stop in Kansas City.

We were at the Kansas City terminal when Stan came up behind us and jokingly stuck his index finger into Don's back, pretending it was a gun. He had no idea about our stings. Fortunately, Don didn't draw on him with his actual handgun.

I desperately wanted to tell my father about our adventures but I didn't. He probably would have told me I was a stupid asshole. Well, he probably would have said that no matter what I had been doing. My mother thought Don was "shifty" and she was suspicious when I told her I was making so much money in real estate deals. But she didn't pry.

I had to tell somebody though, so I revealed my secret life to Andy and my brothers Jeff and Jack, who were now sixteen and seventeen. At the hotel, I opened my briefcase in front of them and they were amazed at the bundles of cash and a couple of Kukhri knives, nasty-looking weapons with curved blades. I strutted around the room with my .38 in my unusual shoulder holster and reenacted scenes with J.D. and Hondo, the bikers and the Greenblatts, and all the rest. To them I was a rock star.

Andy, who really could have been a rock star, had instead become a heroin addict since I had been gone. He had also been in a couple of car wrecks, including one that sent him through the windshield, scarring his face. He also now walked with a limp. For some people, the high point of their life was when they were in high school. Sadly, Andy was one of those people.

I gave each of my brothers $500 as a gift, which impressed the hell out of them. I didn't realize that they would spend it on heroin. Andy had introduced them to the drug. I was livid, and Andy and I would never be close friends again.

"Know any girls?" asked Don. "Let's party."

I'd had a crush on Donna Caruso since high school. She was drop-dead gorgeous, a Sophia Loren type. But I had never gone out with her. Maybe it was because of everything I had been through, and the chutzpah it gave me, but this time I called her.

"Pick me up after school," she said. She was a senior at Shawnee Mission West. "We'll get my friend Carol and go out." I was in Kansas City, my home. I didn't need to bring my gun with me. We were going to have fun.

When we were in New York after the Boston sting, I went to Saks Fifth Avenue and bought some hip new clothes—black high-heeled boots, a white shirt with a wide stiff collar, and a blue double-breasted car jacket that Malcolm McDowell might have worn. I guess I thought I was English and in the rock band Traffic.

That's what I was wearing when I walked down the hallway of the high school.

"I'm looking for Donna Caruso," I asked a trio of football players sitting on a bench.

"Down the hall past the lunch room."

"This way?"

"Yeah. What do you want Donna for?" She was the hottest chick in school. I was invading their territory.

I ignored them and they didn't like that.

"Where did you get those clothes?"

They giggled. Another asked, as a joke, "Are you in a band?"

I tried to brush them off. "Kind of."

"You look like a fag."

The player who said that was an all-state fullback, much bigger than me, probably 200 pounds.

But he had gotten my attention. "What did you say?"

"I said, anyone who looks like that sucks cock." He didn't even bother to stand up from the bench.

The other players laughed. I was nineteen, only a little older than they were, and hardly menacing looking. There were three of them and one of me. I mean, they probably thought, What's he going to do?

I punched the running back in the face. The ring on my hand ripped his cheek wide open. But he was tough. He lurched forward, grabbed me around the waist, and squeezed so hard I could hardly breathe.

I saw Don out of the corner of my eye. He had been waiting in the car.

He ran in at full speed and with one punch leveled one of the players who had risen. Then he nailed the third one. But I still couldn't get the running back off me.

The school bell was now ringing, the classes emptying into the hall. Two other players came to the aid of their teammates as dozens of students gathered around the melee and cheered on their football team.

A teacher grabbed Don from the back. Big mistake. Don turned and, without looking, socked the teacher across the jaw. One of the students yelled, "He hit Mrs. Kendall!" Don had knocked out a female teacher.

The running back had me pinned. Guess he was an all-state wrestler too.

"Give?" he asked.

I knew when I was beat. "Yeah," I said.

He let me up and I scrambled to my feet. Don was still fighting a couple of players. I took him by the arm.

"Don, let's go! The cops are probably coming."

The student body followed us out as we got in our car and took off.

Don was still mad the next day. He returned to the high school and saw the football team jogging around the track. Standing on a small hill, he screamed at them, "I can take all of you!"

Naturally, they came charging up the hill. Don pulled his Kukhri knife from the sheath in his belt and brandished it like a sword.

The players retreated back down the hill.

Don smiled. "Punks."

We couldn't seem to stay out of trouble, not even in Jamaica. Maybe it was because we announced ourselves with a theme song I wrote on the plane and that we kept singing after we landed. To the music of

Dr. Hook's "Cover of the Rolling Stone," which had come out the previous year…

Well we're big dope dealers,
We've got greedy fingers,
And we're loved everywhere we go.
We talk about money and we talk about deals
At 10,000 dollars a throw.
We'll sell you all kinds of pills,
We'll sell you all kinds of thrills,
But the thrill you'll never know
Is the thrill that'll getcha
When we gotcha where we wantcha
And we take you for all your dough.
Rolling Stone, gonna see our picture on the cover,
On the cover of a police portfolio.

I guess we were pretty cocky.

At first, Jamaica was paradise—the sun, the ocean, red bud weed at five dollars a bag, two weeks in Ocho Rios at the Jack Tar Playboy Hotel, and a heavyweight championship fight at the National Stadium.

Frazier was a three-to-one favorite in what they called the "Sunshine Showdown." But Foreman knocked the champ down six times before the end of the second round. "Down goes Frazier!" yelled Cosell. Foreman won the belt with a stunning TKO.

I had bet on Frazier. Maybe my luck was taking a turn for the worse.

We caught the fish, sailed the boat, got the tan. We even hung out with Graham Kerr, famous for his *Galloping Gourmet* cooking show on television, who had a home on the island. He could cook a mean lobster.

But there was no action, no adventure, and no stings. There was no rush.

Then one of the locals told us about a man who sold weed for only three dollars a pound. He put us in touch with the deputy mayor of Ocho Rios, who gave us a tour of the marijuana fields.

"Doesn't the government know about this?" I asked.

He looked at me like I was insane.

"Who do you think is selling the grass, mon?" he replied.

They even had a scheme for exporting the weed. Those large green coconut heads they sold as tourist souvenirs? Each one could carry more than a pound of Mary Jane.

We bought $1,000 worth of weed, stuffed dozens of the silly coconut heads, put them in boxes and went to the post office to mail them to the States. We were only a little concerned when we saw that the post office building also contained the local jail.

"What's in the boxes?" asked the policeman at the post office.

"Coconut heads," I said. "We have a tourist shop."

"What is the name?" he asked. The address I wrote on the boxes was for John Walters, our accountant.

"You wouldn't know it."

He wasn't satisfied.

"What is the phone number, please?"

I made up a number. Little did I think that he would go to a phone and start dialing!

I didn't want to end up in a mud jail. I scooted out of the building and jumped into the Jeep where Don was waiting.

"We could have some trouble. Take off."

We rushed to the airport. But, though we had our return tickets, we didn't realize we needed money for an exit visa. Between us, we only had twenty dollars in our pockets, and it wasn't enough. We couldn't leave the country.

The customs officer looked at the Pulsar watch on Don's wrist. The watch was cutting edge and relatively expensive since it was one of the first to display the time digitally.

"Give me the watch," he said.

"It's worth more than the visa!" Don complained.

"Then we'll have to stay here," I pointed out.

"Fuck." Don gave the watch to the customs officer but he couldn't do it without taking a shot. "Take this and stick it up your ass."

The customs officer slipped the watch onto his wrist and smiled.

We were happy to be going home to the Wild West.

• • •

NOT LONG AFTER we returned to Arizona, we found out that Walters had lost most of our remaining cash to gamblers.

Walters had grown more standoffish since our run-in with the IRS. He wasn't as friendly with us as he had been and neither Don nor I were invited to his parties any longer. Was that any way to treat two guys who had given him a few thousand dollars a week, who brought him from wearing Arrow shirts to Pierre Cardin? We didn't think so.

He had tangled with gamblers who claimed they could fix greyhound races in Miami. They said they could arrange to have the betting line favorites shot up with drugs to make them woozy, just slow enough to lose. All they needed was the cash to make the payoffs. Walters threw in with them as a partner.

Well, the gamblers took his money and never made the payoffs. They won. Walters lost. At least that's the story he told us.

"They got me," Walters said when we confronted him. "They got me good."

"It was our money," Don said.

"I don't know what to do."

"Let me tell you," said Don. "You're going to pay us back."

He promised that he would.

But weeks went by, and instead of us receiving any payments, we noticed that Walters was adding a pool to his house, where he also kept his office. Apparently he had some money somewhere.

We told him to give us the information on the gamblers and we would get our own money back. But he hemmed and hawed and never did give up the info. We became worried he might sell everything he had and bug out, disappear, and we would have no chance at getting our money.

"He's more afraid of them than he is of us," explained Don. Walters didn't take us seriously. I guess he thought it was just Don and I, since we were the only guys he ever saw. We decided to show him he was wrong. Don, Big Red, Bucky, Digger Dave, and I arrived unannounced. Walters wasn't home, so we broke in. As we made our way to his office, his dog, a huge Great Dane, attacked us and tried to rip Don apart. Don shot him with his .38. We found $5,000 and took it. We also left Walters a message.

We put the dead dog in Walters' bed, à la the horse head in *The Godfather*.

Within a few hours, Walters called. He was angry about the dog but said he was willing to settle up with us.

"I have your money," he said.

The five of us again went to his place. Walters was clearly nervous, we assumed because five guys were now confronting him.

"Let's talk in my office. Just you," he said to Don.

In Walters' office, Don got to the point.

"Where's our money?"

"You killed my dog."

"Listen, I'm sorry. But I didn't have any choice."

"Who are the other guys besides you and Craig?"

"Part of the crew. Now where's our money?"

Walters hesitated.

The phone rang and he picked it up. The conversation was one-sided, with Walters agreeing to whatever was being said.

Don sensed that something was wrong. He slapped Walters across the face and quickly headed down the hallway.

"It's a trap! Get out!" he yelled.

The others went out the front; I went out the back. From around the side of the house, I could see the squad cars gathering on the street. Even though I was wearing my fancy high-heeled boots, I took a running start and climbed over the eight-foot concrete wall around the pool. Coming down on the other side, I tweaked both ankles.

I could hear Walters shouting, "One of them went out the back!"

I limped through the housing development, much of which was still under construction. When I came upon a group of Mexicans digging a ditch, probably for a sewer line, I jumped into the hole with them.

"Policia!" I said.

They nodded, and threw me a shovel. I tossed some dirt on myself and started digging.

A police car drove up and an officer asked about a fugitive.

The Mexicans, who couldn't speak English, just shook their heads.

When the car was out of sight, I walked to a house where two kids were playing in the front yard.

"I've been in a car accident," I told them. "I need to use a phone."

"Our mother isn't here," said one of them.

"This is an emergency! Please!"

They let me in and I called a cab. As I finished, their mother arrived.

"Excuse me, young man, what are you doing?"

"I was in an accident."

"That's why those police cars are around?"

"Yes."

"Then we should tell them you're here."

"No, it's okay. I called a cab to pick me up."

Waiting for that taxi was the longest ten minutes of my life. Down the street, I could see a tow truck hauling off my yellow Ford and the police going door-to-door.

I had the cab take me to our fixer lawyer's office. Woodbeck and the others had been arrested at the scene. Green sent me to a hotel while he arranged for the bail money I would no doubt need. Then he had me surrender to the police.

But Walters was now so scared of us that he refused to testify at the preliminary hearing. No doubt he didn't want to reveal anything about what he had been up to either. Without his testimony, there was no case. All of the charges were dropped except for concealed weapons violations for Don, Bucky, Red, and Digger. They paid their fines and walked out the door. But the newspaper article about the incident was the first time any of us were named in public. *The Arizona Republic* even noted the "bizarre twist straight from *The Godfather*," adding that there "was no apparent motive for the alleged break-in and the assault."

Yes, there's no such thing as bad publicity—unless it can put you in jail or in the ground.

· · ·

IN THE SAME instant I saw Don jerk his head up, I felt the cold steel of a gun at my neck.

Don, Milwaukee Jim, and I were having dinner at the Salt Cellar restaurant. J.D. stood to the side, next to me, his gun poking out from under his denim jacket. He and two of his goons—jeans, black work boots, plaid bandannas around their necks—had managed to come around a corner and get the drop on us.

Don would always say "Whoever gets this," tapping the gun in his shoulder holster, "here first," tapping his head, "wins." J.D., suddenly, swiftly, had won. Even with the three of us armed, we were at his mercy.

"Make a move, Woodbeck," said J.D., "and he's dead," meaning me.

"You don't have to do this," Don said.

J.D. tossed a sheet of paper on the table. It was a list of everything he said we had stolen from his operation.

"You owe us $500,000. You have twenty-four hours or we get rid of your little buddy."

Don scanned the list.

"Jesus Christ, J.D., we didn't do *all* of this!"

"Kid, you're coming with us." The larger of his men picked me up by my arm and lifted me out of the booth.

"Bring cash." J.D. smirked. "Or else."

Don started to stand but the younger of J.D.'s men put his hand inside his shirt, onto his gun, and shook his head. Don slid back down.

"That's not enough time to get that kind of money."

"We're not fuckin' around," said J.D.

Woodbeck nodded. "All right." He looked at me. "Sorry, ole buddy."

Sorry, ole buddy? What the fuck did he mean by that? That's it? Good-bye?

"Hey, Don, there's got to be something…"

Don shook his head. "Sorry, man."

J.D. threw a matchbook at Don with a phone number where he could be reached.

"Call tonight."

Don and Milwaukee Jim just sat there as J.D. squeezed me up against one of his men and escorted me out of the restaurant. No one noticed what was going on.

They pushed me at gunpoint up the stairwell to the parking lot and a waiting white Chevy Chevelle. I hoped J.D. would drive and then maybe I'd have a chance to overpower the smaller, younger Mexican.

But the other Mexican now popped open the trunk.

"Get in," said J.D.

"Like hell." I knew that if I got in, I would never come out.

"Get in or I'll plug you right here."

I was hoping someone would drive into the parking lot or someone else would leave the restaurant and get their car. Maybe then I could make a break for it.

The skinny guy holding me was about my age, about nineteen. He began to force me down into the trunk.

I heard the slap of a leather strap.

"Hey, J.D., ya ole horse thief!" Don walked towards us.

"Back off," said J.D.

Slap.

"Hey, come on, let's talk about getting you your money." He slapped the leather against his leg again and kept taking those long strides of his in our direction.

J.D. didn't stop him, so Don kept talking … slap … walking … slap … talking…

He was within just a few feet of us when he slapped the leather again, pulled out his .25 from his back pocket with his other hand, and shot the kid holding me between the eyes.

The kid didn't make a noise. I reached for him but he went limp. I let him go and he crumpled to the ground.

Holy shit.

I had never seen anyone actually shot and wounded before.

J.D. and the other Mexican jumped into the car.

Don tried to aim but I was between him and them.

"Get outta my way!" he yelled.

But J.D.'s car blasted over a concrete curb and sped away.

The kid on the ground had one eye open and the other closed.

"He's dead," Don said. "Let's go."

"We have to find the shell," I told him, not wanting us linked to a murder, even if a jury might decide it was in self-defense.

We looked around for a minute but never found it.

"Let's go, let's go," Don insisted.

We went to a motel and hid out, watching TV. But nothing about a shooting ever appeared on the news. We assumed someone found him. Maybe it wasn't much of a story—some unknown Mexican shot and killed in what was probably a drug deal. I guess he didn't matter.

I felt bad about the kid, later. But if it wasn't him, it would have been me. Don called J.D. and offered a deal. J.D. wanted the weed. Don said all we wanted was the money—and emphasized that we already had both. But if J.D. would give us $50,000, we'd give him his weed back and we'd leave the area. It would be our getaway money. We'd be done. J.D. didn't say yes, didn't say no.

Don told him to go to a shopping mall phone booth the next night. We would call that number at a certain time and give him the exact location for a rendezvous.

"Do you think he'll come?" I asked.

"Don't know," Don said. "But if he does, we have to be ready."

"We're going to rip him off, right?"

"Hell yeah."

I didn't like the sound of his voice—cold, deadly.

"Just a rip-off, right?"

"What do you think?"

"Listen," I said, "I don't want to be part of a hit."

"His men kicked your ass! Remember? That's what got you here with me."

"Yeah, I know. Maybe I should have just moved on and let it go."

"And he was going have you killed at the Salt Cellar."

"Yeah, I know, goddammit!" The Mexican kid had died because of that.

"I was there for you, college boy," Don said pointedly.

He was right. He had saved my life.

"Are you in or out?"

We had been headed toward a shootout at the O.K. Corral ever since I met Woodbeck. I didn't know that then but I knew that now. Sometimes a choice is not a choice.

"Let's do it," I said.

We gathered everyone except for Lewis and Jack the Ripper. We planted ourselves inside and around the storage building behind Janet and Joanna's Mesa house, where we had stashed a few hundred pounds of weed. We told the girls to leave.

At about 10 p.m. we called the phone number. One of J.D.'s men answered. We gave him the address.

I was inside the storage building with Digger Dave and Partridge; Big Red was on the roof of the house and Milwaukee Jim in the bushes out front. Bucky was in the house with Woodbeck, who would bring

J.D. into the storage building. We'd take him down as soon as he opened the door.

Two of J.D.'s men showed up. No J.D. He wasn't as stupid as we had hoped. Don brought them to the locker anyway and opened the door. Digger, Partridge, and I had our guns in their faces.

POP! POP! POP! POP!

Shots came from everywhere.

J.D. had snipers all around us.

Partridge and I hit the ground and the two men at the door ran. Digger chased after one of them and wrestled him down but the other made it into the living room of the house. But he wasn't there long. Bucky threw him through the sliding glass door.

I fired back at the gun flashes.

Suddenly, a black Mustang at full speed crashed through the rear wooden gate and landed in the backyard.

Don, his .38 in hand, ran straight toward it. The driver fired at him through the windshield, smashing the glass. Don jumped onto the hood and shot twice through the windshield at the driver—it was J.D.

The Mustang spun around and Don slid off the hood. J.D. blasted through the fence on his way out.

In a moment, all was quiet. J.D. and his men were gone.

Don calmly walked out of the darkness.

"Everybody up. Let's get out of here," he said. We could hear police cars speeding our way.

"Anybody hit?" I asked.

Blood was filling Don's right shoe.

"Bullet?"

I took a look at his ankle. "No, glass."

"I got him," Don said. "He can't be far."

"There's no time."

As we sprinted to the street in front of the house and hopped into Don's Grand Prix, the Phoenix police arrived, their cars screeching to a stop. I jumped out and badged them.

"Go, go, go!" I yelled. They tried to ask questions but I kept waving them in the direction of J.D.'s car. "That way. They're getting away! Take them!"

We fled in the opposite direction, passing several police cars and an ambulance, their sirens wailing.

We heard they found J.D.'s car a few blocks away and that there was a lot of blood inside. Woodbeck swore he shot him point-blank twice. But the police did not find J.D. and we never heard anything about him being killed.

Getting my revenge on J.D. didn't happen the way I envisioned it. I was glad Don shot him but it wasn't clean, wasn't tit-for-tat, wasn't the end of the story. It was dirty and messy. I thought I would feel satisfied.

Instead I felt lost.

• • •

IT WAS THE summer of 1973 and I was twenty years old. During the previous two years, Don and I pulled off about thirty stings, from Arizona to Ohio, Boston to Las Vegas. Guns had been fired and I had survived. Barely.

During one otherwise uninteresting sting I frisked a middle-aged man. He wasn't packing so I cuffed his hands in front instead of behind his back. Cuffing in front still allowed him to use his hands a little. Over and over, Don had me practice cuffing someone behind his back.

This time I screwed up. The guy was no more than ten feet away from me when he opened fire. He had hidden a small gun in his underwear, near his dick. I hadn't checked him there. Another mistake.

He missed. I don't know how he could have but he did.

Woodbeck drew his .38 and was about to shoot him.

"Don't!" I yelled to Don.

I knocked the man's arm back and took his gun.

Don pushed him to the floor, called him a "Cocksucker!" and kicked him. But he didn't shoot. He could have killed him but he didn't.

I had been lucky. So far. But like they say about riding horses: It's not if you fall off but when.

The crew had been falling apart for a while. Some were doing too many drugs. Most had stopped studying the scripts. After the J.D. shootout, Red said he was tired and ready to quit; Bucky wanted to visit his family in Chicago; Partridge did leave, taking a job in Milwaukee as a DJ; and Digger Dave said he was going to spend the rest of the summer back in Bisbee.

But Don wanted to keep on truckin'.

"We got J.D.," I said. "It's over."

"I've got a line on a museum in Tucson that they're opening and we could rip it off," he said.

"A museum? You're kidding."

"We go through the roof, steal the artwork, and make a fortune."

I couldn't believe my ears.

"We don't do museums," I said. "We rip-off drug dealers."

Some of those dealers were pissed too.

First we heard from Janet and Joanna that the Mexican Mafia had put a price on our heads. Then we heard it from Lewis.

"How much did they offer?" I asked him.

"Five thousand dollars for Craig, ten thousand for Don."

I must admit I was a little insulted that Don was worth twice as much as I was.

Lewis said it was an open contract, anybody could claim the reward.

"Did you overhear these guys or what?" Don asked.

"Not exactly," Lewis said.

"Then how do you know for sure?" I wanted to know.

"Because they offered the deal to me."

We would never again be able to trust even some of those in our own crew.

The cops were closing in too. The word on the street was that they were tracking us. When we started, we took Polaroids of all the people we would sting. I put them in a scrapbook so we could study their faces and try to avoid stinging them again and falling into a trap ourselves. But we never saw that scrapbook again after the Feds raided our condos. If they had that information, then sooner or later they would put two and two together—and we could be in prison for a long, long time.

Two months after the J.D. shooting, I quit. Don couldn't talk me out of it. The movie was over.

I called Stan.

"What have you done now?" he said.

I just told him I wasn't in school anymore.

"Well, if you're in trouble, come on home."

I wasn't sure I wanted to live with him though.

I loaded up a U-Haul for the drive back to Kansas City. I wasn't leaving with much more than I came with. Yes, I had grown up, in a way. I had proven myself to myself. I had won a few battles too. But maybe I had lost the war. The only thing I had to show for the past two years was a lot of great stories to tell.

"Look me up if you ever come my way," Don said.

Zana was pregnant, and the two of them were moving to Fort Collins, Colorado. I couldn't imagine him settling down with a wife and kid but stranger things have happened.

"How will I find you?" I asked.

He laughed. "Just look for trouble."

We shook hands. I figured we'd never cross paths again. Part of me didn't want to cross paths with him again.

My life of crime was over. I'd never do anything like that again, I told myself. From now on, I would live a "normal" life, whatever that was. I was done with stings and playing cops-and-robbers.

But I did take my guns with me—because you never know when you might need them.

7

Undercover Cop

You've got to have people working as agents who know the drug trade.
We're not dealing with a bunch of Sunday school boys or Boy Scouts.
—Vern Miller, Kansas attorney general,
The Kansas City Times, July 4, 1974

"MR. CRAIG GLAZER, may we have a word with you?"
John Eckhart and Jack Hartman, two agents from the
Kansas Attorney General's Office, stood at the door of my cousin
Lenny's Kansas City apartment, where I was staying. I had been
back only a few months and was taking classes at the University of
Missouri at Kansas City. I was bored with my everyday existence but
I was determined to try to lead that "normal" life, one without movie
fantasies made real. Now it looked like my criminal past had followed
me home. Their badges were the genuine articles. I was in trouble.

"Is there something wrong?"

"We've been told about your activities in Arizona," said Eckhart, a
small, thin man with the greasy vibe of a door-to-door encyclopedia
salesman.

"And what were those?" I asked innocently.

"Stinging drug dealers."

Shit.

"We're pretty impressed."

Impressed? What?

"Maybe you can help us and we can help you," he continued.

"No, no, no. I won't roll over on my friends."

"That's not what we want."

"I won't roll over because there's nothing to roll over about." I wasn't going to give them even the slightest opening.

"That may or may not be true."

"So if you want me to be a snitch, forget it."

"Mr. Glazer, you have the wrong idea," Eckhart said. "We're talking about making you a special agent for the attorney general of the State of Kansas."

They had to be kidding.

. . .

MY UNCLE MORT owned the Glazer Chemical Company and was also a private pilot. Besides flying around the Midwest for business and performing as a stunt pilot at air shows, he'd take his friends up for fun. He would occasionally fly with Vern Miller, the former Sedgwick County sheriff who was in his first term as the attorney general of Kansas.

"I just received a dossier from the FBI on someone named Craig Glazer," Miller told Uncle Mort before one of those flights. "That's not a common name. A relative of yours?"

"It's my nephew's name, but he's going to college in Arizona."

"Well, this guy worked out of Arizona and is now in Kansas City." Miller showed him part of the report.

Uncle Mort was stunned. "It's him. I'm sorry."

"Sorry?" said Miller with a laugh. "He doesn't have any convictions. I might have a job for him."

When he ran for attorney general in 1970, Miller's campaign promise was to clean up the campus of the University of Kansas or, as he put it, "leap into the drug-ridden hippie communes of Lawrence with both feet." He did. On February 26, 1971, he led twenty-two seven-man teams of law enforcement officers in what was believed to be the largest bust in state history and one of the largest single raids ever carried out in any city in the United States. Accompanied by reporters from *Life* magazine, whom he had conveniently tipped off, Miller's assault netted thirty arrests. There were no big dealers among them, just student potheads, but he got the publicity he wanted.

He was not above using unconventional headline-grabbing tactics. Once, he leaped out of a car trunk to make an arrest. Another time, he nabbed a suspected dealer, put on his clothes, and went to a party where the suspect had been expected in order to gain information. Miller was one of the most outrageous and flamboyant attorneys general any state had ever seen.

"Hippies" weren't his only target either. The other drug—alcohol—was also on his hit list. Kansas was nearly the driest state there was—only liquor stores and private clubs could sell anything besides 3.2 beer. Miller took the prohibition to the extreme by having his officers raid Amtrak trains to stop illegal liquor sales. He even forbade airlines from serving liquor while flying in Kansas airspace. Johnny Carson got a few laughs in his *Tonight Show* monologue from Miller's antics.

Now Miller, a Democrat, was running a tough law-and-order campaign for governor. If I was the same person he had been reading about in the FBI files he had been sent—common practice when persons of interest moved to another state—maybe this was just the lucky coincidence he needed that would help move him into the governor's office.

· · ·

I FINALLY TOLD my father what I had done in Arizona. I expected him to tell me what a fuckin' idiot I was, like always. But he didn't say anything. I think it was the first time he had ever been proud of me. Of course he didn't say that. There was a lot of "What the fuck?" and "How the hell?" But I could see he was impressed by my adventures.

That they were outside the law only made them more colorful because that made them more dangerous.

He was amazed that his son, Larry Lardbutt, had become the Errol Flynn character, the pirate hero, he had always wanted to be. I think he was surprised that I hadn't fucked up, that I was never caught. I was a bad boy, and I was good at it, even better than he was.

He knew I wasn't bullshitting either. You can't bullshit a bullshitter.

•   •   •

ECKHART SAT IN my cousin Lenny's apartment and made his pitch. "The life I lead is pretty cool," he started, and then went on to explain that there were only eight agents attached to the attorney general's office, each of them with a different territory to cover. They were the glamour boys because they were allowed to carry guns. They were the ones who saw action. Then they would deliver the evidence to the Kansas Bureau of Investigation (KBI), the forensics investigators and lab technicians.

"The pay is shit," he sneered, "but we get lots of 'buy money.'"

"What's that?"

"If we need pot to play a part, the state gives us the money. Anything we need for our job. An apartment, a motorcycle, clothes." He gave my long hair and jeans the once over. "Of course you'll have to do eight weeks of police school at Hutchinson."

"Seriously, you want me to be a narcotics agent?"

"The attorney general would like to talk to you about that."

"I guess I can do that at some point."

Hartman, a big redneck, stood up. "Right now," said Eckhart firmly. "If you've got the time." Within minutes, I was in their car driving the ninety miles to Topeka, the state capital.

As we waited in a corridor of the impressively governmental Memorial Hall, Eckhart continued to sell me.

"You know, there's talk of a special narcotics unit that'll cover four states—Kansas, Missouri, Iowa, Nebraska. With federal funding, it could be huge. If you can help me make cases, that'd go a long way to convincing the powers-that-be to put me in charge. I can bring you with me."

All I could think was: Are they nuts? Sure I had been in the drug underworld and done some crazy things. But I was still just twenty years old. This suit needed me to advance his career?

He introduced me to the chief of Miller's narcotics division, Gary Porter, a tall redhead in his early forties who wore a hairpiece, and another agent, Jerry Federgreen, a small, dark, fifty-year-old with glasses who looked like a high school geometry teacher. Federgreen was Jewish, which struck me as strange since Jews and badges don't usually go together in Kansas. If I did go ahead with this, maybe being of the same tribe would help me out.

Like Eckhart and Hartman, they too carried guns. I might like packing heat as a genuine cop, I thought to myself, instead of as a pretend one.

Apparently an agent had recently been fired. He was well liked but perhaps too well liked by one of the young girls he busted. The word was that he had been sleeping with a lot of his female informants. The narcotics division of the attorney general's office was looking for a replacement. That's when my dossier found its way to Miller's office. Now so did I.

Miller sat behind a massive desk, the American flag on one side of the room, the Kansas flag on the other. The sleeves of his white shirt were rolled up above his elbows and he broke into a big smile when we shook hands, even though he remained seated behind his desk. He reminded me of Jimmy Cagney, a compact fireball of energy.

"Damn glad to meet you," he said. I was surprised he was so friendly. I had heard nothing good about him. After all, busting hippies didn't make him a favorite of my generation.

He dismissed Eckhart from the room.

"I expected you to be much bigger," he told me.

Having read of my exploits in Arizona, he assumed I'd be an imposing tough guy—not a twenty-year-old college kid. I wasn't much different than the students he had made a crusade of busting—long hair, bell-bottoms, mustache. Hell, I looked like one of those "hippie freaks." "Is this stuff true, what I've read in these reports?"

Jeezus, this was a state attorney general! I hedged my bets.

"People tend to exaggerate."

He stared hard at me. "Off the record, is this true?"

"Some of it may have happened," I said tentatively.

"Let's get to the point, son. I've got police intelligence files on my desk on just about every member of the legislature. You should see some of the things that people have alleged about some of them. But no one in this building has the qualifications and experience you have. How would you like to wear a gold badge?"

Months earlier I was in a ditch hiding from the police and now the Kansas attorney general was offering me a job as a cop. Not just any cop either. I'd immediately be given a gold badge, signifying an agent of a high rank. Silver shields were given to patrolmen. I'd be the equivalent of a gold-shield detective. Unbelievable.

"We can help you graduate college if that's what you want. There's a future with us for a man like you."

That seemed promising because I was looking for a future. "But what would I be doing?"

"The attorney general enforces the laws of the state. I may not agree with all of those laws. But drugs are evil. I'd put my own kid in jail if I found him smoking pot. I want you to help me put drug dealers in prison."

"I'd be undercover?"

"That's right. You can handle yourself in a scrap, can't you?"

"I think so," I said modestly.

"Then you don't need eight weeks at Hutch. You just need to pass the pistol course." I wouldn't have any problem with that. I already had a pretty good teacher when it came to marksmanship—one Donald Woodbeck.

Miller pushed hard. "You sign up as a contract agent and we get you an apartment in Johnson County, where you live, and you go to work. I want big cases, big dope busts. I need the hard stuff—coke, heroin. Can you get those for me, son?"

"I think I can." Given that Porter and Federgreen looked, dressed, and acted like cops, and Eckhart and Hartman acted like cops even though they looked like your average dirtbag, I could see why they hadn't scored any major drug busts. Weed, coke, pills, and heroin were bought and sold everywhere, if you knew where to look. They didn't.

"You weren't any better than the people you stung, were you?" asked Miller, not expecting an answer. "But if you become part of the government, you can change. And the only way to change the system is to get in the system. Sign up and put a badge on. I'm not fuckin' around. I need you to go to work."

He pulled a twenty-dollar bill out of his pocket and gave it to me. "And here, get yourself a haircut." The state's highest law enforcement official didn't understand the drug world. He didn't understand that my long hair was a different kind of badge.

A few days later, I was sworn in as the nation's youngest special agent. I was sure I was the youngest because all law enforcement officers permitted to carry guns had to be twenty-one years old. I was only twenty. They had me lie about my age, just like a Hollywood actor.

They had never hired anyone like me before, from the other side of the law. I was flattered and honored. Here was a chance for me to be James Bond, Wyatt Earp, and Jesse James—the secret agent, the sheriff, and the outlaw, all rolled into one. And just like the lawmen of the Old West, the line between the good guys and the bad guys was just as blurry. Just like back then, sometimes the only difference was who was paying.

I spent a week at Eckhart's side but I received no formal police training or instruction. "Anything you don't know, I can tell you," he assured me. I admitted to him that busting kids for drugs was not something I wanted to do. I wanted to get bad guys, super bad guys, off the street.

"You can pick your targets, Craig," he said.

"So if there's a guy who's raping and robbing and shooting and I can manage to get him on a drug charge any way I can…"

Eckhart smiled. "Now you're thinking."

My job, it seemed, was pretty much what Don and I had been doing. Take down people like J.D., people who were worse than us. Only this time, I couldn't keep the money or the weed. Only this time, I would officially be the good guy because the badge would be real.

Eckhart wanted to be the top cop. If I could help him make cases, the chances of him rising to power would improve greatly. Miller wanted to be governor. If I could make those big busts, he'd be a crusading, crime-busting hero the voting public would sweep into office.

Me? I just wanted to be famous, even at the cost of being infamous.

. . .

WHEN I TOLD Stan I was made a special agent, his eyes grew big.

"You?"

I showed him my gold badge. Finally he believed me. But he didn't seem happy. I learned that his honorary deputy sheriff's badge had expired. Now I had one and he didn't.

He asked if maybe I could introduce him to Vern. His brother Mort had never done that for him, but I did. Within two days of their meeting, he received in the mail a badge making him an honorary special agent.

If the attorney general ever needed to form a posse, Stanford Glazer would be called to serve. In the meantime, he'd be badging any cop who stopped him after he ran a red light.

. . .

IT DIDN'T TAKE long before I was making more undercover cases, twenty-one in one month, than anyone else in the attorney general's office.

120

The normal procedure was that the undercover special agent would make the first and second buy, then the third transaction would be a KBI buy-and-bust. I did not follow the rules. I thought there were no rules when it came to bringing down drug dealers. I also knew that the easiest way to bust a big dealer, not a neighborhood peddler, was to pretend to be another dealer, not a buyer. So instead of playing the buyer, I played the seller. A dealer would never suspect that a cop would supply him with drugs. I don't know if I was the first cop to do that but at the time I didn't know anyone else who did. The practice of informants giving dealers or buyers drugs and then the dealers or buyers being busted became commonplace in the years that followed.

I went all over town proclaiming that I was a dealer and setting up sales. It was like shooting fish in a barrel. Easy. But Eckhart and the other agents grew jealous. They didn't like how young I was. They didn't like how I operated. They didn't like my cocky attitude. Mostly, they didn't like that I was showing them up. I saw it as doing my job. I didn't know they weren't making twenty-one cases in a whole year. Oh, and they didn't like my long hair either.

It was soon clear to Eckhart that my success wasn't going to help him as much as it was going to help me. I quickly became his competition for the top cop job with the proposed four-state squad. I even brought in my own friends, like Mike Banks, a mortgage broker, who was made a contract agent; and Joel Weinberg, who played lead guitar in the band Morningstar, and my old pal Marc Mackie, whom I had made unpaid special agents.

In early 1974, I was even invited to a meeting at Winstead's restaurant with Joseph McNamara, the new chief of police of Kansas City, Missouri, and former chief of police Clarence Kelly. McNamara would move on to become chief in San Jose, California, for fifteen years and then a best-selling crime novelist. He also became an advocate for some version of drug legalization. Kelly, at the time of the meeting, was the director of the FBI, appointed by President Nixon the previous year.

The meeting was necessary because a firestorm had ignited over a drug bust I led that collared the Hudson brothers on Missouri soil. Crossing state lines has been a sensitive subject between Missouri and Kansas since before the Civil War. In Kansas City, the border separating the two states is a busy street. As law enforcement, we had permission to cross it if a case took us to the other side but we were supposed to call the other state's officials to let them know. I didn't. McNamara and Kelly preached cooperation between the various agencies.

The Drug Enforcement Administration, formed only the year before, had noticed me. Despite its name, the DEA was full of agents who were neophytes in the drug world. They didn't have a clue how dealers talked, dressed, lived, or operated. They had a lot to learn, and in our meetings before a surveillance, I taught them a few things. One: Wearing a heavy Army jacket when it's eighty degrees outside just might be suspicious. Instead, I would wear a tank top, but have my gun in an ankle holster. Two: Do not walk up to a car and ask to buy a "lid." The word had become obsolete. They might as well have C-O-P stamped on their foreheads. They had to know the jargon on the street.

Once, on a stakeout on a coke case with them, I found the agents themselves snorting coke!

"What the hell are you doing?"

"We've got to stay up," they said. "Hey, it's not like we're selling the shit."

I was more disillusioned being on the law's side than I ever had been on the criminal side. I guess I expected more from the "good guys."

Unlike other agents, I didn't "sell" my cases either. The Kansas Attorney General's Office wasn't the only law enforcement agency having a hard time making big drug arrests. So was the DEA. So state and local agents would sell them their cases. They would set up the arrest but give it to the DEA for the actual execution. That way the DEA would get all the credit. The DEA agents would then pay the state or local agents anywhere from $500 to $1,500 for each case. They made more money than the state and local cops. They could afford it.

I kept my cases for myself. I wanted everyone to know how well I was doing. That pissed off Eckhart even more and he tried to set me up for a fall.

At my apartment he saw a girl with my brother Jeff passing a joint. Eckhart bagged it and went back to Porter with the idea of developing a case against Jeff and the girl. For a joint! Miller called me into his office and asked why I hadn't stopped Jeff and the girl.

"I have the right to protect my cover," I told him. "Besides, you might arrest your son for that but I'm not going to arrest my brother."

Miller knew this was penny-ante and shrugged off Eckhart.

But someone else not enjoying my success was far more dangerous— Mrs. Margaret Jordan, the Johnson County district attorney. She was determined to help fellow Republican Bob Bennett, the former mayor of Prairie Village, defeat Democrat Miller in the governor's race. The bearded Bennett, known for wearing cowboy boots and a cowboy hat, was way behind in the polls for the 1974 election.

Jordan, a dominating, heavyset woman who reminded me of Angela Lansbury's character in *The Manchurian Candidate*, also wanted some of that federal drug-squad funding. She was doing exactly what Miller was—having her own narcotics division try to reel in spectacular drug busts. Drug war? They could care less about getting drugs off the street. For them, it was all about scoring political points, about winning elections, about gaining power. Anything that made Miller look good made Jordan and her candidate look bad. I was making Miller look good.

One night I was chumming the drug-filled ocean for dealers at Chapman's, an after-hours private club. Three guys inside had been giving me shit over a girl I was hitting on. But it was 1 a.m. and I was tired. So I left. They followed me to my car. I was in no mood to get into a fight. I spun around and drew down on them. They backed away. But, not knowing I was an undercover cop, they went to a police station and filed a report.

The next day, Johnson County sheriff's deputies arrived at my door. I offered to show them my licensed gun but they swarmed into the apartment waving a search warrant.

"I'm a special agent with the attorney general's office," I said, and flashed my gold badge. They didn't care. They found my gun in a secure weapons box. They also found weed and coke in my evidence case, along with a testing kit.

I angrily told them, "You're interfering with law enforcement!" That just made them mad. They put cuffs on me, arrested me for aggravated assault, and took me to headquarters in Olathe.

Captain Roy Miller, no relation to Vern, knew I was a special agent. When I arrived, he ordered an officer to remove the cuffs.

"Let's have a business meeting," he said. "The charge will be dismissed."

He brought me into a squad room. On the wall was a chart with several red dots next to the names of his detectives. At the bottom were lots of black and blue dots waiting to be claimed.

"How do you meet so many dealers?" he asked.

"I get around. I have informants."

"We can use someone like you."

Jeezus, this was one helluva way to get me in for a job interview!

"Looks like your guys are doing okay. Those red dots are cases, aren't they?"

"Pot. The black and blue dots are for heroin and coke." None of his detectives had any of them.

"Hmmm, I've made a lot of those cases." I rubbed it in.

Enter Margaret Jordan.

She was the closer. She was a powerful speaker.

"Why are you helping Topeka, Mr. Glazer? You grew up here in Johnson County. This is your home."

"I'm already working for the attorney general."

"You know, the cases you're making in Johnson County have problems. You being the seller instead of the buyer. That's tricky. We can make those problems disappear if you come over to our side."

"I thought we were all on the same side."

She didn't appreciate the criticism.

"Are you staying with Vern then?"

"Yep."

Her voice turned icy. "Then we cannot be friends." She did not smile when she added, "Hope to see you again soon."

After I left, I went to see Vern Miller and told him what happened at Chapman's.

"Why didn't you duke it out?" he asked.

"I wasn't up to fighting three guys by myself."

"I thought you were a tough guy," he said disappointed. "Why didn't you at least badge them?"

"I don't want everyone to know I'm a cop!"

Spunky Vern Miller wanted action, wanted headlines. "I want my guys to fight back if cornered," he said, "and, if you have to, I want you to shoot back too. Understand?"

"Yes, sir."

Then I told him about my meeting with Captain Miller and Mrs. Jordan.

His response was swift: "Fuck 'em."

But the Johnson County authorities were about to fuck me.

A couple weeks down the road, a heroin junkie named Danny Cline was arrested for robbery. Cline bought from a bad dude named Darrell Stephens who ran with the Pennet Brothers, Tom and Dennis, and John Eisman. I knew them all as kids. When they grew up they became dopeheads and made a specialty out of knocking off drugstores. Along the way they shot and killed a couple of people behind the counter. But they had never been caught. By buying heroin from them, I infiltrated their gang.

Cline was in jail being interviewed when the Johnson County officer just so happened to ask, "Ever run with Craig Glazer?"

"No," said Cline, "but his brothers, yes."

"You know Craig's undercover for the attorney general?"

Cline was surprised. "Didn't know that."

As soon as Cline was released, he went to Stephens and told him.

Stephens then called me to say that a new load of heroin was in. Was I interested? I went to his house in Prairie Village and his crew was all there, everyone armed as usual. Stephens was six foot four, mid-twenties, tattooed, and emaciated. He had black bags under his eyes and wore motorcycle gang regalia, including the leather vest and the buck knife. He was a scary guy.

"I see you buying," he said, "but I never see you using. I'm not sure we trust you."

"Come on, Darrell. You think I'm a narc?" When in doubt, get in their face.

"We can square that," he suggested.

They put a few grams of Mexican mud on the table.

"I'd rather not," I said.

"Rather you would," said Stephens.

I was in a bind. If I didn't shoot up, my cover would be blown and I'd probably be blown away. On the other hand, I'd done heroin before, and even though I had a bad experience, I figured I could survive it. But I still couldn't do it myself. So I let Stephens shoot me up. "All right," he said, seemingly satisfied. "We're still on, brother."

On my way home around midnight, I stopped at a convenience store and saw in the parking lot a Prairie Village cop I always talked to, Sergeant Stewart, who knew I was a special agent.

"You know Darrell Stephens and the Pennet boys?" I asked.

"I'm afraid so. Nasty."

"They shot me up."

"Man, you shouldn't..."

"Each in our own way," I said. "But what's weird is that I don't feel anything. Nothing."

He gave me his business card. "You have a problem, you call me."

I went home to write my report. Twenty minutes later my feet and legs went numb. I fell and began crawling on the floor. In seconds, I could barely breathe.

I had been poisoned. They meant to kill me.

I knew what had happened and I freaked out. My girlfriend of the moment did too. She called an ambulance. I gave her Sergeant Stewart's card and she called him too.

He was there in two minutes, followed by the Johnson County drug squad.

"What'd he do?" asked one of them.

"OD'd on his own shit," said another.

"No, assholes," said Stewart, "he risked his life."

I was getting worse. The ambulance still had not arrived. Sergeant Stewart picked me up and raced me to the hospital. The doctors immediately flushed my system with saline and I came around. I had been minutes away from dying. Sergeant Stewart saved my life.

He also called Vern Miller, in the middle of the night, and told him, "Give this guy protection."

When I recovered, I talked to the attorney general and he said he'd get me whatever or whomever I wanted. Vern had grown fond of me. I had been doing his election campaign a lot of good.

There was only one person I wanted.

"What about Don Woodbeck?"

"The guy I read about in your dossier?"

I didn't know where Don was, but Miller would be able to find him. The next day I heard back from the attorney general. Woodbeck was in prison in Florence, Arizona. He had been caught conspiring to sell marijuana, which apparently had gone well since he was carrying an unexplainable $50,000 in cash on him. With that money he then tried to bribe a Border Patrol officer to let him go. Bad move. He was serving the first year of a two-to-three year sentence.

"I can ask the governor of Arizona to let him out on a bond," Miller offered. "If he cooperates, maybe we can work out a pardon."

He arranged for me to call Don.

"What are ya doin', ya ole horse thief?" Don said on the phone from prison.

"I've got a badge. I work for the attorney general of Kansas."

"Jeezus, that's like giving Dillinger the keys to Fort Knox."

"I'm serious."

"You mean they know all about you and they still made you a cop?"

"That's why they made me a cop. And they'll make you one too if you can help me work on cases out here." Officially, he would be a CI, confidential informant. Unofficially, he'd be my partner again.

"Buddy, if you get me out, I'll take down Russia for ya."

Woodbeck was released on the order of the governor of Arizona and put on a plane to Kansas City at the request and under the supervision of the attorney general of Kansas. When he arrived, I showed Don my gold badge with "Glazer" on it.

"I don't like cops," he said. "But in your case I'll make an exception."

Vern brought us into his office.

"No monkey business," he warned. "You are not a cop and you cannot carry a gun."

Don put up his hand to stop him. "I'm not doing this without a gun. That's suicide."

"Like I said, you cannot carry a gun. If you do," Miller added, "then I don't know about it."

He didn't wink but he might as well have.

Then he gave me a twenty-dollar bill.

"Didn't I tell you to get a haircut?"

. . .

WHEN I TOLD Don what Stephens had done to me, he said, "I'll take care of that."

A few days later, Stephens was killed in a hit-and-run accident. The vehicle was described as a red El Camino. Don drove a red El Camino. I never asked him if he was my avenger.

Next up were the Pennet boys and Eisman. I took care of them myself.

I joined them on a drugstore robbery in Missouri. Their plan, I suspected, was that in the midst of the action they would shoot and kill me.

We walked into the drugstore. As they prepared to go to the counter, I hung back a few steps and leveled my gun at their backs.

"Turn around and you're dead," I warned.

I waited for the Missouri cops and other agents I had at the ready to run in and make the arrest. No one came. They were supposed to give me ten minutes inside but we had been there only three. I didn't have a panic button. So I waited.

Finally, twenty cops flooded in. One of them came up to me and said, "Put down the gun! You're under arrest!"

"I'm a cop, you idiot." I badged him and walked right out the door.

Eckhart had told some of them a different story about the setup. Maybe he too was trying to get me shot and killed, "accidentally" of course.

But at least, I thought, I had paid back the Pennets and Eisman. They would be spending many years in prison.

• • •

WHILE ON THE job, Miller was also on the campaign trail. Like most politicians, he had lots of enemies. One of the first assignments he gave Don was for him to accompany me for a couple of weeks as part of his security detail during campaign appearances around the state.

Vern was good. He'd eat corn dogs and watermelon at some grange meeting, then roll up his sleeves and hop onto a picnic table in front of fifty farmers. By the time he finished talking they thought he was the second coming of Abraham Lincoln. I thought he was more like Huey Long.

In Topeka, Miller publicly bragged about the busts I was making, but he also privately pushed for a really big one. "I want kilos, not ounces," he insisted.

Don wanted to get out from under his Arizona sentence and set up a bust as soon as possible.

"What would be big enough?" he asked me.

"A half pound would do it."

"I can get that," said Don.

While he was working for J.D., Don had transported hundreds of pounds of weed and some cocaine on a regular basis to Greg Houston, who supplied the college kids in Lawrence. But Don didn't want to give up Houston.

"Let's get the drugs from him but take down the runners instead," Don suggested. When I told Miller about the switch, he went berserk.

"I want Mr. Big!" he shouted.

"Vern, listen, here's the deal. Let's get these little guys first. We'll land the big one later." I reminded him that earlier when I wanted to bust Stephens with four ounces of heroin, it was Miller who asked, "What if we let him keep it?"

"Then the next time," I told him, "he'll try to sell us a pound."

"Now you're talkin'!" Vern had said. Whatever would look more spectacular in the newspapers is what he wanted.

"Where do you want to do this?" I asked him about the Houston deal. "I can make this land anywhere."

"How about that Margaret Jordan bitch's backyard, Johnson County?"

"Good, we'll kill two birds with one stone."

"I like that," said Miller. "Sure do. Go ahead, take 'em down."

So Jordan and her squad wouldn't get wind of what we were up to, we headquartered outside her territory, booking rooms at the Crown Center Hotel, across the border in Kansas City, Missouri. Houston drove into town with the coke and speed, and also stayed at the hotel. Don took the drugs to Marc's house, where he cut it with powdered lactose. As a gift, he gave Marc some coke in a plastic container, which Marc would later regret accepting.

At first, Don said the runner would be a white male from Wichita, then a baseball player from Topeka. I passed on the info to Vern's office. One night, our special agents and the DEA waited for anyone to show up at Room 161 of the Western Hills Motel in Merriam, on the Johnson County, Kansas, side of the border. No one did. I was embarrassed that we were coming up empty.

Don needed results too. Finally he had Houston contact two black men, James Bonds and Larry Johnson, who were dealing weed and coke in the inner city in Missouri. Don also knew them from running weed years earlier. But they balked about going into Kansas. Don offered them $500 each and a cut of the deal to make the delivery with him.

On the night of Sunday, June 23, they went with Don to the motel. Inside Room 161 was special agent Banks, playing the buyer. I was in the bathroom, waiting.

When Don pulled up with them in his car at about 10:15, Bonds and Johnson suddenly got cold feet. They didn't want to carry the brown paper bag. Don grabbed it. "I'll bring it in." The deal went down as usual. As soon as Banks counted out the money, about $14,000, and the exchange was made, I jumped out of the bathroom and, with Banks, drew down on Bonds and Johnson. I waved a cab driver hat in the window and the other agents rushed in to arrest the two men. Mission accomplished.

Bonds and Johnson were charged with selling drugs. The next day, Miller praised the bust in the press as the largest cocaine seizure in the state since he had been in office.

But Miller had felt compelled to tell Jordan about the bust before it happened. She had Roy Miller put us under surveillance at the Crown Center Hotel. It was cops watching cops. What they saw was Don, not Bonds or Johnson, walking in with the drugs. Something seemed wrong.

There had been rumors flying around that an agent was selling drugs. My name was mentioned. Miller rightly dismissed them, explaining later that, "Well, you know the agents in order to make contact often indicate they are also pushing drugs ... I can see how somebody would get the idea he was a dealer. They've got to give indications along those lines in order to get to the people we're trying to arrest. That's standard procedure."

Even Vernon Meyer, regional director of the DEA, told a newspaper, "I don't want this taken in the context that Glazer was involved in any wrongdoing."

As far as I was concerned, we had arrested a pair of drug dealers. It was a good bust. Then all hell broke loose.

Federgreen told Roy Miller to ask Bonds and Johnson if they thought they had been framed, that they were fall guys. Not so amazingly, they saw a way out of their predicament and said yes. No, they were not dealers at all, they said. They were Woodbeck's bodyguards, and that's why they were given $500 each.

I heard about Federgreen's inquiry and went to interview Bonds and Johnson in their jail cell. Everything they said I had on tape.

"What is your story so far? What did you tell them—you guys get set up or something like that?"

"It looks like what happened," said Bonds. "That is what happened."

"There's somebody behind the thing," I said. "That's who we want, you know. You were just sent over there to deliver the drugs. We want the guys at the top." They were small potatoes. I wanted to get a bigger bust, but someone other than Houston.

"Well, you see, we weren't even supposed to deliver," said Johnson, "like we were going with that other dude"—meaning Don.

Unbeknownst to me, I didn't have the only tape recorder in the cell. Under the bed, Roy Miller had put another one. Bonds and Johnson were now cooperating with him—to get me. Thanks to Roy Miller's surveillance at the Crown Center Hotel, they also tracked down Houston, our "Mr. Big." Caught red-handed for supplying the drugs, Houston scrambled to get himself out of the hole he was in.

Eckhart, Federgreen, and the other agents basically laid out what they "suggested" might have happened. If Houston did not comply, they were going to press charges. He would either get immunity for testifying or go to prison.

Houston told them that he, Don, Weinberg, and I discussed setting up a drug raid to promote my career, make Miller look good, and get Don a letter of recommendation to ease his Arizona sentence.

Houston would then get protection through me on drug deals in the Kansas City area. Houston alleged that he was to get $1,000 as his payment. Nothing would happen to the people arrested because I would arrange for the charges to be dropped.

But, Houston said, he was unable to find fall guys. And when he did, he wasn't so sure the charges would be dropped, and told the guys not to do it. Yep, he was a regular Mother Teresa. Finally Don told him to forget about it because he had found a couple of guys on his own. That was Houston's story.

I was called into Vern's office in Topeka. Jordan, Porter, Federgreen, and others were present.

Miller asked me if Don had created a deal where there was no deal.

"Come clean now, Craig," he said. "If Woodbeck did something wrong, now is the time to give him up."

"I'm not going to do that."

Jordan and the others left the room. It was just Vern and me.

"Do what's right," Vern said.

"Don did what I asked him to do," I said. He was a confidential informant and CIs often manipulated deals the way he did. "If it's a problem, drop the charges on the two guys and let's move on." It would hurt Miller's election campaign if I was arrested. I figured he'd find a way to prevent that.

I thought the storm had passed until two days later when my father called. "They're talking about you on the radio," he warned.

I tuned into a talk show. Someone said that an indictment was about to be handed down against a couple of Miller's agents, badasses who used to rob drug dealers in Arizona. They described everything about us short of mentioning our names.

The next day I called Vern but never got through to him. I was more worried about getting fired than about an indictment. How could they charge me with anything when I was just doing my job?

I had moved into a new townhouse on the ninth hole of the Brookridge Country Club, and Don was staying with me. I confronted him about the motel bust. The fact is that I had never met with Houston. I had no idea what Don might have done.

"You fucked up!" I yelled.

"You got me out of jail. Hey, thanks. But you're the one taking the leap because you now have a badge. I'm not you."

He was right. But it wasn't that I was better than him. It was that I thought I had a chance to truly be a good guy. He didn't realize that's what I always wanted. I hadn't changed at all.

"I figured that if you're a cop and I'm a cop," he continued, "somewhere down the road we might do stings again."

"That is not going to happen," I said forcefully.

"This is your fault," he charged. "You pushed me to get a deal and you pushed the envelope. It's not all on me."

He was right about that too.

We had dates that night and went to pick them up. But returning to my place I didn't want them to know where I lived. They were one-night stands and there were too many drug dealers wanting to do me harm. So on our way back they agreed to have us tie pillowcases around their eyes. They kind of enjoyed the danger and mystery.

But as I parked and we got out of the car, we were swarmed by the KBI and sheriffs from Johnson County. I was sure we were about to get busted for kidnapping the girls.

"Listen, we didn't…" Then I realized that's not why they were there. It was about the motel bust.

Don ran and rolled down a little hill. He came to his knees with his .38 aimed at the cops. They wouldn't have had a chance.

"Don, Don, Don!" I shouted. "Give up, give up, give up!"

He thought for a moment and then dropped his gun. The cops cuffed him.

Federgreen took my .38 and my badge and put me in the backseat of a squad car. I told the girls to call my father.

"What do you think I did, Jerry?"

"You're a crooked cop." As far as law enforcement was concerned, the only way to explain how I was doing my job so well was that I had to be cheating.

"Tell me, what did I do?"

He started to talk about the Arizona stings.

"That was before I was a cop."

"I hope they cornhole you in prison," Federgreen said with frightening bitterness.

"Jerry, when I get out, I'll see you on the street."

"You'll be in for twenty years."

"I don't think so."

I was the first law enforcement agent in America ever charged with conspiracy to distribute cocaine because I supplied drugs to informants or dealers as a means of gaining their convictions.

They had wanted to get me—and now they had.

Deals were made or charges dropped for everyone—Mackie (whom they arrested for having the coke Don gave him), Weinberg, my brother Jeff, Bonds, Johnson, Houston, and even Woodbeck. Everyone except me. They peeled away every witness that could help me. I was surprised Vern went along with the indictment. Maybe he didn't understand how much it would affect him.

As if Jordan's vendetta wasn't obvious enough, she appeared at my bond hearing. Not only was it rare for her to appear in any court but it was extremely unusual for her or any county district attorney to show up at a bond hearing. When the judge reduced my bond from $50,000 to $10,000, she advised against it, saying, "The gravity of the charges and implications for the law, the prosecution, and law enforcement in general in the state of Kansas, would certainly indicate the seriousness of this charge, and the implications that it has for the entire system are such that assurance of this man's presence is of the utmost importance."

My lawyer pointed out my ties to the community and that flight would be a crime equal to the one I was being charged with. He also noted that there were guys in jail in Kansas for murder who didn't have a bond set as high as $50,000. The judge ruled in my favor.

I stood trial alone. I was the one left holding the bag. I was front page news.

The trial was a political powder keg. It was Miller v. Jordan, not the People v. Glazer. It wasn't about the drug war or about right and wrong. With one prosecution, Jordan could eliminate Miller's top agent, deflect any revelations about the lack of results in her own office, and help Bennett. Miller would say later: "She used it for all it was worth ... Oh, there was politics being played." At stake were the governorship and the careers of several politicians. Glazer, Woodbeck, Bonds, Johnson? We were just pawns in a political chess game. Miller supported me, privately and in the newspapers. He said of the charges, "You're still not going to get me to believe that until they prove it in court ... Glazer was one of our best agents. One of the reasons I didn't pay any attention to the police report on him was because he was doing such a good job."

He said it again years later: "It made me absolutely sick when Craig was arrested. He was a bright young man and had been doing just a super job. I don't believe Craig meant to do anything wrong."

But the press was out to crucify Miller and ate up everything fed to them by Jordan's camp. In the gubernatorial debates that followed, Miller was castigated for hiring unsavory characters, such as myself, to be agents. But the attorney general continually defended me: "It takes a special kind of policeman ... It takes a person who doesn't mind getting right down in the filth of the operation."

He knew there wasn't a big difference between the guys I was after and myself. To be one step ahead you have to be in step with. Sometimes the best cops make the best criminals, and vice versa.

Even Curt Schneider, the candidate for the attorney general's job, who later won, said, "We would much rather have the testimony of a police officer on the stand but drug dealers aren't stupid ... they can smell a police officer a mile away."

Strangely, I enjoyed the notoriety. I was excited to see my name in the news. Being famous was what I always wanted. I was no longer obscure. But, on the other hand, I was painted only as a villain. No one was on my side. For my generation I was a narc. For the older generation I was a drug dealer. Other cops thought I was a traitor. I was a defrocked undercover agent.

I was nobody's friend and everyone's enemy. It was not a good place to be. I was now also a target. And I no longer had a gun to protect myself. I was naked. I was more frightened about being in public unarmed than I was about the trial.

My lawyers would not allow me to talk to the press or to testify. They were afraid that everything I had done in Arizona would be brought up, further incriminating me.

It happened anyway. Don did it. I didn't blame him for testifying against me. He either had to say what they wanted or he was going to prison, not just in one state but two and for some serious time. That was a calculation Don was always aware of—what's the time for the crime?

Most of what he said in his testimony, and how he said it, didn't hurt me. What did hurt me was him opening the can of worms that was Arizona. For the first time, our names were officially tied to the stings there and elsewhere. The prosecutor, Dale Hartung, an assistant district attorney, could ask, "Didn't you rip off guys for years? How was what happened on June 23 any different than that?"

Bonds and Johnson testified that in Room 161 Don had to prompt Johnson, saying, "Ask 'em about the money." They said that I then asked them the price for the drugs but that they didn't know. So Don whispered it to Johnson, who repeated it. They said that I then took a roll of bills from my pocket and threw it in Bonds's lap—and that's when we drew down on them and arrested them.

They lied. The only way their Scenario made sense is if they had never made a drug deal in their lives. They were veteran pushers and, in my book, deserved jail—for agreeing to the motel deal if nothing else. Even Hartung admitted that some of the prosecution's witnesses "shouldn't be allowed to walk the streets. But the state cannot pick and choose its witnesses."

Still, I was the one facing prison for dealing drugs, even though I was "dealing" drugs in the line of duty.

But who would believe my story of corruption? That's not how law enforcement worked, was it? No, it was a lot simpler to give it the "good cop gone bad" spin. In my case it was even easier because they could make it "bad criminal stays bad."

Probably the smartest thing anyone said during the trial came from one of my lawyers, Randolph Austin: "It's getting to where you can't tell the good guys from the bad guys in this area of drug prosecution."

Judge Harold Riggs smelled a rat. He was aware that, no matter what I did, the attorney general not only had to know about it but had to approve it. Besides, how could an undercover agent who was posing as a dealer to get busts for law enforcement be charged with conspiring to sell drugs?

But somebody had to pay and it was going to be me. I was convicted and sentenced to one to five years in prison. My attorneys pointed out, however, that I had been exposed as a narcotics agent. If I were to go to prison, my life would be in grave danger. Prison was one thing. Being afraid for my life was another. The judge agreed and I remained free while the case was appealed.

Woodbeck pleaded guilty to the conspiracy charge and was also sentenced to one-to-five years. But he was immediately placed on probation and allowed to serve his time concurrently with his Arizona sentence. In essence, he received no jail for the Kansas offense. With Woodbeck shipped off to Arizona, I was sure that this time really would be the last time I would see him.

Regrettably, all of the cases I was involved with as an agent for the previous several months, many of them ready to go to trial, were dismissed out of fear that my conviction would make them unwinnable for the prosecution. Even the drugstore robbery.

I wasn't alone in my fall from grace. No one won. Those who set me up paid a heavy price too.

Margaret Jordan was publicly scolded for misconduct by Judge Riggs, who said that her "holding press conferences and granting television interviews and the like ... (about) the credibility of the defendant and the witnesses in the case and ... the guilt of the defendant, the evidence and the merits of the case ... (was) prohibited by the code of professional responsibility." He called her actions "most unethical and most reprehensible." In the next election, Jordan was defeated in her attempt to remain Johnson County DA by Dennis Moore.

Captain Roy Miller was disgraced and his job was taken by Lieutenant Lew Hoskins, who became a friend of mine. Eckhart didn't get the top cop job he coveted. We should all be grateful for that. In a subsequent court case, medical records obtained by subpoena from the High Plains Comprehensive Community Mental Health Center revealed that he had been diagnosed there as a psychopath and pathological liar, and previously had been diagnosed as schizophrenic at a Veterans Administration hospital.

Vern Miller suffered a surprising upset in the gubernatorial race as Bob Bennett came from behind to win the election. Said Miller in a *Kansas City Star* article in 1979: "(Glazer's arrest) was political dynamite ... I only lost by 3,000 votes. You bet it had an effect."

Miller had all of the charisma and savvy needed in politics. If he had become governor, who knows where he might have gone from there. He was a very convincing guy. I even finally cut my hair on his twenty dollars. Who knows, but the governor's office might have led him to become president of the United States. I might have cost America a lot of entertainment.

Years later, after he was no longer governor, I came across Bennett at Stanford & Sons, the restaurant my father had opened, and we talked.

"I had nothing to do with that case," he said. "What a crock of crap that was." Yeah, I know.

There was some good, though. Under the next attorney general, the Kansas Bureau of Investigation launched a probe into the existence of the 300 to 400 files on private citizens as well as legislators that Miller said he had seen. Eventually a decision was made to destroy those not related to criminal activities. There was also a much-needed public debate over the system of special agents, contract agents, and confidential informants.

Though in 1978 my appeal was denied two to one by a three-judge panel, another three-judge panel by the same vote immediately reduced my sentence to five years' probation. "This case has gone on so long," I said at the time, "that yesterday I felt like Muhammad Ali in the fifteenth round with thirty seconds to go and you're getting your head bashed in with no hope to win. And then he (the assistant district attorney) turned around and said they didn't want me to go to prison. I couldn't believe it."

Hartung snidely said, "I'm sure he'll never do anything wrong again."

Well, I was going to try.

I went straight. I quit doing drugs and barely drank. As part of my probation that began in 1978, I was ordered to present myself to the Johnson County sheriff's office in Olathe for three nights a week between the hours of midnight and 4 a.m. It didn't matter if it was twenty below zero. At around 2 a.m. every one of those nights, after closing Stanford & Sons, which I was helping to manage, I drove the forty-five minutes to the station. I was never late. I did that for three years.

One snowy night that first year, nearly falling asleep at the wheel, I decided that the time had come to tell my story. The time had come to make my movie.

8

Outlaws and Outsiders

We deserve what we get. It took years of living and risking to get here.
—Don Woodbeck, *Los Angeles Herald Examiner*, August 22, 1982

THE POWER TRIP I had been on, whether as a sting artist or a cop, was intoxicating. Now I was on probation from crime and punishment. For the first time in years, I did not, and could not, carry a weapon. For the first time in years, I could not make a living from either side of the criminal divide.

I also felt on probation from life, like I was in a sort of limbo, just waiting. I was "the kid who shot down Vern Miller," according to one newspaper. And I was Stan's son, the little boy who couldn't seem to stay out of trouble.

I had experienced the highest highs and lowest lows. Day-to-day life paled by comparison to the feeling I had after the Boston sting. How could I go to work in an office after that?

Stan had lost the large auto auction business he owned and was scrambling around again too. His quest to be accepted into society continued. He didn't want to be a member of the largely Jewish Oakwood Country Club, but rather the exclusive "no Yids" Kansas City Country Club. But only after golf great Tom Watson resigned in 1990 to protest the club denying membership to his friend Henry Block, of H&R Block, did the KCCC relent and allow Jews to join.

My father and I were both local celebrities but we were also both outcasts. Maybe because of that we became closer than we had ever been before.

My photo had been in the newspaper so much, people recognized me on the street. I could see them whisper and point—and I knew it was not out of admiration. There was no glory in being a villain. On the other hand, the organized crime mobsters I'd cross paths with in bars and restaurants would say hello. But they didn't trust me either. After all, I might still be a cop.

Following the trial, I didn't have a job or money. Marc and I even went to work for a computer dating company.

"So how much is a dinner and movie for you and a date?" I'd ask some poor homely schmuck way out in the sticks.

"Oh, about forty-five dollars. That's with gas."

"It's a long drive, isn't it?"

"Gas'll eat you up. Not to mention the wear and tear on the vehicle."

"Not to mention," I'd commiserate. "And what's it gotten you? I don't see a woman around here that'll love and take care of you and maybe, if you're lucky, want to marry you."

"No."

I'd draw a "0" on my pad. "This is your social life—a big, fat zero."

Just before he was ready to either strangle himself or me, I'd ride in on my white horse.

"Well, I'm here to change all that. At Computer Date Match, I can provide you with ten beautiful women who will fulfill your every need and desire. How do I know that?"

"How?"

"Because you will be compatible. The computer will make sure of that."

His eyes would brighten.

"The amazing thing, my friend, is how inexpensive happiness can be."

I drew a "2" and a "5" in front of the "0." "Just two hundred fifty dollars: a hundred dollars down and another hundred fifty later." It was pathetic.

"Know what I've always wanted to have?" Stan asked me one day. "A restaurant. We're both good-looking guys. We can talk to people. Maybe we can get investors together and open a restaurant."

He had seen a bar called Kelly's Irish Pub in a rundown building in the decaying Westport area of Kansas City attract hundreds of people each weekend night. His idea was to turn it into a restaurant with San Francisco Embarcadero décor. He gathered ten investors, promised them they'd eat there free for life, and gave each a 20 percent stake. Hopefully they wouldn't eat at the same table and start talking about their deal.

I suggested we call the place A Fistful of Dollars, after the Clint Eastwood spaghetti Western. But we settled on Stanford & Sons, its name a play on the TV show *Sanford & Son*. Jeff, Jack, and I were the "sons." My father got top billing as usual. He deserved it. He loved to take the big gamble, make the splashy move when everyone else said he was crazy. "What's the point doing it like everybody else?" he would say.

Stanford & Sons was a gamble that paid off right from the start. Anyone who was anyone came to eat there and be seen there. Our guests included sports heroes such as boxer Muhammad Ali; baseball's George Brett, Bob Gibson, and Roger Clemens; football players Len Dawson and Otis Taylor; and, during the 1976 Republican national convention in Kansas City, Barry Goldwater, President Gerald Ford, and future President Ronald Reagan.

But, outside of Ali, the guest I was most interested in meeting was Clint Eastwood, who came in with actress Louise Fletcher. I went up to him and lamely said, "How's your food?" Before he had a chance to answer, I told him I had a movie idea. "It's a modern day Western," I began, starting to tell him the story of my adventures.

"Excuse me," interrupted Fletcher, who played hard-nosed Nurse Ratched in *One Flew Over the Cuckoo's Nest*, "but we have another appointment and need to eat and run." I had been given the Hollywood brush-off.

In the late '70s, I was the Kansas City Tony Manero, John Travolta's character in *Saturday Night Fever*—by day working seventy hours a week at a dead-end job at my father's restaurant, by night enjoying a life of rotating disco balls and rotating girlfriends.

Once upon a time I used to brag about how many girlfriends I had and show other guys my black book. Now I had three or four and didn't tell anyone. Servicing them wasn't fun, it was work. Seriously. Trying to keep them all satisfied, going from one to the other to the other, sometimes all in one night, was exhausting not just physically but emotionally. When one would say she loved me and expected me to say the same to her, I would never answer. I'd just show up the next night.

In *Saturday Night Fever*, Manero said, "Fuck the future!" His boss at the paint store snapped back, "No, Tony! You can't fuck the future. The future fucks you!" If my future was as an employee for a father who never gave me any credit, I'd be fucked for sure. After the first couple of years, Stan would never refer to Stanford & Sons as "ours" but rather "mine." I was always the senior assistant or senior manager but never the general manager. He made sure to put someone else between him and me in the hierarchy. The day would never come when he would let me take over.

There are dads who spoil their kids and give them everything. There are dads who give their kids what they earn. Then there are dads like Stan, who treat their sons so badly that the staff can only imagine how he'd treat an employee if they screwed up.

Stan was the cock of the walk. Stanford & Sons would soon open a second restaurant, at the Plaza in Kansas City, Missouri, and then a third in St. Louis. My father was building a new home by a lake and driving a Porsche.

I was slaving away at the restaurants and driving the '68 Cutlass that Grandpa Bennie, as usual, loaned me.

I was depressed and increasingly desperate.

I asked to meet with Vernon Meyer, the regional director of the DEA, at their headquarters in downtown Kansas City, Missouri. Meyer knew about my undercover work and never publicly criticized my actions.

"I want to continue doing what I was doing," I told him. "I'm even willing to go overseas." Maybe he had some connection with the CIA. I could go from special agent to secret agent.

"Why?"

"Because I'm good at this." It was the only thing I was good at-besides women.

"We're interested," he said, "but let's see what happens." Losing my appeal and the finalizing of my felony conviction in 1978 put an end to that hope.

My need for action grew so extreme that I wrote a letter to my great-grandmother who had befriended Moshe Dayan, the Israeli military leader. Maybe she could recommend me for the Mossad, the Israeli spy agency. I never heard back.

My brothers were in trouble too.

Right after Stanford & Sons opened, the FBI was at my door. They weren't looking for me; they were looking for Jeff and Jack, whose hundred-dollar-a-day heroin habits had turned them into criminals.

My good-looking brothers would pick out a cute bank teller and have her open her cash drawer for some transaction. Then one of them would distract her by asking for information about a fictitious bank account. The teller would have to leave her drawer and, occasionally, would forget to close it. Jeff or Jack would then quickly reach over and grab a stack of bills. At the end of the day the teller thought she had simply made a mistake, that she had miscounted. Until they robbed Shawnee State Bank. Not only was it our own bank but it was one of the few banks in the area at the time that had surveillance cameras. The bank president saw them "tapping the till" on tape and instantly recognized them. He called the FBI.

For the $2,000 they were charged with stealing, Jeff and Jack were sentenced to prison for three years. Both were out in little more than a year and put on parole. But they would continue to steal and commit street crimes to feed their drug addictions. A bevy of girlfriends would help them. Eventually they served their full sentences because of parole violations.

They even stole from Stanford & Sons. The waiters and waitresses would slip their cash into a money slot in a wall. Jeff and Jack tried to put their hands down the slot but it was too narrow. So they shoved a small plastic bag into the slot. The cash would be dropped in and later all they had to do was pull the bag out through the slot. The waiters and waitresses would be accused of short-changing the restaurant, until one day we found the bag attached to the slot. Jack would never hurt a fly and Jeff, who was a bit tougher, wasn't mean either. But heroin killed and made people killers if not thieves.

In 1976, Andy Thomas called. We had been estranged ever since I found out he had hooked my brothers. He wanted me to come over and talk. I drove to his apartment and went up the walkway. At the front door, I saw something out of the corner of my eye lying in the grass, maybe a dog. I knocked.

He answered very calmly and I walked in.

"What do you want?"

"Didn't you see?" he asked.

"What?"

"I killed him."

I noticed a rifle lying on a bed.

"They tried to rob me. I shot him. The cops are on the way."

The words had barely left his mouth when the squad cars arrived. The police quickly covered up what I had seen outside—the dead body of Mark Whitsitt. Andy said Whitsitt had ripped off two grams of heroin from him at the apartment. Then Whitsitt threatened him and laughed. Andy picked up the rifle and shot him between the eyes.

He was charged with first-degree murder but was acquitted on the grounds that he acted in self-defense. He was, however, sentenced to a couple of years in prison for possessing the heroin.

At one time, Andy was my very best friend. I always thought it would be him and me going through life and having adventures together. It was sad to see what heroin had done to him.

My only solace, as usual, was the movies. This time, though, I could watch them at home. HBO had premiered and would replay movies over and over, movies I loved like *Bonnie and Clyde*, *The Godfather*, and, of course, *Butch Cassidy and the Sundance Kid*. I couldn't wait to get home to watch them.

Serpico, though, only made me mad. I had already done more than Frank Serpico. I had been a cop too. But I had also been a hood.

I wanted everyone to know my story, the whole story, the story of the stings. I wanted everyone to know that I had taken down badass drug dealers, that I had outsmarted them, and that I had almost gotten killed along the way. I wanted people to know that I was brave. Everyone was looking down on me, while I thought some of what I had done was actually heroic. I wanted everyone to know that part. I wanted my life to actually be a movie.

So after a snowy late night on my way back from my probation appearance in Olathe, I took the next step and had a friend of a waitress help me write down the main idea. The story was about a college student who teams up with a Vietnam vet in the seamy underworld of the drug trade. I called it *Outlaws*.

Stan found out I was writing my story and was typically supportive. "I don't want to hurt your feelings," he said, "but no one gives a shit. That ship has sailed. You're wasting your time." Maybe he was right. But I had to give this a try. I was twenty-eight years old. This would probably be my last chance.

Other people have that little voice in their head that says, "Hey, that's a pretty big jump into the unknown. Maybe you should just be satisfied with what you have." My little voice always said, "You can have more! GO FOR IT!!!" That fuckin' little voice had already gotten me into so much trouble.

I had no idea how a movie got made. So I put together a list of fifty literary agents I found in a copy of *Writer's Market* and sent each of them a query letter.

The rejections flooded in. Stan loved that. The staff would open the mail and yell out, "Another rejection!" They were like the wicked stepsisters in *Cinderella*.

The only person in my corner was Terri Westbrooke, a waitress working at Stanford & Sons. I remember her Italian boyfriend Jerry introduced her to me, saying, "Keep the guys away from her."

He had good reason to be jealous. Terri was five foot ten with chestnut red hair, green eyes that would turn blue, and a Playboy body. She was also sweet as sugar and somewhat quiet. What made her unusual was that, unlike many women who are room-stoppingly beautiful, she lacked any arrogance about her looks. She carried some baggage, however—an infant daughter, Michelle, by her high school sweetheart, whom she had divorced. We began to talk but I wasn't interested in her as a girlfriend. I didn't need a woman with a baby. Besides, it seemed the guys she dated were handsome older men who were fast on their feet, flashed big money, and talked real nasty.

Yes, I was aggressive but I never used foul language to get a woman in bed. I was more upfront: "Here's the deal: If you want, you can come to my place."

Terri had a very different come-on: "Wanna see my baby?"

We became friends. Soon she confided that Jerry was not going to be the man she married. Still, we didn't sleep together for quite a while. When we finally did, we had "nooners." Jerry was occupied during the day. She did not want to be caught by him and have him cut her off before she was ready to leave.

"Did you actually do what you write about?" she asked after reading my concept for *Outlaws.* I said yes. "What are you going to do with this?"

"Go to Hollywood, play the lead in the movie about my life, and be a movie star and a producer," I said matter-of-factly.

Craig's mother Rita at her home in Prairie Village, Kansas.

Stan Glazer's outtake shot from his "4-Aces" cologne commercial.

Stan and Rita Glazer in Las Vegas on New Year's, 1955.

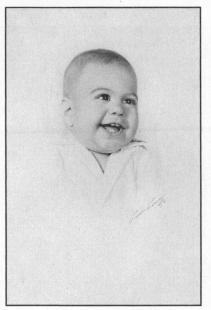

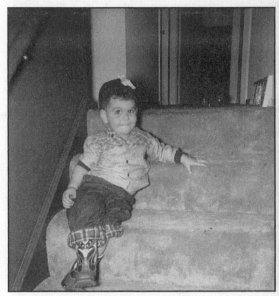

Craig, a few months old.   Craig in 1955, age 3 (note the cowboy boots).

Rita Glazer with sons Jeff and Craig at their first home in Prairie Village, Kansas.

"The Glazer Bunch" (left to right): Craig, Stan, Jack, and Jeff.

Craig with his mother Rita.

Jeff, Grandpa Bennie, and Craig at Stanford & Sons Comedy Club in Kansas City, Missouri.

Don "locked and loaded" in Phoenix, Arizona, ready for the next sting.

Craig stabbing the air on a boat somewhere off the coast of Miami.

Don Woodbeck and Craig Glazer, just after arriving in L.A. to begin their Hollywood careers.

Last photo taken of Don, in Craig's L.A. condo before he was shot to death.

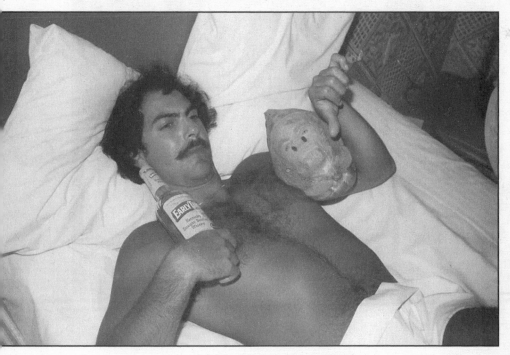

Craig drunk in bed during the Jamaican adventure.

Don and Craig at a Hollywood photo shoot in 1981.

Craig and Hollywood agent Harold Moskovitz at Craig's Brentwood condo.

(left to right) Grandpa Bennie, Jack, Jeff, and Craig. At the Missouri State Penitentiary in Jefferson City, visiting Jeff and Jack.

By a pool in Las Vegas.

Interviewed on *Good Morning L.A.*

In studio dressing room of *Entertainment Tonight.*

"Just Arrested." Stan visiting Craig at Terminal Island, Long Beach, California shortly after Craig's arrest.

Craig's fiancée Terri with Academy Award winners Orson Welles and Warren Beatty.

With Maria, Terminal Island.

At the weight pile in the Lompoc prison yard.

Craig and Jeannie the phone operator, Federal Correctional Institution at Safford, Arizona.

Movie premiere of Craig's film *Latin Legends* at Station Casino, Kansas City, Missouri with boxing announcer Michael Buffer, Chiefs' All-Pro kicker Nick Lowery, and other local celebrities.

Exterior of the newest Stanford & Sons at Legends, Kansas City, Kansas.

With former heavyweight champion Joe Frazier.

With comedian David Brenner.

Connie Glazer with comedian Tommy Chong.

With comedian Lewis Black.

Craig and wife Connie at an American Cancer Society event in Kansas City, Missouri.

She thought for a moment. "Then that's what you should do!"

Others belittled my try at grabbing the brass ring. Terri was happy for me. "It's your dream," she said. "I'll do anything I can to support you."

"But if this works out you might never see me again."

"I don't care. This is for you. You'll never be anything but your father's son if you don't try." She was something. I guess I had never experienced such selflessness before. She really did care about me.

Harold Moskovitz didn't write, he called from Los Angeles. Only much later did I realize how lucky I was that any agent had responded positively to a letter from a complete stranger, someone without any track record and without any connections in Hollywood.

Harold wasn't the most powerful agent in town but he was at a small firm, The Agency, working with the Louis L'Amour estate on his Western novels and had recently helped sell the movie rights to the horror novel *The Howling*. Most importantly for me, he was involved with selling *Catch Me If You Can*, a book based on the true story of Frank Abagnale Jr., a con man who took on different identities during a 1960s crime spree. As far as I was concerned, Abagnale's adventures playing doctor and airline pilot and forging checks couldn't begin to compare with mine. I had faced the wrong end of a gun in the hands of guys who wanted to blow my head off.

My hard reality was so unbelievable that it hooked Moskovitz and eventually many others in Hollywood. But Harold said I needed more—to put the story together and sell it I had to come to Hollywood. He had a question too.

"What became of Woodbeck?"

I didn't know. I hadn't spoken to him since the trial a few years earlier. But Harold said having Woodbeck with me would turn us into a new *Butch Cassidy and the Sundance Kid*. That would really grab Hollywood.

I called Digger Dave. He said Don had been in jail again.

. . .

WOODBECK WAS A friend of Eric "Joe" Ramirez, whose Mexico-based family owned marijuana fields and a used car business that was a front operation. After serving the remainder of his sentence in Arizona, Don went back into the drug delivery business, along with Milwaukee Jim, as usual. They bought two private planes, twin engine Beechcraft Bonanzas, and began transporting hundreds of pounds of weed from the Ramirez plantation to remote areas of Arizona and Southern California. The operation became so well known that it was proudly dubbed the MAF, Marijuana Air Force, by *High Times* magazine.

On October 23, 1977, Don and Milwaukee Jim were about to land in the Palm Springs area with 600 pounds of grass. Suddenly they noticed a San Bernardino County Sheriff's Department stakeout waiting for them. As soon as Don touched down, he hit the throttle and took off again.

But they had not gotten away. A handful of government aircraft, fixed wing planes and helicopters, were in hot pursuit. Don and Milwaukee Jim frantically dumped marijuana bales from the plane. Don even tossed his .38 out the window.

The chase turned into a bizarre dogfight. At one point it appeared Don tried to bring down a helicopter by clipping its tail rotor with a tip of his wing. He also seemed to try to ram one of the prop planes. An astonished agent in the plane fired his shotgun through the windshield at the Bonanza. The blast forced Don to land in a field and surrender.

The next day, a retiree in Palm Springs was surprised to find a .38 embedded barrel-first in her front yard.

Don served some eighteen months at the Arizona State Prison in Florence, presumably transferred there for violating his parole in that state. During his time in Florence, Don began to study transcendental meditation and yoga. He thought maybe they would change his life. He certainly already believed in karma. Every day he spent in prison he knew he was paying for his crimes both known and unknown.

After his release, Don joined Milwaukee Jim in Santa Barbara, where they worked at a restaurant and also as salvage divers. Digger Dave gave me their phone number.

"How ya doin', ya ole horse thief?" Don asked when I called.

"I'm selling our story to Hollywood, Don. Told you one day I'd make us famous."

"I don't know, college boy. We tried the sting thing, tried the police thing. It never happened."

"Now it is. I got us an agent and we're going to be movie stars."

"You said 'we,' right?"

"Yeah. We're going to tell them everything we did."

"Everything?"

"Except we'll be Robin Hoods," I said. "We'll be hippie vigilantes."

"But we weren't."

"That doesn't matter. It's a great story."

"I don't know," he said. "I'm as famous as I want to be."

I played the Bronson card. Don liked Charles Bronson.

"The story is like *Death Wish* except there's two of us."

Don still wasn't saying yes.

"Just come on out to Hollywood with me," I said. Then I pushed the same button that had worked on him playing pool that fateful night at Fridays & Saturdays in Phoenix when I was eighteen years old. "We can make some real money."

"Well, guess I don't have anything better to do," Don said. He thought it was a crazy idea to try to get a movie made, but if he could make some money on it then why the hell not.

"I got a red El Camino. How do I get there?"

• • •

I FLEW TO Los Angeles and met Don in Beverly Hills at the Beverly Rodeo Hotel, where Harold got us rooms.

I had only been to Hollywood once before, in 1971 with Steve Asher. He had his mom's credit card and we drove from Phoenix to see the Rolling Stones at the Palladium. He also had family connections that got us onto the set of *The Mary Tyler Moore Show*, and we were able to chat with Moore, Ed Asner, and Cloris Leachman. I thought that just meeting me they would offer to make me a star. My childhood delusions were a constant companion.

When I saw Don again, he looked none the worse for wear despite having done a couple of stints in prison since we had last seen each other. I was glad to see him. I guess our friendship was like when guys go through a war together. You're connected, forever, no matter what. And we had certainly been in a few battles together.

He showed me the issue of *High Times* with his MAF mentioned on the cover. He was proud of that. For all of his "Aw shucks, I don't give a crap" attitude, Don liked being in the spotlight just like anyone else.

But I was different than he remembered. I was no longer the scrawny kid he could dominate. I had jumped on the '80s bandwagon of going to the gym and lifting weights. I was bigger and stronger than before.

When he grabbed the gold fist pendant I still wore around my neck, he pulled it and the chain broke. I wasn't happy, and somewhat playfully, somewhat seriously, I started to wrestle with him in the hotel room. Maybe we needed to test each other, like bear cubs.

Don got me in a headlock. But I pulled out of it and held him at bay. I had grown up, and I sensed a new respect from him. This time, I would take the lead and Don would follow.

We were set to meet Harold at a restaurant. I told Don that I would come in by myself and sit with Harold. He was to come in later and sit a couple booths away.

"Why?"

"So he can discover you on his own." I would direct this scene and I wanted Don's entrance to be as powerful as possible.

Harold was a smart, educated West Coast flower child who, in his early thirties, was learning to balance business with a '60s philosophy. The short, glasses-wearing lover of books was part owner of his family's string of Hollywood and Beverly Hills dry cleaners, which served a celebrity clientele. The counterculture, antihero vibe of *Outlaws* echoed for him, as it did for me, the spirit of movies like *Easy Rider*.

I sat with Harold and described the scenes—my run-in with J.D. in college, my shooting lesson with this tough guy that was Don Woodbeck, the Boston sting, the battle with the bikers … Suddenly he stopped me. He was looking over my shoulder. "Is that him? Is that Woodbeck?" Don smiled at him.

"He's just like in your story!"

Don came over and together we acted out the highlights from *Outlaws*, dialogue and all. We never rehearsed them. We just fell into the rhythm. I guess it's not that surprising considering that we had lived those scenes. We had been there.

When we finished, Harold was bursting with excitement. "That is the greatest story I have ever heard. And you guys are great telling it. You ever thought about playing yourselves in the movie?"

Bingo.

He told us to come back in two weeks and he'd send us around town to pitch the story to movie producers. Harold hyped both of us up: "This is going to be one of the biggest sales for a story in Hollywood history."

When we returned, he put us up at the Marina City Club Hotel and even paid for Terri to come with me. Foolishly, he gave Woodbeck a credit card with an $8,000 limit. Don bought every drink in every bar and every cowboy hat and pair of cowboy boots in every Western store he could find.

We were there the night in December 1980 that John Lennon was shot. Everyone who grew up in the '60s remembers where he was when he heard the news. In many ways it was the end of a generation's innocence, but I had lost mine a long time before that.

"An Outlaw makes a statement about his era," I wrote in the *Outlaws* concept we submitted to the Writers Guild a week later. "A statement dealing with people's political mood, feelings about their loyalty to their community and country, and last, but certainly not least, the

153

morality that surrounds them. Make no mistake that an Outlaw does break the traditional, technical laws of the society in which he lives. Oftentimes he has gone outside of the law because of his disagreement with society. Unlike a criminal, the Outlaw usually has the support of some, if not most, of his or her community, state, or country. Only history and time can tell us whether or not each individual Outlaw becomes a hero or a villain."

I was changing the camera angle on my story, turning us into the kind of rebel hero I always wanted to be. That was the kind of story I wanted to see in a movie, even if it wasn't exactly the story I had lived.

But I also believed every word I wrote. There were two worlds in America during those years—the culture and the counterculture. Every kid wanted to be part of the underground, the counterculture. Our heroes were those who broke the law, whether they were dragged away during a protest against the Vietnam War or were openly getting high at a rock concert, not the people who upheld the law.

The big-time dealers and organized crime? They were nobody's heroes. They were criminals. People like Vern Miller couldn't see the difference. The response to drugs from him and the rest of the establishment had made otherwise decent people into lawbreakers. While he was wasting his time busting college kids selling dime bags—which would have little effect on the drug problem—those pushing the hundreds of kilos and making the big money, people like J.D. and Charlie Costa, were free to do business.

In the black-and-white world of the Vern Millers, we were all the same. My generation, today's baby boomers, knew differently. That's why it was called the "generation gap."

. . .

HOLLYWOOD LOVED OUR story.

We made the rounds of producers and executives, sometimes three or four in one day—Warner Brothers, Paramount, Universal,

CBS, NBC, and on and on. We'd wear Western garb, like tan leather cowboy vests, to emphasize my point about a "modern Western." We didn't have a screenplay or a treatment. We just acted out our gritty adventures in their sterile corporate offices.

Not only was our story exciting, not only was it true, but the main characters were right there in their office. These execs and producers had never been around anyone like us. They were used to make-believe. If this were the 1930s, it'd be like Bonnie and Clyde walking into the office of legendary Hollywood studio head Louis B. Mayer and saying, "Would you want to make a movie about us?"

For the first time, there were two Craig Glazers. I started to talk about myself in the third person, talk about the "Craig Glazer character." In meetings with Hollywood executives, I'd say things like, "Craig wouldn't do that." There was the real me and there was the character I had created. When most kids grow up, their fantasies fade away. Mine came to life and became a movie script.

Here we were handing Hollywood true crime mixed with all-American action. None of the crime movies that had come out could compare. *Serpico*? Hollywood had to stretch to get an action scene from the actual events. *Midnight Express*? Hollywood had to stretch to make Billy Hayes seem even vaguely courageous. In fact, we met with the producers of *Midnight Express* and that film's Oscar-winning writer, a guy I had never heard of by the name of Oliver Stone, long before he made *Natural Born Killers*, a movie about the media glamorizing crime.

Another meeting, with Peter Saphier at Universal, turned into a three-hour extravaganza of storytelling, food, and drinks. Saphier had discovered the novel *Jaws* and would later coproduce *Scarface*.

"Your story is great! You guys are great!" he said as he put his arms around our shoulders and walked us to the elevator. "We'll call you on Monday." We were ecstatic. He was going to buy *Outlaws*!

"Hey, you want to go to Chippendales?" he asked. "Lots of lonely women. Come party with us." He was developing a film about the male striptease revue and Universal was throwing a party at the club.

It was my first big Hollywood industry party. He was right about the women. There were 300 of them and almost no men besides those on stage. The women were all over Don and I. This was Hollywood. This was great!

The next Monday, there was no call from Saphier. We never heard from him again. Having talked drug dealers out of their dope and their money, I thought I was a good bullshitter. I had nothing on the guys in Hollywood.

But I wasn't worried. Everybody loved Don and Craig.

Hollywood didn't have a problem with whether we were good guys or bad guys, though a few execs thought we should dial down the drug aspect, maybe make the stings about jewelry or gold instead. Others were worried that Don and Craig not only didn't pay a price for being outlaws but were rewarded.

The script, I suggested, would end with us being introduced to Vern Miller:

VERN MILLER

Raise your hands!
Don and Craig raise both hands, ready to surrender.

VERN MILLER

No, your right hands.

And he swears us in as special agents.

Most, including David Sontag, an independent producer who had a deal with the relatively new CBS Theatrical Films division, just rolled with the punches and punch lines. *The Kansas City Star* asked him about us and the reporter wrote: "Sontag said he will have no problem working with two men with shady characters. 'Those are actually pretty good qualifications for Hollywood.'" Before we left L.A., he too said he'd buy *Outlaws*.

But again, we heard nothing.

Back in Kansas City, everyone who knew I had gone to Hollywood to sell my movie, including Stan, thought I was full of crap. Everyone, of course, except Terri.

We had just started to book stand-up comedy acts into Stanford & Sons on Sundays and had transformed one of the other Stanford's into an *Urban Cowboy*-ish nightclub called, appropriately, Outlaws. Stanford Glazer and his sons were doing very well. "Hollywood phooey," said Grandpa Bennie. "It's good you stay at home. You have a nice business here."

But my chance at what I really wanted—fame and fortune in Hollywood—had apparently vanished.

One night, two months after leaving Hollywood, I was at a poker game when Harold called.

"Are you sitting down?" he said. "I just sold your story for $150,000."

It's funny but I didn't immediately jump up and down for joy. My first thought wasn't about the money either but rather, "Okay, I'm going to be famous. Just like I said." The orgasmic joy I felt after the Boston sting had to do with winning in the end. When it came to Hollywood, I knew the game was just beginning.

I went to tell Terri but first we had sex. In the glow afterward, she said, "You've never told me you loved me."

I broke the news about the deal to her: "I'm going to Hollywood."

Completely nude, she stood up and blocked the bedroom door.

"What makes you think I wouldn't come with you?" she asked.

So we filled up a U-Haul, hitched it to the '78 Cadillac my father was making payments on for me, invited Grandpa Bennie along for the trip, and headed for Hollywood.

When Grandpa Bennie took his turn driving, smoking a smelly cigar, hunched over the wheel, and chugging along at a whopping fifty-five miles per hour, Terri and I rested in the backseat. I looked at her napping and thought to myself, "Maybe she's the one." Even though I never told her, I fell in love with her on that trip.

Stan, however, was pissed that I left Stanford & Sons. He was mad because I was accomplishing what he had wanted for himself. So he stopped making the payments on the Caddy. Eight weeks later, in L.A., it was repossessed. "That stupid fuckin' movie deal is going nowhere," he said.

But I had already been through rip-offs and gunfights, a drug overdose and a major arrest on the front pages of a newspaper. Hollywood couldn't possibly be that tough.

9

Going Hollywood

"Our acting coach asked us, 'Can you act?'" Woodbeck says. "I said in our line of work when our scenes failed shots were fired. You don't have any gun, so let's do it."

—*Los Angeles Reader*, June 11, 1982

I WANTED A chance not only to have my story on the big screen but actually to be the guy on the screen. Sontag said we would be given that opportunity. Acting wouldn't be a stretch for Don or me. Hell, we had acted for years, with our lives on the line.

Harold enrolled us in Sal Dano's acting class. Dano was a husky, DeNiro-ish "let me tell you how it is" character with an acting studio on Robertson Boulevard. Most of his successful students were physically big, action-oriented men.

Our classmates included Tom Selleck, who was starring in the first season of *Magnum P.I.*; Lou Ferrigno, the bodybuilder who was in the middle of his run as the Incredible Hulk; and Sonny Landham, an imposing, rough-looking Indian who always played bad guys and was about to star as one of the villains in *48 Hrs.* with Eddie Murphy and Nick Nolte. Also in class were Robert Hays, who had just hit the big-time in the summer of 1980 with *Airplane!*, and Priscilla Barnes, who was about to replace Suzanne Somers on *Three's Company*.

Dano tried to impress the rest of the class by introducing us as having been on *The Tonight Show* and giving us a lot of other credits we didn't have. It was all lies but nobody cared. In Hollywood you get used to being conned by con artists. Yep, we would fit in nicely.

Don and I became fast friends with Sonny. I guess "badasses" liked to stick together, even if Sonny only played them in the movies. We also tagged along with the rest of the Hollywood bad boys, like Gary Busey, who had exploded as the lead in *The Buddy Holly Story* a couple years earlier, and Mickey Rourke, an edgy actor whom the public was beginning to notice after he played the arsonist in *Body Heat*. All we needed to be friends was coke, and thanks to Don's connections, we certainly had that.

Terri and her daughter moved into an apartment with me on Alta Loma, off Sunset, across from the Playboy office. Living the high life not too far away, at Sunset and La Cienega, was Richard Hellman, whom Harold introduced us to soon after we arrived in Hollywood.

Hellman was a very proper, aristocratic, British-born movie producer with gray hair and steel-blue eyes. Supposedly Marilyn Monroe had once lived in his apartment, but just about everyone in Hollywood said that about where they lived. His greatest claim to fame was *The Great Escape*, for which he was not only assistant producer but also appeared on screen playing the French waiter at the cafe where the German soldiers were gunned down by the Resistance. Don and I would hang out at the coke-and-backgammon parties he hosted at his apartment. We reveled in meeting stars like Burt Reynolds and Jaclyn Smith and directors like Hal Needham. Hellman would tease the Hollywood crowd with our adventures and show us off—"the outlaws"—to his movie star friends. We were the real things in their fantasy world and they became the fantasy come true in mine.

I went Hollywood. Gym, acting class, meetings with producers, coke at a hundred dollars a gram. What people outside Hollywood don't realize is that the people who party are the ones not working. If you have to get up at 5 a.m. to be on a set, you are not dancing the night away. The partying comes between jobs. If you get that wrong, you're not working for long, unless, of course, you're already a star.

We were babes in the woods. We judged producers by how nice their offices were and looked down on those who operated out of trailers on the lot. We didn't know that being in a trailer meant they were actually working and that sometimes those who had offices had little else.

When we met Mike Fenton, we didn't comprehend that he was one of the biggest casting agents in town, a partner in Fenton-Feinberg. He could make or break an acting career.

"You have the looks," he told me, "but you're a little young to play an outlaw." If only he knew the truth!

He liked Don, though. "You have that Bronson thing going for you." That made Don's day.

He told him there was a part available for a tall, blond, blue-eyed, strong-looking soldier in a movie being shot. The film was about the Nazis trying to find the Ark of the Covenant in the Middle East. We walked away laughing. What a stupid idea for a movie, we said to each other. Don blew off the audition. Of course, the movie was *Raiders of the Lost Ark*. Fenton never called us back for another audition.

• • •

FOR ACTING CLASS, Dano gave Don and I a scene from *The Odd Couple* to perform, Don in the Walter Matthau role as Oscar and me as Jack Lemmon's Felix. A reporter from the *L.A. Times* was writing a major story on us and Harold invited him to the class. But Don and I hated to memorize anything. Studying got in the way of partying until four in the morning.

Neither of us knew our lines. So we improvised. We were funny and our classmates laughed their asses off. Not Dano.

"Take a seat," he ordered. Then he dressed me down, just like my father would. It was a big league embarrassment in front of the whole class. He was never as hard on Don. Maybe because he was one of those big guys he liked to be around.

Our antics didn't bother the reporter, Peter Brown. The story he was writing was about the national controversy we had ignited.

There were rumors that CBS Theatrical was about to go under. I wanted to make sure my movie got made and figured that national attention would help. So in early 1981 I told Harold to contact all of the top talk and news shows and offer to set up a drug sting for them to film. Jon Alpert, a highly respected, award-winning TV journalist from the *Today* show, was intrigued. Alpert had led the first American TV crew into Vietnam after the war and during the hostage crisis in Iran was the last newsman to gain entry into the embassy where the captive Americans were being held.

He came to L.A. to meet us and see if we were legit. We proposed that he follow us with a hidden camera as we planned and executed a sting on a heroin deal in Kansas City. This was reality TV à la what crusading journalist Geraldo Rivera had recently been doing.

Alpert liked the idea and the *Today* show flew us to New York on the red-eye to consult with Steve Friedman, the show's producer. Friedman thought it was "a dynamite story" from "one of his best correspondents." Though Tom Brokaw, a cohost on the show, was supposedly nervous about the story, we never met with him or the other cohost, Jane Pauley. Nevertheless, Friedman was stoked, saying, "These guys have such charisma and dope is such a hot topic that it makes it a natural for the *Today* show."

But I needed to cover my ass on the legal side. My five years of probation had only begun in 1978. I had to stay out of trouble for at least another year. I'd be breaking the law with this drug buy and I knew it. I did not want to go to jail.

I called Lieutenant Lew Hoskins, who had become the top drug enforcement officer in Johnson County after Roy Miller's exit. I explained what Don and I were up to and that we would then make a citizen's arrest of the dealer.

"Craig and I are good friends," Hoskins said later, "and I can appreciate what he's trying to do … I steered them away from trouble and made sure they didn't get hurt … They told me in advance what their plans were and I appreciate them telling me … I wanted to know what (heroin) was out there and my unit had been unsuccessful in finding and buying any heroin." Hoskins told us he wouldn't take any action to stop us and that if we helped him find heroin we would not be arrested. But he advised us not to make a citizen's arrest because it might complicate any possible arrest of the dealer by law enforcement. The special agent in charge of the Kansas City office of the DEA, Charles Sherman, defended Hoskins' approach: "I don't think Lew Hoskins did anything wrong. If these characters planned to do this anyway, what more could he do?"

Publicity wasn't my only motive. I also wanted to help my brother Jack.

"I believe Craig was honest in wanting to break up an alleged heroin ring," said Major Lloyd Cooper of the criminal investigation division of the Kansas City Police in Missouri, whom I also told what was happening, along with the Johnson County district attorney's office. "He tried to make a deal at first to lighten the load on his brother who's serving time on drug charges. But we had to say no."

The buy was set for the afternoon of May 4, but was delayed a few hours because Friedman realized he needed union cameramen to be present with Alpert. He turned around a Lear jet carrying a couple of NBC staffers so they would arrive later that day. While we waited, we recreated our sting routine, with unloaded guns, for Alpert in a room at the Crown Center Hotel, the same place we had been headquartered before the ill-fated motel bust years before. Finally, the clandestine heroin buy went down after hours at, conveniently, Stanford & Sons. In view of a camera hidden in a briefcase on the table, Don and I tried to buy a gram of heroin from a bearded, long-haired biker type with large tattoos on his arms, though it was hard to make out his face. When we questioned the quality of his merchandise, the asshole told us to fuck ourselves. We went back and forth for about twenty minutes before we gave him a hundred dollars for the gram. We then went to Hoskins's office and watched as he tested the gram to verify that it was heroin. It was.

We also demonstrated on camera how one of our stings might have gone, using an assistant manager from Stanford's and, as the dealer, a guy who worked for my old friend Marc, who had settled into a comfortable suburban life as a plumbing contractor. That portion of the tape would be clearly labeled a dramatization.

We told reporters in Los Angeles and Kansas City what we had done and newspaper articles began popping up. Getting a buzz going was exactly what I wanted. What I hadn't expected was that local law enforcement officials would be pissed. They figured the public would ask, "How could these two guys make a buy when our police are unable to find any dealers at all?" As for me, the more controversy the better—as long as it got us in the news.

Worried that the story would make them look bad, the authorities asked for a copy of the footage, presumably so they could identify the drug dealer, track him down, and arrest him. But there was about as much chance of getting that footage from NBC as there was of getting the notebook from one of their reporters or the names of his sources. It wasn't going to happen. They tried to get it from Alpert too but he made sure that wasn't possible by dropping out of sight.

That made the cops angrier. "I guess we'll have to make our own copy when it shows on *Today*," an annoyed Major Cooper told one newspaper. "And that's a fine way to get evidence, isn't it?"

Dennis Moore, the post-Jordan Johnson County DA, threatened to throw me in jail for violating my probation. Even before this incident, Moore had asked a judge to deny my request for an early end to my probation. Now he was incensed. "I don't think someone on probation ought to be out there making a heroin buy," he said. "I don't like it, and I'm going to look into the possibility of whether Craig Glazer's probation can be revoked."

Two days later not only did Moore not follow through with his threat but he did the opposite—he recommended I be freed from probation immediately!

He tried to explain his about-face to the public by saying that many people "have their probations terminated early. So I decided that I wanted this probation handled like any other probation." I didn't buy it.

Was he suddenly grateful to me because he might never have gotten his job if the motel bust case hadn't soiled Margaret Jordan? After all, he became the first Democrat to hold that office in more than thirty years. Probably not. The only reason I could figure for him changing his mind was he realized Don and I might actually come off as heroes for exposing the heroin underworld to a national TV audience. He wanted to be a hero too. Putting me in jail and trying to justify it on camera wouldn't be the way to do that.

The story was scheduled to air on July 15.

But as the newspaper stories—all of which mentioned some of what Don and I had done in the past—actually began to appear, Friedman grew uncertain. After all, we were admitted con men. Were we conning NBC too? One article charged, "Woodbeck and Craig Glazer are attempting to pull off what could be the biggest scheme in their long careers in con artistry." "I didn't mind that they wanted to make their lives in the movies," Friedman said. "But I resented all this hype—leaks to newspapers and public comments from their agent. I began to think, 'Maybe this whole thing is just staged for us from top to bottom.'"

Every article about the upcoming *Today* show talked about *Outlaws*. "Today the *Today* show, tomorrow the movies?" asked one headline.

"I think they were trying to use us more than we should be used," said Friedman. He wanted a purity that didn't exist in television then and doesn't exist now. Alpert knew that and said so at the time: "Most people involved in television have some type of motive."

But TV news was reeling from questions that had recently arisen about the credibility of Geraldo Rivera's reports. His opening of what was supposedly mobster Al Capone's vault earlier in the year on a massively promoted two-hour special resulted in absolutely nothing being found. Had the public been scammed? Questions about the use of "dramatizations" and "recreations" were flying around.

Finally, on July 14, the day before it was supposed to air, the *Today* show killed our story.

The cancellation had us all over newspapers around the country, from *The New York Times* to the *L.A. Times* to an article by Tom Shales in *The Washington Post.* We took as much advantage of that as we could, always mentioning our movie. But it was a huge disappointment that the story didn't run.

Did we almost sting NBC? Did Friedman have reason to question what was on film? Was it an actual heroin buy?

Here are the facts, which I have never revealed before:

Yes, the heroin was real.

Yes, the heroin dealer was a real heroin dealer.

But the buy was staged, scripted by me. We guaranteed the pusher that the camera would be placed so that no one could identify him. Alpert didn't know about any of this.

Would airing the story have done some good in the drug war? Maybe. But in truth we did it for the sensationalism, for the publicity.

I'm guessing Geraldo would have done the same thing.

• • •

BEGINNING WITH THE *Today* show fiasco, my vision of a Hollywood future started to fall apart. Even our relationship with Harold suffered.

"You and Don owe me some money," he said, reminding me that Woodbeck had put $8,000 on the credit card Harold had given him the first time we were in town. He was especially annoyed since Don had bought silly things like tennis rackets. Don was naturally athletic and had started playing regularly with Fleetwood Mac's Stevie Nicks, as well as with Bo Derek of *10* and her husband, John.

Don didn't consider the money a loan but an agent's cost of doing business. After moving to L.A., he thought he was pretty smooth when he squeezed another $20,000 from Harold. He figured Harold was a pushover, and Don had no respect for wimps.

But when we received our first check from Sontag, it was less than we expected. Harold had reimbursed himself for at least some of what he had given us. When our next check arrived, it was even smaller— Harold had taken nearly all of Don's share.

Don was furious.

"I ought to throw you through the window," he threatened.

From that moment on, Harold kept Don at arm's length.

Meanwhile, Sontag wrote the first *Outlaws* script. It was horrible. He wrote it as a comedy! His version opened with a "Ballad of Craig and Don," performed by someone like Waylon Jennings, that would be heard throughout the film, like in *Cat Ballou*, the Lee Marvin classic.

He consulted very little with us and then submitted the script to CBS Theatrical without telling us. Not surprisingly, the script did not encourage the company to start filming. In any case, CBS Theatrical would fold in just a couple of years. We were in trouble.

Were our fifteen minutes of fame over already? I did everything I could to make sure it wasn't and kept the publicity machine primed.

In July 1982 we were on the cover of the *Los Angeles Reader*, a free weekly, dressed up as Old West gunslingers. The headline read: "Reeling & Dealing: Can Two All-American Outlaws Sell Their Story of Drugs and Double-Crosses to Hollywood and Live Happily Ever After?" The paper came out on Thursday afternoon and we went to Tower Records on Sunset Boulevard to pick up a few copies. We walked over to two cute girls who were standing there reading the article.

"That's me and him," I told them proudly.

They looked us over. "No it isn't."

"Yes it is."

"But they're drug dealers."

I shrugged. "It's a long story."

They wanted nothing to do with us and walked away.

"Sure glad we're on the cover of a newspaper," said Don with a smirk. "Boy, am I gonna get laid now."

The next day, while working out at Bally's in Hollywood, Mr. T, who had just starred in *Rocky III*, came up to me.

"You're one of those guys in the newspaper." He shook my hand. It felt good to be recognized by someone who was on the big screen.

In Kansas City, I was different. In Hollywood, as long I was on the front page, I was one of them.

. . .

EVERYTHING WE HAD been promised evaporated.

Having lost its heat, *Outlaws* was in "turnaround," put on the backburner. And I now knew that no one in Hollywood ever meant it when they entertained the idea of us playing ourselves in the movie. Soon we were no longer being introduced to Burt Reynolds but to a friend of Burt Reynolds, not to a producer but to an associate producer. Woodbeck and I were just two more wannabe actors in Hollywood waiting for the phone to ring.

I had gone through all of my money for the movie option. Don was restless and wanted some action. He started mumbling about stings again. I started to listen to him. We met Harry Reems, of *Deep Throat* porno fame, and he invited us to the Playboy Mansion, where Don talked to him about ripping off a coke dealer. But that part of my life was over. Wasn't it? The script to the movie that was my life had been written. I didn't think there ever would be anything more to add.

Terri overheard Don and I talking about the possible sting. She didn't like Don, thought he was dangerous, especially to me, or rather to us. Earlier, when we were at home in Kansas City, I had asked her to marry me. I gave her an engagement ring at Marc's house and she said yes.

But while she had signed on for Hollywood and my fantasy life, she had not signed on for a lifestyle of stings and snorting coke.

I came home from the gym one night and found a note: "I love you. I hope your life works out. I believe in your movie and I believe in you. Follow that path, but it can't be with me."

10

Blood in Redondo Beach

They write novels about cases like this.

—Rick De La Sota, Los Angeles County deputy district attorney,
The Kansas City Times, February 12, 1983

I WAS STUNNED. As I read the note, Terri was driving Michelle back to Kansas City. I called her mother but she was not encouraging. I had succumbed to Hollywood, was doing too much blow, and now my chance for a real family life had picked up and left.

I had spent a couple of crazy years betting my life on being able to read someone's eyes. Are they scared? Are they scared enough to give up their gun? Are they too stupid, too strong, or too high to care? The eyes don't lie. When Terri would say she'd leave me because of Don, I'd tell her, "When you can look me in the eyes and say you don't love me, then I'll be the one to go."

There were times she tried to look me in the eyes and say that. But in the end she'd turn away. That's why she wrote a note and left. When I flew to Kansas City to convince her to come back, she wouldn't even see me. She knew she couldn't look me in the eyes.

I went so far as to ask my mother to have lunch with her, to see if there was any hope of us getting back together. She said there was none. I even had Marc talk to Terri. Still she refused to see me.

"Hey man," Marc advised like a long-time buddy should, "move on."

169

But I had lost my rock.

At the same time, with *Outlaws* dead at CBS Theatrical, the Hollywood paychecks had stopped. When we occasionally auditioned as bit players in TV action dramas, there was no payoff there either.

I tried out for a role as a lifeguard in an episode of one series; my line was, "Get out of the pool!" A thousand guys could do that. But there was one more requirement. "I can get you the part," said the casting assistant, "if you can get me some blow."

In the early '80s, coke was currency in Hollywood. He wanted $1,000 of coke so I could get a one-line gig paying about $300. He might as well have asked me to bend over. I said no. We were also told we could play racecar drivers in a sci-fi flick starring Mick Jagger. The movie, *Freejack*, finally came out ten years later, in 1992. We weren't going to wait that long. We couldn't wait that long.

Maybe because of his growing coke habit, Don was on edge more often. He flew off the handle like never before. When reporters questioned our motives, when he was challenged in interviews or he read an article in the paper that doubted we did what we said we did, he'd get royally pissed.

UPI reporter Vernon Scott wrote that we had sold our story of "wildly improbable drug robberies … to the movies in what amounts to their easiest and most lucrative con job … How much of their story may be unadulterated poppycock apparently doesn't bother CBS Theatrical Films."

"Maybe we ought to just show them," Don said.

He lost faith that we would get any more money from Hollywood. I think he lost faith in me too.

"You think there'll be a movie someday?" he asked.

"Yeah."

"Well, I don't give a fuck."

"But then no one will hear our story."

"We're not Robin Hoods. We didn't give the money back. We kept it, dude."

"But they were worse than we were," I insisted. I thought that meant something. He didn't.

He needed money. He suggested we rob a bank. I said no because how would that look in a movie? We ripped off drug dealers, bad guys. Robbing a bank didn't fit my image of who I was.

I was a mercenary for the money *and* for the fame. Everyone is out for himself in this world. Sports heroes? Sure they love the game but at the end of the game they get rewarded if they win—with money, with praise. The same in business. The same in crime. I had put myself in front of gun barrels, played at the highest stakes there were. I wanted to get something out of that, money and something more. I wanted Woodbeck and Glazer to be legends, folk heroes like Jesse James or Black Bart.

"So your idea is that when you're dead," Don said, "you'll be famous?"

I wanted to be alive and famous. But, yeah, he was on target. If nothing else, I'd rather be dead and famous than dead and forgotten.

"Okay, then make us famous," he said, "but pay me now."

I couldn't.

• • •

MY COUSIN LENNY knew a quasi-mobster and bookie named Buzzy Schultz who had an office in L.A. and seemed to be in the business of selling cars and boats on the "warm" side, i.e., probably stolen. Buzzy kept his own yacht at Marina del Rey and Don and I would go deep-sea fishing with him. Like everyone else, he loved to hear our stories about the stings.

He had a gorgeous English woman for an assistant—Stephanie, a thirty-eight-year-old Linda Evans type but with dark hair. Several years older than me, she had two teenage boys from a previous marriage, lived in a nice home in Tarzana, and drove a Mercedes 450 convertible. Other than screwing him, how she assisted the chubby, balding, middle-aged Buzzy was uncertain. But she was smart enough not to rely solely on

Buzzy. She was also having an affair with singer Tom Jones. In other words, Stephanie was that rare former Hollywood bimbo who had succeeded. She understood that in Hollywood the used become the users.

She invited me to lunch in Beverly Hills.

"Maybe I can help you with your wardrobe," she said, knowing I was low on funds. She wanted to buy me clothes? I was offended, not because she insulted my fashion sense but because I had never taken money from a woman. I was not a gigolo. But I was hurting over Terri and maybe I wanted to use and be used too. Stephanie and I began to have sex about once a week, but only on certain days and at certain times. I'd have to clear out before Tom Jones showed up. I guess I was his opening act.

One night we were watching *The Tonight Show* in her bed when she took a phone call. The husband of a girlfriend of hers had been indicted for trafficking in coke. Her friend, Rosa, was frantic. Hubby had gone down in a multiple kilo bust and was looking at a decade or more in prison. Knowing that Stephanie was attracted to shady characters, I had given her a thumbnail sketch of my sting adventures. Now she asked if I could help Rosa.

"Uh, I might," I said, and in that instant concocted a storyline. I told Rosa that I knew a federal agent named Ed who might be able to fix her problem. She asked for his last name but I refused to tell her. When she asked how much it would cost, I told her it would be expensive. Even as a kid I wondered why no one seemed to recognize that Clark Kent looked exactly like Superman but with glasses. Stephanie knew that taking money from drug dealers had been my specialty. I guess she didn't think I was the same person.

I hadn't done a sting since Arizona, ten years earlier. If I did one now, I'd be getting back in the business. But this would be a soft sting, no gunplay, and I'd be hurting a drug dealer. Even better, the dealer was already in jail, being held without bond. It wasn't likely he'd be getting out anytime soon. So why the hell not do it?

Which is what one guy says to another guy about jumping off a cliff. Terri would have been the "why not." But she wasn't around.

"Ed the Fed," of course, would be Woodbeck. When I told Don about my plan, he was more excited than he had been about the movie deal. He was especially happy because the sting involved a lot of acting and he would get to be the main character for a change. Not only that but, unlike most of our past stings, I would play the sleazebag and he would play the good cop. Finally we would be Hollywood stars, even if it were just in our own little drama.

We rehearsed like never before. Don even came up with some physical shtick for his back story. He would have a limp and walk with a cane because he had been shot in the leg during a drug bust. As a result, he was a DEA agent about to retire. I truly had to stop him from wearing an eye patch.

We discovered that times had changed when we had trouble getting a DEA badge. We didn't have any connections anymore and visited every pawnshop in town without luck. After two days, we went to a costume shop and bought an FBI badge that looked like it was from the '50s. I felt like a retired boxer who decides he's going to make a comeback and doesn't realize that, while he still has the power, his punches have lost some speed.

I first met Rosa alone in the late afternoon at Ben Frank's, an all-night coffee shop on Sunset Boulevard. Ben Frank's was the classic Hollywood hangout where in one pan of the camera you would see Hell's Angels, wannabe rock stars, famous actors, not-famous-at-all movie executives, cops, and hookers.

"I'm only doing this because you're Stephanie's friend," I told the overweight Latina after we ordered coffee.

"How do you know this Ed?"

"When I was an undercover drug agent in Kansas, I worked under him. He's a straight-up guy. But I told him you could give him leads on other cases. If you do that, he'll call a buddy of his, an assistant to the U.S. Attorney, who can pull some strings and help your husband."

Don made his entrance, suit and tie, carrying a black briefcase, limping, and very nervous, just like a DEA agent doing something he shouldn't.

"I don't like drug dealers," Woodbeck said as he sat down. "You and your husband should both do lots of time."

Rosa looked at me like "What the hell?"

"You want my help or not?" asked Don sharply. "I don't care."

"Yes, yes, please."

It's amazing what people will believe if you just take charge and overwhelm them. They don't have a chance to stop and think that something might not be right. Like in the movies, they suspend their disbelief because they want to believe.

"I need to check if you're wired," Don said, and immediately reached across the table with both hands, grabbed her large breasts and began feeling around them. She was surprised but didn't stop him. Maybe it was because Don made sure his jacket fell open so Rosa could see the .38 in his shoulder holster.

I didn't know if anyone in the place saw Don groping Rosa but at Ben Frank's the regulars would have shrugged it off. They wouldn't have even thought it unusual that Don then took her into the women's restroom.

We had to be sure she was not with the cops, not looking for a way to get hubby off by trapping someone else in a criminal act. We also wanted to impress her with how serious we were. So, in the restroom, Don told her to pull down her underwear. Ed the Fed was strictly business. But Don had to work hard to keep from laughing. Her pussy wasn't wired either.

By the time they returned to the table, Rosa was not a happy camper.

"I told you he was the real deal," I whispered to her.

"How will you do this?" she sneered at Ed the Fed, wanting to get this over with as quickly as possible.

Don looked her in the eyes. "Half the money…" He paused for effect. "Goes to my friend in the U.S. Attorney's office." Ed the Fed stared at her stone cold.

"How much?"

Don took a pen from his jacket pocket, wrote "$30,000" on a napkin, and shoved it across the table to her.

"The money's not important to me," he said. "Craig gets the other half. Fifteen upfront and the rest when your husband walks out of jail. I want the information you have."

She winced reading the amount.

"You have forty-eight hours," warned Woodbeck, "or your husband will end up in Terminal Island Federal Penitentiary and you will not see him for a very, very long time."

She nodded.

When the waitress came with the check, Ed the Fed said, "I got it."

He flipped open his wallet so Rosa could see his gold badge but not enough so she could see it read "FBI" and not "DEA." He also left Rosa with some advice: "Tell your husband to never deal coke again."

Two days later, Rosa returned to Ben Frank's. I went inside while Don, as Ed the Fed, waited in the parking lot. She gave me $5,000 good faith money.

I went to Don.

"Just like old times," he said.

A few days after, Rosa delivered another $10,000. She wasn't going to give us anything more until her husband was free. But that decision would have nothing to do with us and wasn't going to be made for a very, very long time.

We had made $15,000 for one little acting job, more than most members of the Screen Actors Guild made in a year. I knew I had fallen back into the mind-set I had a decade ago when I realized that my next thought was, "How can we get more out of her?"

I didn't have to come up with anything fresh. As with many soft stings, the victim came back to give us another opportunity.

It turned out Rosa was as big a coke dealer as her still-in-jail, still-awaiting-trial spouse. "I need to shovel some snow," she said. She wanted me to set up a buy for several ounces, about $15,000 worth. We would share in the profit.

My cousin Keith, a guitarist in a rock band called The Reds, had moved to L.A. to make it in the music biz and looked like the quintessential longhaired rocker. We gave him $1,000 to pretend to be the buyer, a roll of show money—which was actually from the same stash Rosa had given us—and put him in Don's apartment. Don was in the process of moving to Brentwood so Rosa knowing the location wouldn't matter later.

Unfortunately, Rosa was not alone when she arrived. Stephanie had come with her, much to my surprise. I didn't want her involved but there was nothing I could do.

As Keith weighed the coke, he cranked up the radio—our signal—and "Ed the Fed" and I blew in through the front door, our .38s drawn, a limp still in Don's step.

"DEA! You're under arrest!"

"What are you doing?" Stephanie asked, looking at me. "You betrayed me?"

Of all the stings I had done, I felt worse about this one than any other. It was a bad emotional scene. Maybe because it was personal.

"I told you not to deal coke ever again," Ed the Fed chastised Rosa.

"Ed, can't you lighten up?" I offered. "She might help us down the road. Know what I'm saying?"

He thought for a moment. "Young man," he said to Keith, "on the floor, hands behind your back. We're taking you into custody." He told the women, "You too, on the floor."

He handcuffed Keith and brought him to the door.

"What about my husband?"

"You have your own problems," he said. "Stay down. Other officers are on their way to take both of you to the station."

He and I hustled Keith down the hallway and out of the building.

As soon as we were gone, Rosa and Stephanie bolted. Rosa had been fully stung. She would never see us again. Don kept the coke and gave me some of the profit for whatever he sold rather than put up his nose.

The day after the sting, I had Keith call Stephanie and explain to her that I had no choice but to be a CI for Ed the Fed. She told

Keith she did not want to date me any longer. I could understand that.

• • •

DON LOOKED LIKE someone who had been in tough spots and come out in one piece. I trusted him—often with my life. Even complete strangers were willing to trust him.

I remember him calling me from the Los Angeles airport after visiting friends in Phoenix. He had such a story to tell that he couldn't wait to meet up at my apartment. I had moved to Brentwood too, only three blocks from his place.

"You're not going to believe this," he said.

The man sitting next to him on the flight into LAX looked like a shoe salesman, but he was sweating bullets. Don chatted him up, telling war stories about Nam. The man leaned over and softly said, "I'm scared to death. Can I trust you?"

"You sure can, pal. What's the problem?"

The man put his mouth to within an inch of Don's ear. "I'm flying a kilo for a friend. Can you help me get it off the plane?"

Obviously, he had never done anything like that before, or he would never have told someone he didn't know that he had $30,000 worth of cocaine on him. Talk about your bad luck days. Of all the people he could have sat next to, this day it was Woodbeck.

"Yeah, right, you're just fuckin' with me," I told Don.

"God's honest truth," he said.

He asked the scared passenger, "Why don't you just walk it off like you brought it on?"

"I think maybe the cops might be looking for me. They might grab me when I step off the plane."

The guy was about to pee in his pants.

"What do you want me to do?" Don asked.

"The stuff is here." He patted his jacket. "You take my coat and go to the restroom and take it. Then we'll meet later and I'll give you $500."

Don took his coat and felt for the kilo. He suggested that after they land they meet at a particular restaurant outside the airport.

The frightened man shook hands with Don. "Deal."

In the airplane toilet, Don stuffed a half-kilo plastic bag of coke into each cowboy boot. Back in his seat, Don was cool as could be for the rest of the flight. The worried courier calmed down.

They ignored each other at the terminal and exited separately.

Don never went to the restaurant.

He was laughing on the phone as he finished the story.

"I tell ya, buddy, I don't look for it but sometimes it just comes to me."

I wondered how long the courier waited at the restaurant before he figured out he had been swindled. Yes, you could trust Don—as long as you weren't someone he thought he could get one over on.

Don arrived to my apartment and pulled out a bag of coke from each boot.

"Let's party!" he yelled. He put one of his big bear claws of a hand into a bag, scooped up a tremendous amount of blow, and snorted it. It was Christmas in June and the snow was falling in Southern California.

I could see that his coke habit was affecting his judgment. For example, there was his new girlfriend, Debbie Brewster. She was in her early twenties, pretty in a trailer park sort of way, and very wild. She and her stripper friends thought Don was cool because he had blow. They would do anything and anyone for coke.

After one party at Don's apartment, I smelled something burning. Like skin. I found one of Debbie's blown-out girlfriends in his bedroom. She had passed out while masturbating with an electric dildo. A hot part of the pocket rocket ended up settling on her pussy lips. The Steely Dan kept on going. We had to take her to the emergency room.

Debbie wanted more coke and asked Don to rip off her ex-boyfriend who stored kilos at his Hermosa Beach pad. She arranged for us to visit his apartment, where the short, chubby, twenty-something with long curly hair, T-shirt, and jeans said he was waiting for some Colombians to bring over the kilos.

We were armed and ready.

In the meantime, the ex showed us his stamp collection, then his baseball card collection. A fat friend of his also came to visit. Don and I were getting bored.

"Oh, and I also collect derringers." Now that was something that interested Don.

"They're in my safe." Our eyes widened.

The ex had a floor safe and he used his hand to shield us from seeing the combination as he opened it. How very cautious of him. After all, you never know who might want to rip you off. Inside the safe we could see a few derringers—and $40,000.

"I think this is good," I said to Don.

We pulled out our guns and went through our sting arrest routine. We took the derringers, about five ounces of coke, and the forty grand. It was the easiest score of our entire career.

"Let's wait for the Colombians," said Don.

"Nah." He was getting greedy. "Let's get out of here."

"But we can get a couple kilos!"

"Let's go!" We left but Don wasn't happy. He thought I had wimped out.

Two days later, I heard loud banging on the door of the condo next to mine. I looked out the window and saw the ex and the fat friend. Don had told Debbie what had gone down. When the ex called her, knowing that we had come over to his place on her say-so, she admitted everything and told him where I lived.

I jumped quickly into the hall and drew my silver .38 on them.

"Police officer! Freeze!"

"You're not a cop!" said the ex. "Debbie told us all about you."

What now? I never wanted to shoot someone but if these two guys went for me I'd have no choice.

Who should just so happen to show up? Yep, Woodbeck. He read them the riot act.

"If you ever come around either of us again, we'll fuckin' kill you!"

He smacked the ex across the face and kicked the fat guy's ass as they ran off.

I was pissed and nervous. Maybe next time they'll hire some muscle instead. I would have to move again.

• • •

MEANWHILE OUR HOLLYWOOD life took a turn for the better.

Paramount optioned our life story rights. Walter Hill, who hit the big time directing *48 Hrs.*, was supposedly interested, with Eddie Murphy playing me. Hollywood didn't care that I wasn't black—and I didn't either. There was also talk of Tom Hanks playing Craig Glazer and Jeff Bridges or Harrison Ford playing Don Woodbeck.

Our new producers were Tony Garnett and John Heyman. Garnett was a well-known English TV producer-writer-director trying to break into the Hollywood movie world with low-budget films about gritty subjects, movies such as *Prostitute* and *Handgun*, which was about a rape victim who gets revenge. He wasn't afraid of tough subjects. In 1978, his BBC miniseries *Law and Order* upset many people because of its radical idea that professional criminals operated like, and weren't much different than, any other group of enterprising businessmen with profit as their primary—and usually only—goal. So I wasn't surprised he was attracted to *Outlaws*.

Heyman was a German-born Jew who grew up in England and in 1979 had produced *Jesus*, which some claimed was the most-watched film of all time. But his feature credits went all the way back to 1964 when he produced Richard Burton's *Hamlet*. Having taken on those two lofty subjects, obviously he was very arrogant and very sure of himself.

Also on board was screenwriter Nicholas Kazan, son of famed director Elia Kazan (*On the Waterfront*). Not many outside Hollywood knew about Nick. *Frances*, starring Jessica Lange, about the tragic life of actress Frances Farmer, wouldn't be released until the end of the year. He would then write *At Close Range*, starring Sean Penn, about a notorious crime family. Years later he'd earn an Oscar nomination for penning *Reversal of Fortune*, about Claus von Bulow's successful bid to overturn his conviction for the murder of his wealthy wife. True-life drama was Nick's specialty and the frail, balding writer loved our story, even though at first he thought we were just a couple of thugs, no different than the scumbags in *At Close Range*. But when he started to interview me for the script, he discovered we had something in common—he had a difficult time growing up with his father much as I had with mine. Maybe we could be friends.

In the background was an assistant to Garnett, a smart, hard-working, ambitious recent UCLA grad named Amy Pascal. She would go on to become chairman of the Sony Pictures Entertainment Motion Picture Group, run its Columbia Pictures division, and rank as not only one of the most powerful people in Hollywood but one of the most powerful women in the world. But that would be twenty years later.

This was the summer of 1982 and *Outlaws* was back on track.

On the other hand, I went to sleep with my .38 under my pillow because there might be people trying to kill me.

. . .

DEBBIE KNEW SHE needed to make up for her blunder. She did it the only way she knew how—she gave up a big weed dealer.

Maybe it was the coke to stay up and the downers to go to sleep but Don just wanted to rip people off, as many as possible as soon as possible. He didn't even want to continue the sting scenario.

"Fuck, I don't need any badge! All I have to say is, 'I'm Don Wood-dick! Freeze, motherfuckers!!!'" He thought everyone he had come up against or would come up against was a stupid punk. I worried that his confidence had become overconfidence, and that was very dangerous.

There were times that summer I really hated Don for the first time. I heard during those weeks that, during an argument with Debbie, he pushed her out of his car and hit her. That's something he never would have done before.

We met Debbie's weed dealer one night at his house in the hills above Hollywood. We were going to scope out the situation and see what they had before setting up a sting for later. He was there with three of his friends. They didn't look very tough. They didn't even have a lot of weed, only about fifty pounds.

"How do you want to play this?" I asked Don out of their hearing.

"They're nothing. We're invincible. No one can touch us. I'll show ya."

"Don, don't…" But I couldn't stop him. He no longer cared.

He stood up and yelled, "LAPD! Hit the floor!" He didn't flash a badge or draw a gun. One of the guys bolted down the hall for the bedroom and I ran after him. I cocked my .38 and saw that I had accidentally taken Don's gun—and that it wasn't loaded. Don hadn't even bothered to make sure it had bullets.

The guy asked, "If you're a cop, show me some ID."

I didn't have any. I guess I had gotten pretty sloppy myself.

"I'm a black belt," he said, summoning up his courage.

I squared up behind my .38 and aimed right between his eyes.

He threw his hands up.

We didn't have any handcuffs either. So I ordered him into the living room with the others. They were all scared and willingly lay down on the floor. We took their weed and left. I didn't like what we were doing, nothing more than a strong-armed robbery. There was no style, no movie drama. We were just big and bad and they were not. This was not what I wanted. I was determined that it would be my last sting.

Don didn't see it that way.

"Fuck Hollywood," he said. "This is how you do it. I can do whatever I want. I can do this all the time."

He wasn't the same Don Woodbeck I had known.

. . .

KAZAN WANTED TO interview us for the script at his Santa Monica beachfront house. But Don hated doing that. He didn't like people he thought were judging him, were looking down on him. Kazan looked down on Don, and Hollywood looked down on both of us. We were outsiders. And Don thought they were pussies.

"If you can't carry the football," he would say, "then sit down and shut the fuck up." He had grown tired of telling the same stories too. I would sit in Kazan's living room talking to Nick but Don would walk around, sulky and disinterested. At least until we got to a part where he could play his role in a sting. The action scenes would bring Don to life.

The fact that both of us were up late doing coke hardly helped with getting the script done. We'd do a couple of grams apiece, three nights a week, partying from nine at night to four in the morning. To then have to sit down with Kazan and recite our life story at 9 a.m. was a problem. We would show up at least an hour or two after our scheduled meeting times. Kazan would be furious.

Once we were so late that Kazan left before we got there. I took a twenty-dollar bill and wrote on it, "Sorry we missed you." I tacked it to his door. His reaction? He couldn't believe we would just give twenty dollars away like that. He had been raised with money and was living in an expensive home but he thought leaving a twenty-dollar bill behind was ridiculous.

I guess he still didn't believe we were the outlaws we said we were.

● ● ●

I WENT TO visit Harold and who should be sitting in his office waiting for Don but Milwaukee Jim. He told me that he had been ripped off by Colombians for a quarter million dollars.

I thought he was joking. "You had a quarter million dollars?"

He was serious. He said he had a make on a connection being supplied by the Colombians and that he had come into town to set him up and get some of his money back.

His name was Mark Armantrout. He was a Vietnam vet and a Bronze Star winner, just like Woodbeck. A little smaller than me, with short, sandy blond hair that was thinning and a scraggly beard and mustache, he was a college graduate in theater and had been a surfer when he was younger. Now he claimed to be a freelance photographer. But in truth he was a full-time coke dealer.

I joined Don and Milwaukee Jim down the street at Barney's Beanery. In the parking lot, Jim opened the back of his van and showed me the several handguns he had.

I said, "Let's cool it. If they're Colombians, then that's hardcore." I searched for any excuse to not do another sting.

I appealed to Don. "Let's wait and see about the movie and the script. You don't have to do this right now."

Don relented. "Okay, but let's go meet him."

The next night, Don, Milwaukee Jim, my cousin Keith, and I met Armantrout at his apartment on the Esplanade in Redondo Beach. Don and Armantrout hit it off right away, comrades in arms who had survived Vietnam. Armantrout knew all about the stings Don and I had pulled. He had read about them in the newspaper. It didn't seem to matter to him. We were all doing lots of blow and drinking beer. Don and the wild-eyed Armantrout were talking real fast to each other, coke talk, and even singing songs together. It was strange. Don and Armantrout were so wired that while they were talking, they would soul shake, then circle each other, and then repeat the sequence again and again, as if they were dancing.

By 3 a.m. I wanted to go home and go to bed. As I left with Keith, he said he too noticed their dance. "Yeah," I said, "like a dance of death." I felt very uneasy.

Don and Jim in Woodbeck's red El Camino were going to follow us until Don had another idea.

"Let's get a motel for the night and take them out tomorrow," he said.

"No," I said. "I'm not going to do it. I'm done. No more."

"Well, I don't care what you think," Don said. Milwaukee Jim was now by his side, just like he was before they ever met Craig Glazer at that bar in Scottsdale.

I saw Don and Jim pull into a motel and I drove Keith home.

The next day, Saturday, August 7, at around noon, Debbie called. "Where's Don?"

I told her he had stayed down in Redondo. They were going to rip someone off but I wasn't going to join them.

"Pick me up," she said. "Maybe with both of us we can talk him out of it."

I wedged a .38 long barrel in the back of my gym pants, found Debbie at Woodbeck's apartment, and drove with her to Redondo Beach looking for the motel they had crashed at. At about 4 p.m. we found his red El Camino in a motel parking lot. Don and Jim had major hangovers, from the drugs and booze, uppers and downers. We woke them up.

"Don, we're back on with the movie. We've been lucky with these stings out here. Let's not do anything right now. It's not worth it."

"Don't be a grandpa," he said angrily. "I need the money. Your family has money. If you're going to punk out, fine, but don't tell me what to do, you fuckin' Jew!"

I was shocked. Don had said something like that only once before to me and never with such viciousness.

"What the fuck's wrong with you?" I asked.

"You're scared, that's your problem," he said.

"I'm not scared. Never have been."

"Bullshit. Why don't you get the fuck out and take that bitch with you."

Debbie had been too frightened of Don to say a word. I took her hand and we left. We watched Don and Jim get in the El Camino, presumably to drive to Armantrout's.

"Are you going to let him do this?"

I was angry and frustrated. "What choice do I have?"

"Please, Craig! We have to stop him!"

She was crying. And I didn't like the way I had left it with Don.

We caught up to them in front of Armantrout's apartment building. It was about 5 p.m.

"Hey man," he said, "I'm sorry for saying what I did. You're right." He had calmed down and sounded reasonable.

"So you're not going to hit this guy?"

"No. We'll just go up there and stop for a minute."

"Promise?"

"Craig, if I wanted to take him out, it'd be easy. Like popcorn."

"You're coming right back down?"

"You can wait if you want."

"Nah, we're going to leave."

Don and Milwaukee Jim headed upstairs to apartment number 523.

After a few moments, I pulled out of the parking lot and headed home with Debbie.

Suddenly she had a brainstorm. "Do you think I can get a gram out of that guy? Can we go back?" I turned the car around.

When we returned, there were half a dozen Latinos around the El Camino. They didn't look like car buffs to me. Maybe they were the Colombians with Armantrout.

"You stay here," I told Debbie. "I'll go warn Don."

I took the elevator up to the second floor apartment. As soon as I stepped into the corridor, I heard the sound of a fight going on and someone, Armantrout, I thought, yell: "Man, this ain't right!"

An instant later, two Latinos crashed through the apartment's window screen and landed on the floor. They started toward me.

I put one hand on my .38 but didn't draw.

"I'm the apartment manager!" I yelled. "What's going on?"

"Nothing, man."

"Okay, then let's go back down there and see."

I walked to them. I was within fifteen feet when I heard…

POP! POP-POP! POP-POP-POP!

One of the Latinos jumped over the railing and hit the concrete ten feet below. The other ran full-speed in the opposite direction from me.

I thought, "He shot somebody. Shit, Woodbeck's probably killed somebody! That would definitely make us bad guys. How could Don screw up like this? That fucker's ruined the movie."

People in the apartment building started shouting to call the police.

If I entered the apartment now, I would be involved. If I left, I wouldn't be part of anything that had happened.

I went to the elevator and hit the down button.

As I hustled to my car, police vehicles and an ambulance were screaming up the street.

"I think your fuckin' boyfriend shot somebody."

And all she said to me was, "Did you get anything?" That's what coke did to people. Debbie couldn't think of anything else but the blow.

We drove off before the cops arrived and I took her to Don's apartment.

"Clean up the place in case the police come," I instructed her. "Get rid of any drugs. Okay?" She looked everywhere Don might have hidden any coke she didn't know about, because she could sure use some. She came up empty and then gathered what little money she could find and got out.

I sped back to my apartment, where I loaded another weapon, my Colt .25, and filled my wallet with a couple grand. I wanted to be prepared for anything. I didn't know what I might be doing next.

I drove to the house Keith was renting. I could hide out there as long as I needed. I wasn't surprised Don didn't call right away. He probably was busy high-tailing it to Mexico.

I had Keith call Armantrout's apartment. "Is Mark there?" he asked.

"Who's this?" said the man who answered.

"I'm a friend."

"Nah, he's not here." There was a pause. "But he'll be back soon. What's your number and I'll have him…"

Keith hung up. "Sounded like a cop," he said.

But the next day there was nothing on TV or in the newspaper about a shooting.

"Let's go down there," I told Keith.

We slowly drove past the apartment building. The red El Camino was still parked in front. Maybe they got away on foot.

I went back to my apartment. There was no message from Don on the answering machine. I didn't call the police; I called my agent.

"I don't know what Don did," I told Harold, "but I could be in trouble for just being around there."

"There goes our movie deal," he said. "You need a lawyer, not an agent. Get over here right now."

On my way, I stopped to use the pay phone at a car wash. I called the Redondo Beach Police Department.

"Hi, I haven't seen my cousin for a couple days and I wanted to see if anything might have been reported."

"What's his name, sir?"

"Mark Armantrout."

"Hold, please."

The next voice I heard said, "Homicide."

"Um, I was trying to find my cousin, Mark Armantrout."

"Yes, we have him here. I'm sorry to tell you this but Mr. Armantrout is being held for a double homicide."

I went cold.

"Perhaps you could help us identify the victims, two John Does. One was tall, with sandy blond hair, wearing cowboy boots…"

I hung up before he finished.

An overwhelming sadness flooded over me and, yes, guilt too. Did I try hard enough to stop him? Could I have done something so this would not have happened? If I hadn't woken up Don and Jim at the motel, would they still be alive?

There was fear as well. Don didn't believe in much but he believed in karma and he believed in fate. He once said, "If your time's up, that's destiny." Cut and dried. From dust to dust. Don and Milwaukee Jim had been murdered. I was scared. What would happen to me? I drove straight to Harold's office.

"Woodbeck's dead."

"Are you sure?"

"Yeah."

"Oh my fuckin' God!"

It was too much for me to handle. I broke down and cried.

Don and I had been a team, had been in dangerous spots together, had faced gunshots together, had stuck up for each other. He had saved my life once if not twice. You don't forget that sort of thing, even after he turned on me during the Kansas trial. There was a magnetism, an energy, when we were together. He was my other half. We had come to Hollywood and we were going to take over the town. We were going to live the life. Now he was dead.

Harold walked me across the street to a law office that included Richard Rosenblum, the stepson of renowned Hollywood columnist Army Archerd. I told them the story and one of the criminal lawyers said, "We have to call the police now, tell them you might be a witness to a murder and that you want to cooperate. They might give you immunity." I agreed. Within an hour, two LAPD homicide cops arrived.

They showed me the crime scene photos of Don and Jim. I rushed to the restroom and threw up. The scene had been bloody, very bloody.

• • •

THIS IS WHAT I believe happened inside Armantrout's apartment, based on police accounts and court testimony:

> Woodbeck and Milwaukee told Armantrout they were going to buy eight ounces of cocaine from him for almost $20,000. But when they arrived at his apartment, they drew down on him. It was a straight-up robbery.
>
> "Man, this ain't right!"
>
> The two Latinos, who were the cocaine delivery boys for the Colombians, jumped through the window screen and fled.

Our history had always been that if the victim cooperated, there would be no violence—no muss, no fuss. Armantrout must have tried to fight Don and Jim, which is probably why they beat him up and shoved him to the floor. There could have been no other reason.

Armantrout claimed he told them to take whatever they wanted but to stop hitting him. "They didn't say a word. They just kept beating me and I started to bleed a lot," he said. "I was pretty frightened that they were going to hurt me or kill me. I was laying with my head in a pool of blood and it was my blood."

They dragged Armantrout from the living room, down the hallway past the kitchen and the bathroom, and into his bedroom. One of them cuffed his hands to his ten-speed bicycle.

"Like popcorn."

But whoever handcuffed Armantrout made a mistake—the same mistake I had made once back in Arizona. Armantrout was cuffed in front of his body rather than behind his back.

While Don and Jim were searching for more coke and cash in the rest of the apartment, Armantrout dragged himself, still cuffed to the bike, to the bedroom closet and pulled out an M1 semiautomatic rifle.

At the threshold of the bedroom, Armantrout saw Don and Jim in the hallway. They were just three feet from him. They must have been on their way out because when he emptied the magazine into them, every bullet but one hit them in the back. Woodbeck was shot four times, Milwaukee Jim six times. Don and Jim never fired their guns.

When Detective William Wood arrived at the scene, he smelled a "weird odor of sweat, water, and blood." He called out but only Armantrout's caged parrot responded, with a "hello." The detective went to the bathroom and, looking through the glass shower doors, saw what he thought was a man on his knees. Opening one of those doors, there was a body, Woodbeck's, face down in the tub.

Opening the other shower door, he found Milwaukee Jim lying partly underneath Woodbeck. The water was still running over them.

According to the police, Armantrout had dragged their bodies into the bathroom, put them in the tub, and turned on the water. Woodbeck didn't die right away. He bled for a good while first. He was a fighter. He wasn't the kind of guy who would just let go.

On the floor of the apartment, the police picked up the M1, a .45, a .38, and a pearl-handled derringer, one of those Don and I had taken from the collector. They also found eight ounces of coke in Armantrout's camera case and two more ounces in his knapsack. The key to the handcuffs was discovered in Don's El Camino.

When the police arrived, Armantrout was still handcuffed to the bicycle.

• • •

ARMANTROUT WAS CHARGED with two counts of murder. The cops quickly understood that I was not directly involved. I was granted immunity and testified for the prosecution. The trial took place two years later.

There was little sympathy for Don. One defense witness, a former Ventura County sheriff's deputy who had helped arrest and convict Woodbeck and Milwaukee Jim in San Bernardino after the airplane shooting, told the *L.A. Times* outside the courtroom that "they should give this guy (Armantrout) a medal for killing those two guys." Of course, this being Hollywood, he had also written a book about the incident and happened to mention that he was trying to get it published. He hoped it would lead to a movie deal.

Don was not a model citizen by any measure. But he understood that killing was messy and, unless in self-defense, unnecessary. Don thought like a criminal, not a killer. Don and Milwaukee Jim were each shot in the back. They were on their way out. If Armantrout had not shot, they would have just left.

They did not deserve to die.

I remember when Donna Caruso set up a sting for us a year after the brawl at the high school. We cuffed and tied up our victims and of course did the same to Donna, or else everyone would realize she was the insider who was with us.

One of our crew got a leer in his eye and made a move to fondle the helpless girl.

"You touch her," Woodbeck warned him, "and I'll break your arm."

That was cool and I never forgot that incident.

Don wasn't a bad guy and he wasn't a good guy. He was just born a hundred years too late.

The prosecutor, Richard De La Sota, admitted that events surrounding the double murder were filled with "mystery and unexplainable elements." He said Armantrout's tale of self-defense—that Don and Jim were going to beat him up some more and that's why he shot them—"just makes no sense at all." The biggest mystery, which remains to this day, is how Armantrout, still handcuffed to a bicycle, could drag the bodies of two grown men into a bathtub.

It didn't help the prosecution that I had to come clean about the recent L.A. stings. When Don told the jury in the Kansas undercover cop case about our Arizona stings, it helped to convict me. Now, ironically, admitting that we had ripped off dealers in L.A. hurt the case against his killer.

In the end, it was a "he said, she said" situation. Only one side—Armantrout—was still alive to tell the tale.

The jury had to acquit him. He only pled guilty to a charge of cocaine possession.

Woodbeck never wanted a Hollywood ending, but he got one anyway. When he was killed and officials were trying to identify his body, someone gave them that June's *Los Angeles Reader* cover story where Don and I were photographed dressed as Old West gunslingers. The day he was murdered, he was wearing those same fancy cowboy boots.

Like the outlaws of the Wild West, Don Woodbeck died with his boots on.

11

No Trust in Tinseltown

The terrible thing about this tragedy is that the people in Hollywood didn't like their heroes in a drug story going on their merry way. It's cold-blooded, but now they have the ending they wanted: a tragic one.
—Craig Glazer, *Los Angeles Herald Examiner*, August 22, 1982

IN MANY WAYS, Woodbeck was the big brother I never had, the one who shows you the ropes and gets you in trouble but also the one you can count on in a tight spot. He was also my best friend and partner in crime. When I did something well, he'd say, "Man, you pulled that off." If I hit the bull's-eye at target practice, he'd go, "Good shot." My own father never did that.

If I hadn't insisted on us going to Hollywood a couple years earlier, maybe Woodbeck would still have been alive. Okay, he probably would have been in jail or on the run, but he still would have been alive. Probably.

Now I was on my own.

When the press in Kansas City heard about the murders, they thought I was the other man killed with Woodbeck. I called a reporter there and told him that Jim Wojt was the other man killed. I was still alive.

But was the movie still alive? Woodbeck was fearless and seemed indestructible. His dying was not in the script, on paper or in my head. Real life was rewriting my storyline. You don't see Butch Cassidy or the

Sundance Kid blown to pieces at the end of their movie—even though you know that's probably what happened after the freeze-frame.

I realized why Hollywood had such a love-hate relationship with us. The movie studios never did like the idea of two outlaws who win—*Easy Rider* didn't have a happy ending either. Besides, this was 1982, the year comedian John Belushi overdosed with a speedball and died, freaking Hollywood out and overflowing rehab centers everywhere. This was the year maverick automaker and loose cannon entrepreneur John DeLorean went bust and got busted for smuggling coke to try to save his company.

After the good times, it was payback time.

Woodbeck had finally lost. One of us had paid a price for our sins, the ultimate price. For Hollywood, maybe that would be a better ending. Our original story was a no-harm-done adventure. Now it had taken a more serious turn.

As the final scene faded to black, I imagined a card would come up: "Don Woodbeck attempted one last sting in August 1982. He was shot and killed."

Then another card: "Craig Glazer is a movie producer in Hollywood."

Don's girlfriend Debbie moved to Hawaii after the preliminary hearing. His brother Tom came to get his El Camino. Woodbeck's father, Robert, would later describe his son as a "real happy-go-lucky kid. He had to be doing something all the time. The hotter it was the better. He just diddled his whole life away."

I was struck by how little Don left behind after all those years. Dust to dust.

I asked Harold, "Do you miss Don?"

"I miss the drama," he said. "But Craig, you're one of us. Don wasn't. He was a gun-totin', six-shootin' outlaw. I tried to befriend him but I never could."

"Are you saying you're glad he's dead?"

"Glad? No." He hesitated. "More like relieved."

. . .

I CALLED OUR acting teacher to tell him what happened.

"I don't want you back in class," Dano said.

"Why not?"

"There might be a contract on you and I don't want some innocent student shot."

"That's ridiculous."

"Whatever."

Some of my classmates did call with condolences. Oh, and they were just wondering if the rights to the story were available because, if the movie were their vehicle, they would want to play Don.

One overly imaginative detective, L.A. County Sheriff's Department Sergeant Stan White, at one point thought I had Don killed so I would own all the rights to *Outlaws*. White would go on to be a technical advisor on police matters for movies such as *JFK*, *Midnight Run*, and *Year of the Dragon*. He also played a cop in those films. He believed owning a script could be a motivation for murder.

In Hollywood, the line between fantasy and reality was razor thin.

As expected, Kazan too expressed no sympathy toward Don.

"Sorry," he said, "but your friend was a major asshole."

Suddenly he reminded me of Rabbi Margolies.

"Live by the sword, die by the sword," Kazan told me.

He could think what he wanted but no one should have said that to someone about a recently dead best friend. I wasn't surprised that Hollywood was a cold, cruel place. I was surprised that it was so holier than thou.

Don's murder did put an end to the credibility questions. There were no longer any doubts about whether our stories were true—even though we admitted they were colored to make us look better. Now I put as favorable a spin as I could on his death.

Just four days after the killings, we made the top of Army Archerd's *Daily Variety* column, the morning must-read for everyone in the industry. He called Don and I "a pair of modern day Robin Hoods" whose "motive was strictly non-profit ... They continued their amazing saga of derring-do for the good of the community for ten years.

Their exploits make some vidshows look like kindergarten games …
Last Sunday, Woodbeck was about to try and break up a major cocaine
deal in Redondo Beach. But something went wrong." Army laid it on
thick.

Only in Hollywood would a story about a murder end with: "Agent
Harold Moskovitz reps *The Outlaws*."

• • •

ARMY PUMPED UP our story because of his stepson, Richard
Rosenblum, who became my lawyer. After our meeting upon Don's
murder, Rosenblum tagged along with me to parties and we became
friends. Army and Rosenblum's mother would ask Richard to dinner with their '50s- and '60s-era power group—Robert Wagner, Jill
St. John, etc.—and I'd join him.

A couple of years after Don died, Army was given a star on the
Hollywood Walk of Fame and he invited me to sit at the head table
with him at the black-tie dinner. Don Rickles was there to roast Army
with his insult comic shtick.

Rickles strode to our table.

"Army, am I a big star?" he asked.

"Yes, Don."

"I'm a major comedy star, right?"

"Of course you are."

"And how long have we known each other?"

"Lots of years."

"So let me ask you a question: Since I'm such a big star, why am I
sitting at that table way over there and not here with you?"

"Don, I think it's because this is for family."

"Family?" He looked at each of us. "Then who's this shmuck?" He
pointed the microphone at me. The whole room laughed. I smiled.

"My stepson's friend."

"Are you in the business?" Rickles pushed the microphone in my
face.

"Yeah."

"What do you do?"

"I'm a movie producer."

"Oh? What movies do I know you from?"

"Well, nothing's been made yet. It's in development."

"Oh wow, in development. Anybody in this room who does not have a development deal, please raise your hand." No one did. They laughed at the inside Hollywood joke.

"Yep, you're special, kid. What's your name?"

"Craig Glazer."

"Glazer? You Jewish?"

"Yeah."

Rickles shrugged his shoulders.

"Okay, then you can sit here."

. . .

I FLEW TO Kansas City a week after the murders. My life had turned upside down. I could barely eat, and lost nearly thirty pounds. I was looking and feeling very fragile. I needed to clear my head. I needed to connect with something, someone, not Hollywood.

I needed to see Terri again.

She had called me in L.A. after hearing about Don's murder.

"I'm glad you weren't killed," she said.

That was a start, I guess.

"Maybe your life will be better now," she added.

"Your" not "our." She refused to see me when I was in Kansas City.

I spent time with my mom and dad and brothers, and they were really sad about Don's death. I had never lost anyone near and dear to me. They knew how much I was hurting. Even Stan, though he was scrambling himself after filing for personal bankruptcy, the result of being $3 million in debt.

After a few days I returned to L.A. and changed apartments. I wondered if I could change my life, if I could stop living my movie and instead just live, if I could be the movie outlaw without being an actual outlaw.

Terri called from out of the blue.

"I miss you," she said. She had been to a Royals game and it reminded her of when we were together at the stadium for a World Series game in 1980. "Maybe I made a mistake," she went on. "I'll give you another chance, if you want."

"I want," I said, very happily.

But she would be the "movie producer's girlfriend" not the "outlaw's girlfriend." Matter of fact, she didn't want to be a girlfriend at all. She still had our engagement ring and she wanted to get married. A couple of weeks later, she flew to L.A. and began moving in.

When Don and I first arrived in Hollywood, we would walk down the beach at Malibu, past the houses of people like Barbra Streisand and Michael Landon. One day, Larry Hagman, at the height of his *Dallas* fame, saw us walking by as he hosted a barbecue at his house. He invited us in. I couldn't believe we were partying with J.R. Ewing. Don and I would talk about someday being filthy rich and moving into their neighborhood.

After he died, Terri and I would stroll down the same beach and dream the same dream. I remember once she started running across the sand, this beautiful girl, and I felt that for the first time I had a woman as my closest friend.

Maybe we could finally create a new life together. I hoped so.

But it wouldn't be easy. Her first day back, she saw one of my guns in the apartment.

"I want that gone," she said. "If I'm going to bring my daughter to live with us, I don't want any guns around here."

I told her I would get them out. In truth, I hid them under the carpet in a closet. You have to compromise in a relationship. But risking my life, and hers, was one compromise I was not willing to make.

· · ·

THE NOTORIETY SURROUNDING Don's death actually gave *Outlaws* more juice. Even "happiest place on earth" Disney became interested in picking up the option if it ran out at Paramount. There was also talk of not one film but three—the first about the stings, a sequel about being an undercover cop, and a third about Don's death.

Of course, we still needed a script from Kazan. He typed away on his old Royal but refused to show me what he was writing.

Paramount offered to pay us for a research trip, to revisit some of the sites I had told Kazan about. In Phoenix, we drove to the Salt Cellar and sat in the booth where J.D. and his boys got the jump on me, Don, and Milwaukee Jim. We went to the parking lot where Don killed the kid who was going to stuff me in the trunk. I took him to the place that used to be Fridays & Saturdays, to The Jewel Box pawnshop that was still there, and on and on. In Kansas City, Kazan met my family and also went off on his own to interview my lawyers.

The trip back in time was somber and nostalgic. I had survived so much.

Finally, on the plane returning to L.A., Kazan gave me his draft of *Outlaws*.

Our story was there, but without any of the raw excitement. It was a cross between a dark comedy like *M*A*S*H* and a hysterically silly movie like *Blazing Saddles*. I guess Kazan thought we had to be pranksters instead of outlaws. That's why he decided that the catchphrase in *Outlaws* would be "Hey, dude!" And the entire third act was about a sting that never happened.

I lit into him.

"This is boring and not funny."

He was insulted, of course.

"What would you write?" he asked, looking down his nose.

I acted out the "you were a gazelle" scene for him once more. I did the same for scene after scene.

Sometime after we returned to L.A., he sent the rewrite to Garnett, who called me into his office. The producer read those scenes, one after the other, aloud to Amy Pascal.

Kazan had used my action and dialogue word for word. I was proud of that. And Garnett loved it too.

"That's pretty much how I told him," I said.

"What? You wrote it together?" Garnett asked.

"Yep."

"He didn't tell us that," said Pascal.

They had had a meeting without me about a script that was about me! That made it easier for Kazan to take credit for what I had done.

I exploded at Garnett. "Maybe I should be in your meetings!"

I never sat down with Kazan again. Garnett would take my notes on the script either in person or on the phone and he'd pass them on to "the writer."

Just like with a drug deal, there could be no trust in Tinseltown.

. . .

IN HOLLYWOOD, IF you don't look like you need the job, you get the job. If you don't look like you need the money, you get the money. And if you don't look like you belong, then you don't.

If I wanted to make it in Hollywood, I needed the sports car, the nice clothes, the lunches and dinners at expensive restaurants, the cocaine. Only the coke wasn't tax deductible. Even though I couldn't afford it, I would do lunch on a regular basis at Ma Maison, Wolfgang Puck's eatery. Another regular, one who presided at his own table, was probably Hollywood's most respected figure—actor-writer-director Orson Welles of *Citizen Kane* fame. A gregarious, generous sort, Welles would often call me over to join him.

One midday, he was entertaining another Hollywood superstar, Warren Beatty—who had starred in two of my favorite movies, *Bonnie and Clyde* and *McCabe and Mrs. Miller*—when he waved Terri and I over to his table.

We were having a grand old time when Terri excused herself to go to the restroom. A minute later, Beatty said he had to make a phone call and got up and walked off. I thought that was strange since there was a phone for customers just a few feet away.

Orson caught my eye: "Your fiancée is very beautiful," he said. He stared at me. It took a second before I realized what he was trying to say but could not because of the unwritten rule between guys about cock blocking your friend.

I found Beatty in the men's room.

"You're a big star," I said angrily, "but that's my girlfriend. Understand?"

"Oh, I'm sorry if I offended you," he said, genuinely polite.

I exited with Terri.

"What's going on?" she asked as we drove away.

"Did he give you his phone number?"

She nodded, took the incriminating piece of paper out of her purse, and handed it to me.

"I would never cheat on you, Craig," she said. "But he is Warren Beatty." She smiled a little.

To me, he was just Warren Beatty trying to fuck my girlfriend.

Then *Entertainment Tonight* fucked me.

Harold received a call from the entertainment news show saying they were doing a report on hero cops who end up in the movies. The feature would include former NYPD cop Frank Serpico, former NYPD narcotics detective Bob Leuci (the real-life Daniel Ciello of *Prince of the City*), and me. Don's death had rocketed my profile onto the front page. When they offered to pay for my appearance I turned them down. *ET* was going to use photos from his murder scene and I didn't feel right making money off Don's death like that.

Reporter Scott Osborne flew to Kansas City to shoot footage and also interviewed me on camera in L.A. The questions grew more and more confrontational as the interview went on. "Do you feel responsible for his death?"

He grilled me as if the police were interrogating me. I became suspicious. Then I heard that Serpico and Leuci had pulled out, if in fact they were ever actually going to do it. Maybe this story might not be very positive, I thought.

They told me it would be a two-parter, supposedly the first the show had ever done. The piece would air twice during the week and twice again on the weekend. Stan put up signs at Stanford & Sons: "See my son on *Entertainment Tonight.*"

So, on national television, *Entertainment Tonight* called Don and I a couple of con men who "managed to turn some top Hollywood sharks into sheep." They made us out to be bad guys who were more Bonnie and Clyde than Butch and Sundance.

They had an agenda, to make a hard-hitting statement about Hollywood cozying up to criminals. They obtained the *Today* show tape, and interviewed Vern Miller, Harold, Margaret Jordan, an unnamed Arizona narcotics cop, and my publicist, John Oldman.

The Arizona cop was asked, "Were you surprised to hear how Woodbeck's life ended?" With his voice distorted and his face in shadow, he answered, "Absolutely not. You work in a violent world, you'll die in a violent world. I'm surprised it took as long as it did."

Jordan, still upset that I had exposed her vendetta and helped stunt her career, managed to take a poke at me by praising Woodbeck: "I'd rather deal with a seven-time loser that doesn't protest his innocence and just says, 'How much skin am I going to leave behind me' … and that's Woodbeck."

Vern was even angrier. He went off the deep end and outright lied. Not only did he claim that I was the one who approached his office about becoming a special agent but he called me a "snitch."

They aired the gruesome photos showing Don in the bloody bathtub but I was the one crucified.

Stan took down the signs after the first show.

. . .

BECAUSE I WAS fearful someone we had stung who wanted revenge, anyone from the Colombian cartel to the Mexican Mafia, might kidnap Michelle, I took extra precautions when I picked her up from school, such as showing up early. She was going to school in Brentwood, alongside the children of movie stars and movie executives, doctors, and lawyers, even though I had no money coming in. Fortunately, Terri had landed a job at MGM in Culver City as a receptionist. She was the one with the Hollywood job, not me.

I was about to get married. I needed to take care of my family. I had to do something. I asked Grandpa Bennie to pay the rent for me and he came through as usual. I wasn't going to go back to crime. Not with Terri with me.

I called Anwar Soliman. He headed a company that owned everything from the El Torito Mexican restaurants to Houlihan's, Baxter's, Coco's, Carrows, Reuben's, and Charley Brown's. Before I moved to L.A., I met him at Stanford's. He offered me a job and said if I went west to look him up.

I did and he sent me to the Coco's/Reuben's in Long Beach to begin a management training program. I would learn the ropes by spending two weeks as a cook, two weeks as a waiter, two weeks as a bartender, etc.

Everyone else in the program was early twenties, several years younger than me. This would be their life. But I had already been there. I was going backward, back into the restaurant business, and it wasn't even my own family's.

"You're hating this, aren't you?" Terri asked.

"Big time."

After eight weeks, my manager called me in. Soliman was at the meeting. They said they were moving me up and sending me to Phoenix. They told me how much money I'd be making this year, next year, and every year after, what brand of company car I'd be given at each level, and where in the country I'd be located as I moved up in the hierarchy. The whole rest of my life was right there on the pieces of paper they shuffled on a desk.

To most people, it probably looked like a sweet deal. Not to me.

"I can't leave L.A.," I said. "I'm in the movie business."

The manager looked around his corporate office. "No, you're not."

"Then I quit."

"You can go out the back," said Soliman.

"No thanks," I shot back. "I'll go out the front."

. . .

I MET MIKE Gable at Mirabelle's, a restaurant and bar on the Sunset Strip. He had managed singer-songwriter Joan Armatrading but had fallen on hard times. We came across each other the way many people in Hollywood did in the '80s—doing blow in the restroom.

Gable was tall and pale, maybe ten years older than me, with prematurely graying hair. He reminded me of Ichabod Crane. He was always sweating too, maybe because he constantly wore the music biz uniform, a black leather jacket.

Along with Peter Brown, the *L.A. Times* reporter, we formed Low Oak Productions, based in an office on La Cienega. We figured we would use the company to develop projects, write scripts, and pitch ideas to Hollywood.

One I wrote was called *Tall, Dark and Handsome*.

A thirteen-year-old boy who is pushed around at school is in love with a cute blonde classmate. He also has a crush on his twenty-eight-year-old teacher. He decides to take a muscle powder to improve his size so he can win her over but the concoction magically turns him into a thirty-year-old grown man, tall, dark and handsome.

He doesn't know how to cope with everyday adult activities, such as driving a car. He wants a milkshake not a cocktail. But his new stature allows him to square off with the mean gym coach and get even with the kids who had been harassing him. He becomes a hero to his former classmates.

But he's confused by sex, especially when his ex-teacher falls in love with him. She eventually lures him to her bed and he's wearing pajamas. Just before they get physical, he turns back into a little boy. The relationship ends, but putting into practice "if I knew then what I know now," he becomes the most popular kid in school.

Hanging out at Hellman's, I crossed paths with Anne Spielberg, sister of director Steven Spielberg. She was trying to be a writer and not having much success. I told her the story of *Tall, Dark and Handsome*. A few years later, in 1988, a movie with a similar premise, *Big*, starring Tom Hanks, was released, cowritten by Anne Spielberg. She was Oscar-nominated for Best Original Screenplay.

Our best project was *The Perfect Season*.

A star college quarterback at the University of Washington gets hit by a blitzing linebacker, crushing his shoulder and ending his dreams of a pro career. In his thirties, he's a used car salesman coaching semipro football. One day, he risks his life to save a woman in a car wreck and again his shoulder is injured. The newspapers reveal who he used to be and he again becomes a local hero.

Meanwhile, the Seattle Seahawks are horrible and attendance is miserable. With the undefeated Miami Dolphins coming to town for the last game of the season, the team owners want to put cheeks in the seats. They agree to give our "Rocky" a tryout, presumably for a cameo on special teams or something else equally harmless.

But after he recovers from his latest shoulder injury, he discovers he can throw the football ninety yards, and accurately too. The coaches take notice.

The Dolphins are mauling the Seahawks when Seattle's quarterback gets injured. Our man comes in to replace him and can't be stopped. Touchdown, touchdown, touchdown. His final throw puts Seattle in the lead with less than ten seconds to play. But Miami returns the kickoff for a touchdown and wins.

When reporters ask his son whether he sees his father as a hero, all he says is, "That's my dad."

But neither project sold.

• • •

I HAD BEEN a Pac-Man junkie like everyone else. Now video games were getting more elaborate—Super Mario Bros. had become Dungeons &

Dragons. Video game parlors were opening on every street corner. Everyone said the business was as good as the boom in baseball cards, where everyone was getting rich.

I saw an ad for a company that would find a storefront and provide the equipment. Many of the machines came from defunct video game parlor owners who leased them out and split the profits with new operators. One of the people running the company was Ed Najarian, a guy in his twenties, of Armenian heritage. He was fast on his feet like me. I liked him.

What I didn't know at the time was that he had been arrested in a San Francisco money laundering scheme involving video games, a very useful all-cash business. It's ironic that the addiction that would pull me back into crime wasn't drugs but video games.

With a $25,000 loan from Grandpa Bennie I bought a video game parlor in Torrance. Video Village, with Michael Jackson and Duran Duran posters plastered on the walls, was right near a high school—location, location, location. It had potential—and it was legit.

I left the day-to-day management to my cousin Keith, but by the time I noticed the high maintenance costs—duh, kids would break the machines—and that employees were skimming off the top, it was too late.

I shut down Video Village after just ninety days. I was glad Najarian agreed to resell all of the equipment for me. He even sold the machines he didn't own but had leased. I certainly wasn't anyone who could get all moral with him. Besides, he knew I was scrounging for money and the $5,000 he handed me for my share was much needed. I was grateful to him.

When I took a temporary job at Silent Radio in Hollywood, I helped Najarian get one there too. The company provided the scrolling ticker messages, and the ads between them, that ran on electronic displays at restaurants and bars. My job was to get those venues to subscribe to the service. I didn't last long.

It seemed like everyone was doing well but me. I was a failure and I brooded over it. I was also snorting coke at two in the afternoon, something I never did before.

I was angry with myself—but I was angry at Terri too. I was angry that she was gorgeous and was being hit on by everybody in Hollywood. Terri was around successes all day and I wasn't one of them. I knew that if I did not make it in Hollywood, I would hate myself and I would destroy my relationship with Terri. But I also knew that if I did make it in Hollywood there would be other women. That was part of the fantasy I wanted to live. It never crossed my mind that Terri might already be seeing someone else. Looking back, I sure can't blame her.

• • •

I HAD TRIED to do everything right, by the book. But I couldn't keep to the straight and narrow because it just wasn't as exciting as a mountain road with sharp curves. Other people enjoyed settling, I never did. For me, it was success or failure, all or nothing.

Tim Sheridan was a dead ringer for Robert Conrad during his *Wild Wild West* days. He was an actor-producer and also a sting artist— guess I wasn't the only one—though he didn't have a movie deal. Sheridan, who knew about my past from Hellman, came to me with a proposition.

"You look like you could be Persian," he said. "Interested in playing a role?"

A woman friend of his had been ripped off by Arab drug dealers in an investment scheme. He wanted to get back at them for fun and profit. He'd do the whole setup; I would just play the buyer. The Arabs would bring the coke and Sheridan would rip them off. He'd pay me $10,000.

I felt the adrenaline rush just thinking about getting on that dangerous road again. Still, I hesitated.

Sheridan had a trump card and he played it. "These guys give some of their money to the PLO. They're funding terrorists who want to wipe Israel off the map. With you being a Jew, I thought…"

He pushed the right button. I was in.

Sheridan introduced me as a wealthy buyer to two Middle Eastern men at a gloomy office by CBS Television City off Fairfax. They were gruff and spoke broken English.

To cover my lack of Mideast knowledge, I told them upfront, "My parents are from Iran but I grew up around Kansas City." They were satisfied with my performance.

The dealers said they would leave predetermined amounts of coke in a locker at Los Angeles airport. Sheridan would make the pickup and deposit the appropriate payment in cash in an adjoining locker.

But the first two times, Sheridan left only half the money he owed. The Arabs weren't happy. Sheridan told them he'd make it up to them on the third exchange.

The dealers arrived at the LAX locker and opened it to deposit their coke. This time the LAPD was there to greet them. Sheridan had tipped them off.

Sheridan received some brownie points from the LAPD. He also told them I had assisted. He kept quiet about the ten G's he paid me. Helping to make the bust didn't improve my standing with local law enforcement; but it had an unexpected bonus later on.

· · ·

I STILL NEEDED a job, preferably one in Hollywood, even if I had to start at the bottom. Harold saw a classified ad about an opening for a junior VP of music for New World Pictures, the home of B-movie king Roger Corman. I made an appointment and met Ken Dalton, a thin, country redneck who had just scored a hit producing the tits-and-ass flick *Hardbodies*.

I didn't have any qualifications for the gig and Dalton had no interest in giving it to me. But when he asked what college I went to, I told him Arizona State and he brightened up. He went there too.

Suddenly I had an office, business cards, a lousy salary, and a nice expense account. In Hollywood that's all you need to pretend to be a success. But bullshitting my way through a job I knew nothing about would last only so long. So I asked Mike Gable to help me. He did know the music business.

What I could do was hold my own nightcrawling the clubs on the Strip—the Roxy, Gazzari's, Whisky, and Troubadour. My job was to snake through the underground music world buddying up to the hundreds of bands who would do anything for a record deal, including selling a song for $500 to be in such cinematic works of art like *School Spirit* and *Women Behind Bars*.

In the early to mid-'80s, the Strip was filled with a new wave of rock groups that played hard and lived hard, bands like Mötley Crüe, Quiet Riot, and Dokken. One of the groups I bought songs from was L.A. Guns, which spawned Guns N' Roses. Coke was my calling card and it said, "I have connections. I'm a player." Having coke was as necessary in Hollywood as having an agent.

Najarian came by my office. He was crying, bordering on suicidal. He was about to get married but no longer had a job at Silent Radio. He needed help. He had done me a favor, so I figured it was my turn. I made him my assistant, even though I didn't need one. But at least I could get him a couple hundred bucks a week.

At New World I crossed paths with film heavyweights such as Jack Nicholson and director Francis Ford Coppola, both of whom earned their first breaks from Corman. Also there was former child star Ron Howard, who made his directing debut a few years earlier with Corman's *Grand Theft Auto* and was about to dive into the big-time with *Splash*. My goal though was to buddy up to Corman himself. Corman was educated and erudite but when it came to films he was pure cheese. He made terrible movies. But, unlike most producers in Hollywood, his movies made money.

One night, Corman had a dream that the next big theme in movies would be World War II. At the same time, he found a financier who would put up the production cost as long as the movie was shot in South Africa. Corman said that whoever gave him the best pitch, that's the movie he would make. It would be between me and a writer who had been working at New World longer than I had.

I came up with the idea of a U.S. Army squad that goes to Africa in World War II. Centered on two brothers, a theme I always liked, *The Lost Patrol* was a cross between *Beau Geste* and *Tarzan*.

Corman loved it.

"But it's the other guy's turn," he said. Best doesn't always win. My big break vanished. It was January 1984 and the Kazan script for *Outlaws* wasn't knocking anyone off their seats at the studios. My movie career was at a standstill.

I was never satisfied with where I was, never satisfied with how fast things were going. If I had only been patient, my life might have turned out differently. But that virtue just wasn't in me. I wanted it all and I wanted it now.

For the first time, Najarian saw me do a line of coke. That led to telling him about the stings and showing him the newspaper articles. I told him the story of *Outlaws*.

"Do you sell coke?" he asked.

I said no.

He thought for a moment. "How much would it cost to make *The Lost Patrol*?"

"A couple million. But I'd rather make *Outlaws*. That'd be ten to twelve million."

"If you had to, could you do *Outlaws* for, say, five mil?"

"Sure," I said. "Absolutely."

"I know people who have that kind of money. They're sitting on it because they need to clean it. They want to meet people with the horsepower to make that happen."

He said these Americans had $5 million to $15 million in profits from transporting cocaine from Colombia to the U.S. through the port of Long Beach. Unless they could launder the money, make it appear legitimate, the cash would have to stay in shoe boxes.

Colombians? Could they be connected to the Latinos I stumbled onto outside the apartment where Woodbeck was murdered? Revenge would make a great motive for the movie character I thought I was. How beautiful would that be to nail them?

At the same time, if I could sting them for $5 million or more, I could finance *Outlaws* or maybe a smaller movie that would lead to *Outlaws*. Putting Don up there on the big screen thanks to money from scumbags involved in his killing, now that would be karma.

If things got too hairy, well, I could just give them up to the cops, like Sheridan did. I'd walk away a hero. The notoriety it would bring, putting me on the front page of every newspaper, would catapult *Outlaws* back onto the front burner.

But I knew only a little about money laundering from my days in Arizona. The object was to disguise the source of criminal profits, usually by putting those profits on the books of a legitimate business. That way you could tell the IRS that the profit was generated from the business. How else could we explain the Mummy Mountain real estate, the luxury condos we had bought? We sure didn't get 1099s at the end of a sting.

John Walters, our accountant, put the scheme together. He claimed he had twenty investors, each contributing between $2,000 and $4,000 apiece every week to purchase property. The truth, unknown to the IRS, was that we gave Walters more money than he claimed, he kept a percentage and returned the rest, supposedly fairly gotten gains on real estate transactions. It worked—until Walters screwed up and got involved with gamblers.

But there's a difference between understanding a concept and executing a plan. So I went to the Santa Monica Public Library and asked the librarian at the desk, "Do you have any books on money laundering?"

She looked through an index and said, "No, but recently there was a major story in a magazine." The article explained all the ins and outs, including what middlemen charged for their services.

The risk seemed small and the return enormous, as long as I didn't get killed. I had never been seriously hurt during a sting. Sure, Woodbeck was dead. But he had made a critical mistake. I wouldn't make a mistake. I'd make sure I covered my ass. I always had. I had it all figured out, from every angle.

. . .

NAJARIAN SEEMED MOST impressed by my connections to the Mafia, guys like Charlie Costa. He said the Americans he knew wanted the Mafia on their side for protection and for diversification. One problem—I wasn't connected to the Mafia.

True, Woodbeck and I had worked for Costa on the Boston sting and Costa too had since come to Hollywood. But we were hardly friends.

True, if you were in business or government in Kansas City you naturally brushed up against infamous gangster families such as the Civellas, Cammisanos, and Speros. The Civella family's influence extended all the way to Las Vegas, where they controlled the Tropicana, Fremont, Hacienda, and Marina.

True, Italian cons and Jewish cons often ran in the same circles. Stan's side of the family had been in auto parts and salvage, a business that occasionally ventured into gray areas of the law. My grandfather Jack made some of his money from buying surplus World War II Army vehicles, refurbishing them and then selling them to foreign countries. That was okay for Jeeps and trucks but he got into trouble with the federal government when he sold 500 armored cars to Israel. His defense against the accusation that he sold implements of war to a foreign country was that they were not armed.

When a congressional committee asked him what he thought the Israeli government was going to do with the armored cars, he replied, "Perhaps they will use them as tractors to pull plows on their fields." The criminal charges were dropped, though his United Auto Parts was blacklisted from doing business with the U.S. government.

And, of course, I knew Mob kids when we were growing up together. They told me lots of stories.

But the fact was that I knew more about the Mafia from *The Godfather* movies than from experience.

I wouldn't be able to pull this off on my own either.

There would be no Woodbeck or Milwaukee Jim. And the rest of the crew was gone too. I heard the Chicago cops killed Bucky Walsh—and that his policeman father was on the scene when he died. Richard Lewis OD'd and was supposedly found in a dugout in Arizona. Jack the

Ripper tried a sting in Reno and was shot down by security guards in a hotel parking lot. Digger Dave went back to his family's funeral business. Jim Partridge and Big Red found other lines of work. The J.D. shootout scared Janet and Joanna all the way to L.A. The only person from back in the day that I might count on was my old friend Marc.

"I'm gonna check this deal out," I told Gable. "I might need someone to help. Are you interested?"

I told him what he needed to hear—that I would take the biggest risk and do the actual handling of any money. He would not be committing any crime and he would not be in any physical danger. I would simply call on him to play his part and then he would exit stage left to be paid.

I also told him what he, and every other rookie I recruited, wanted to hear—that this was their chance to be part of the most exciting adventure they will ever have in their lives.

Gable said, "I'm in."

. . .

I HID MY coke under the rug in my closet along with my guns. One day I went to get a gram or two and there was hardly any there. Maybe I forgot I had already sent it up my nose.

A week later, though, I was going through Terri's purse looking for gas money. When I opened her change purse, I found the missing coke. That's when I knew she was seeing another guy. She was a weekend warrior, not a cokehead. She wasn't snorting with her girlfriends. She was doing blow with a guy—and I discovered very early on that girls who snorted coke with you would also sleep with you.

Just like the girl I was seeing.

Marcia Princia was a beautiful Puerto Rican. A receptionist at Silent Radio, she was five foot two, well endowed, had a bubble butt, and said she was a former Miss Puerto Rico contestant. She married her photographer but they were separated.

Terri and I were still living at the condo but we were no longer together. She preferred the straight and narrow, and I was out on the curves again. I was going nowhere and her new guy, whoever he was, could no doubt offer her and Michelle a more stable life.

I bought three grams of coke, rented a Corvette, and took Maria to a concert at the Greek Theatre for our first date. After the show, we went to a hotel room in downtown Hollywood and shared a couple of bottles of champagne.

Between the coke and the booze, my dick was the size of a peanut. I was so embarrassed in the hotel room that I just threw a towel over my naked groin. Maria played with herself while I waited for my manhood to return to form.

Eleven o'clock became 1 a.m. became 4 a.m. We never had sex.

I drove home. There was no way she'd want to see me again.

Until that day, even though we had drifted apart, I always came home at night to Terri.

She was waiting for me when I showed up at seven in the morning: "Where have you been?"

"I got a DUI and…"

"Liar."

I knew I hurt her feelings—and I knew she deserved someone better than me. By the end of the day she started to move out.

"I had the greatest time." It was Maria on the phone. "Do you want a second chance?"

I guess if people didn't give me second chances I'd have no chance at all.

Maria moved into the condo. And Terri ran into her when she came to pick up some of her stuff. Even though Terri had someone else, she was still hurting and I could understand that. She cried and I went with her to her new apartment. We had dinner and a few drinks. The moment came when we were about to hop into bed one more time.

Terri shook her head. "I think we've both moved on," she said.

She was right. I just wished I knew whether I was moving up or down.

12

Dope and Duplicity

I wasn't thinking, "Let's do the adventure routine" or "Let's get some publicity for the movie." I couldn't do any more to hype the movie and I wasn't looking to get killed.

—Craig Glazer, *Los Angeles Reader*, November 30, 1984

NAJARIAN SET UP a meeting at a sports bar in Long Beach with the people who wanted to launder the money. Vern was tall, in his late thirties, with thinning blond hair. He had a bushy mustache and tied his sweater around his neck over a button-down shirt. Dick was in his late forties, stocky, with grayish-blond hair. He wore a paisley shirt, white shorts, and tennis shoes, just what you'd expect a retired surfer to wear. He said he had a bum ear from a surfing wipeout so he asked me to talk toward his good right ear.

Dick said he was the boss but Vern did almost all the talking. "We're ready to move millions of dollars of product," he said. "If you could help us do that maybe we'll bring you into our business."

"Whoa, I'm not a drug dealer," I told him. "I thought this was about cleaning some money." I needed to know more about Vern and Dick. "How do you know Ed?"

"A couple years ago we tried to move money through his video parlors," said Vern. "The deal didn't work out." He changed the subject.

"Ed says you know some of these." He took a finger and bent his nose to one side. "People who could service our money. People we can do business with."

"Sure, I know people," I boasted. "But we need to go slow. They wouldn't want to meet you right now. You'll deal with me."

Vern cut to the chase. "Dick and I are getting older but our asses are still on the line. We want to get our money cleaned and not have to mess with this anymore. So what can we do?"

"We'll run the money through a couple of Beverly Hills dry cleaners. I'll take…"

"Wait a minute. We launder money through dry cleaners?"

"Yeah, who would think it, huh?" I laughed. Vern and Dick were stone-faced.

We could use the cleaners Harold owned with his family. He owed the IRS and was struggling for money. I told him he'd get a piece of the action. Coincidentally, money laundering earned its name during Prohibition when organized crime hid its profits from alcohol by using coin laundromats. The government could not know how much money was really coming in because it was not about to count every coin deposited. So the Mob cleaned large amounts of cash by claiming hugely successful coin laundry businesses.

I called on what I had learned from the magazine article at the library.

"I want 15 percent plus $1,500 every time we make a move. A few days later, you get a cashier's check for the clean money."

Dick nodded to Vern in agreement. I looked at Najarian. "And what does Ed get?"

"I'm out of this," Najarian said. "I just put you together. That's all. Besides, I'm moving out of town."

Vern was matter-of-fact: "We'll take care of Ed."

Within a week, I met with Vern and Dick again, this time in a downtown L.A. hotel room and this time they brought along Dominic, their accountant. Dominic was small, bookwormish, with balding dark hair and a beard.

I wanted some good faith money and they hit me with $5,000. The adrenaline kicked in, just like old times. I was on Cloud Twenty and ready to roll.

After a few more get-togethers, each one with me asking when the big money drops they promised would start and them asking to meet my "boss," I brought in Gable to play Mike Farino, who, I told Vern, not only owned the dry cleaners but was a Mob lieutenant skimming money from the Teamsters' pension fund to finance Las Vegas casinos.

I felt on familiar turf. Roy Lee Williams, the corrupt head of the Teamsters who was in the pocket of Kansas City Mob bosses Carl "The Cork" Civella and his brother Giuseppe "Nick" Civella, was also from Kansas City. I could bullshit Vern just with the names and stories I had heard.

Gable jumped in with both feet. You bet it attracted him to get involved in my movie when I told him, "I'll pay you to play the Mafia chieftain." He would be someone else, someone bigger than himself. Anybody would want that. Besides, this was "Craig's crazy deal." I was sticking my neck out, not him.

I took "Farino" to meet Vern and Dominic at Filoy Cleaners on Canon Drive, down the street from the famous Nate 'n Al deli in Beverly Hills. Besides celebrity clients like Burt Reynolds, Farino proudly told them that his Filoy's Cleaners also serviced billionaire Marvin Davis, who owned 20th Century Fox. Davis would have his chauffeur and three assistants arrive weekly with loads of laundry—not just clothes, but everything from drapes to cloth dinner napkins. He'd rack up $20,000 a month just in dry cleaning bills.

While the two dealers looked around, in walked Liza Minnelli. They were starstruck.

Seeing an actual business operation sealed the deal. They handed me a brown paper grocery bag. Inside was $50,000. Seven days later, I gave them back a check for $40,500. As Woodbeck would say, "Like popcorn."

That's when Harold got cold feet. He was worried that since the IRS was already looking over his books that any out of the ordinary deposits and withdrawals would throw up red flags. I think too that as much as he wanted to be involved in a sting, reality set in and Harold knew he just was not cut out for this kind of an adventure. He backed out.

I needed a new plan fast.

Hank Whiteman was a friend of Gable's. Once a bookkeeper, his drinking cost him everything and he couldn't hold a job. Like seemingly everyone else in L.A., he was also a failed part-time actor. Now a house painter in his early thirties, he had long blond hair, a mustache, and a creased face that made him look older than he was. Always hustling to make money, he and some others had created a company called Olympic Record Cards in preparation for the 1984 Olympics, which were coming to Los Angeles that summer. They obtained audiotapes of the "golden moments" of past Olympics and transferred them to gold-painted cardboard records. Their plan was to sell them by phone and door-to-door.

It was a disaster. Whiteman was left with the entire stock, thousands of records, in his possession.

I called Vern and said Farino had a better idea than his dry cleaners. We would claim Olympic Record Cards was selling hundreds of thousands of records and run the dirty money through that business. Vern wanted an operation that was already laundering money but he thought this was clever.

I convinced him, Dick, and Dominic to incorporate and they formed Balboa Enterprises, though I was in charge of everything. I rented space in a modern office building in Long Beach, moved in desks, file cabinets, the usual furniture, and hired a secretary.

At the Balboa offices, Farino promised to introduce Vern and Dick to the Civellas and Speros, sometime. Also on stage was Whiteman, who naturally played our accountant. I bought him a suit and made him promise that, while working with me, he would stay off the booze. We were in business.

"How about I make the next delivery to your condo in Brentwood?" Dominic suggested.

I gave him a time when I'd be home. But I was late. When he made the drop, I wasn't there. My South American cleaning lady was on time though. Dominic handed her a paper bag and she put it on the couch. When I finally arrived, she said, "A man come with this for you." I opened the bag. Inside was $100,000 in tens and twenties. It was all there. The cleaning lady apparently hadn't looked inside. Or she had but was amazingly honest.

That night I showed the money to Maria. A bag filled with $100,000 is an impressive sight. Even I hadn't seen that much cash in one spot before. I gave her a couple hundred dollars to go shopping. She was still working at Silent Radio for not much more than minimum wage so the cash raised my stature in her eyes. I was connected and I was cool.

I told Maria generally what I was up to but not too much. Like with Mob wives, she didn't ask questions and frankly would rather not know the answers anyway—as long as I helped maintain her life-style. With Terri, I had a semblance of a family life. With Maria, it was always about the next party. She wanted to dance the night away at clubs. With this new sting operation, I didn't have to be anywhere the next morning. So party on.

I called Vern: "What the hell was Dominic thinking?" Leaving $100,000 with my cleaning lady was pretty stupid.

"Hey, she worked for you. It didn't matter. You got it all, didn't you?" The drops would continue but from then on Dominic delivered the bag to Whiteman and a few days later Whiteman returned a cashier's check to Dominic.

Jeez, these guys will be easy to take down, I thought. Vern didn't seem like much of a badass. He talked tough but that was usually a sign of a wannabe tough guy, not the real thing. Dominic was a mild-mannered numbers guy. Dick was the only one I might have to worry about, even with his hearing problem. He looked more "street," with a couple of scars on his face and the hands of a construction worker. I got the sense that he had been around the block.

I thought maybe Vern was so talkative and pushy because he didn't want me to buddy up to Dick. He would always interrupt our conversations. But I never had a calm and easy feeling around any of them. Despite all the meetings and parties, I never saw them indulge in any coke, a friendly line. Another thing I noticed was that when we'd go out to lunch or dinner to talk business, none of them tipped very well. For drug dealers they sure were cheap pricks. Well, waitress karma would get them, I thought. After the sting, the Colombians would blame them for losing their money, not me. Vern, Dick, and Dom would be in serious trouble then.

Ida, our plain, middle-aged secretary for Olympic Record Cards, had no idea what was going on. I'd have people call and make phony record orders every day just to keep up appearances. She couldn't figure out how we actually did business since she never saw any salesmen. I'd go days without showing up and Ida would just sit there doing busy work. She felt so sorry for us, worried that we were such lousy businessmen, that she offered to put together a business plan for us. But she was getting paid, as were Gable and Whiteman, and so, in the end, she just went along.

The money I kept I didn't spend on a new Ferrari or a vacation in Rio or anything that would draw attention. I kept my eye on the prize—the $5 million payday.

With each drop, I dangled more and more bait in front of the dealers. I promised to get them in on a gold mining operation in Colorado where we could inflate the amount of gold mined. I brought up various construction industry scams. But by the time I had "laundered" $350,000 they were getting antsy.

"I thought you'd be connecting us with players. You keep mentioning big names, but all we've met is Farino," Vern complained. "We want to expand out of this rinky-dink record business."

To keep the sting on track, I arranged a sit-down for Palm Springs. This time, when Farino arrived he would be accompanied by a "Civella" bodyguard. In truth, he was an Englishman named Sean Hoskins and he was a licensed private detective.

Sean was a Richard Attenborough type—a small but stocky bull-dog. I had met him through Harold, who was the agent for a book deal a friend of Sean's had going. Both Sean and his friend were among the British law enforcement folks who nabbed Ronnie Biggs of Great Train Robbery fame. Sean was as sharp and savvy as they come.

• • •

SOON AFTER WOODBECK and I first arrived in Hollywood, Sean took us with Harold to a home off the Sunset Strip owned by George Maharis, the *Route 66* star. It was called "The A-Frame" and it was a swinger party house. Admission for guys was twenty dollars and a girl. The rules were simple: If the girl leaves, you leave. But if you leave, she could stay. I recruited a cute blonde UCLA cheerleader to go with me to "a movie party."

Inside the house, parachute cloth divided the open areas into rooms. Naked people were everywhere. We walked through the house and to the outdoor deck, where a couple was fucking in the jacuzzi. The cheerleader freaked and wanted out of there. I was a little embarrassed myself. You didn't see that sort of thing in Kansas City—at least I didn't think you did. I talked the cheerleader into staying. She started drinking and slowly I got her down to her underwear, not much less than what she showed before 50,000 football fans every Saturday in the fall. But that's as far as she'd go.

"Okay, let's leave," I said. "I'll just get another drink and I'll be back and we'll go." When I returned, she was fucking two black guys, one of whom was a Los Angeles Laker. I couldn't believe it. The two men made it clear that I was not welcome to join them. I walked away. The bouncer came up and said, "Where's your girl?"

"Gone."

"Then bye-bye."

• • •

SEAN WASN'T CHEAP. He demanded a couple grand plus travel and a condo at Canyon, the Cathedral Country Club near Palm Springs. Gable didn't mind an all-expenses-paid vacation either. I also put up Vern, Dick, and Dominic. They ran up huge bills at the Club. Of course, I was paying for their good times with their own money.

At first, they wanted to meet with Farino separately, away from me. "No offense, Craig," said Vern during a "cocktails at night" with Farino by the pool, "but you don't need to be here anymore." I think the dealers saw me as the smart-ass middleman who could just mess things up. They wanted a clear path to the big guys. They treated me like a puppet, not knowing that I was the one pulling every string, writing, producing, and directing every scene.

"We're tired of dealing with the low-level guys like Craig. Even you, Mike. You're higher up, I know, but we need to meet Civella," Vern demanded.

Sean leaned over and whispered in Farino's ear. Just like Don had done with Rosa at Ben Frank's, he let his jacket fall open just enough so that Vern could see the gun in his shoulder holster. Sean was a pro.

"Maybe they don't want to meet you," said Farino. "Maybe if you were smart, you wouldn't want to meet them either." He smiled. Gable had been in enough music business negotiations to know how to play the tough guy.

Vern didn't back off. "We keep talking about Vegas money," he said. "So why are we meeting here instead of Vegas?" Whatever I needed to do to keep the money drops rolling is what I did. You have to give the audience what they want or else they get up and leave. They wanted Vegas; I'd give them Vegas. Same play, different stage.

They wanted a Civella, I'd give them a Civella, specifically Carmen "Butch" Civella, whose father Carl had just been sent to prison. Of course, my Butch Civella was an actor I hired in L.A. He was perfect— in his fifties, six feet tall, heavyset, very New York, always wore a suit or sport coat. He had been in a few TV movies but not much else. He insisted I pay him in cash. I gave him $3,000.

I paid for an expensive suite at the MGM Grand for Vern and Dick, and lied to them that it was a freebie, a favor to me from the hotel's owners, just to show how connected I was. Meanwhile, Gable and I flew into Vegas a day early, rented a cheap room, a $19 special at the Tropicana, and ate at the $4.95 buffet.

I found out who would be working at the MGM the next night— bellhops, hatcheck girls, bartenders, cocktail waitresses, and stickmen. In particular, I wanted to know everyone who would be on duty along the route I would take leading Vern and Dick up to their suite when they arrived. With Gable, I went up to each of them.

"This is Mike Farino and I'm Craig Glazer. I'll give you a hundred dollars now and a hundred dollars later if when we walk in tomorrow around 9 p.m., you recognize us and say hello. There will also be a large, Italian-looking man with us. That's Mr. Civella. Be very respectful to him."

When the bellhop questioned whether I'd be back to give him the other hundred dollars, I took one out of my pocket, tore it in two and gave him one of the halves.

"It's no good to me or you unless I come back."

A hundred-dollar bill works like a charm. Besides, like I said, everybody wants to be an actor.

As Farino, Civella, and I paraded into the hotel with Vern and Dick, the bellhop greeted us: "Oh, Mr. Farino, so glad to see you again."

"Mr. Civella, welcome to the MGM as always," said the cigarette girl, who came up to us as she made her rounds of the slot machine players. "And thank you so much for that nice thing you did for me."

Civella squeezed her arm and winked.

It was like the arrival of Marlon Brando's Godfather himself. All I knew was that our Butch Civella sure as hell wasn't him. All that mattered was that Vern and Dick thought he was. We took them to their suite and ordered champagne.

"What else can you get?" Vern asked.

"You want girls? I'll get you girls," Civella said. Dick's eyes lit up, and I made a mental note to get him a hooker, which I did later.

But Vern had other ideas. "How about some gambling, you know, that's not gambling?"

I interrupted Civella before he could answer. "What do you mean?"

"We put our money on the craps table three times, $1,000 a throw, and we win. Luck that's not luck, know what I'm saying?"

Civella stepped up to the plate. He knew his back story and I'm glad we had rehearsed all of the possible scenarios.

"Our tables are not fixed," he said, insulted. "We have a legitimate operation here."

"So you control the owners who supposedly run this place," said Dick, "but all you can get us are broads and booze?"

"Why do we need to cheat?" said Civella with a laugh. "Have you seen the casino? We make money every second. We're not the ones gambling."

Once again, I bullshitted about what the Mob would do for Vern and company. Once again, Vern wanted more.

"Why are we still getting these checks from Olympic Records?" he asked Civella. "Why aren't we getting checks through one of your casinos?"

I couldn't believe how stupid that was. I told him, "You want to bring attention to us by having the checks come from here? The Feds aren't looking at Balboa Enterprises in Long Beach but they sure are looking at the casinos in Vegas."

Vern was annoyed but he grasped my point. Soon after that meeting, as there was after every meeting, there was another money drop. All I had to do was keep the meetings happening. All seemed to be going well.

• • •

BUT WHEN EVERYONE returned to L.A., Armantrout's trial for Don's murder was finally underway. There it was on the front page of the

Metro section of the *L.A. Times*. Dominic read that Woodbeck's partner was one Craig Glazer, a Hollywood character living out his fantasies and writing about his exploits setting up criminals and drug dealers for stings.

Vern called me: "We have a problem."

We met at the Balboa offices.

"So you ripped off dealers and now you're making a movie about it?" He was angry.

"That's Hollywood," I said. "Hey, you knew my name. You could've found out who I was anytime. I wasn't hiding anything."

"So here's the question: Are you trying to rip us off?"

"No, no, no," I said quickly. "That's all in the past."

"I'm supposed to take your word on that?" Vern shook his head. "No more money until we get something more solid."

I could see all of my work, all of the money, all going down the drain.

I had by this point received $750,000 to launder. I returned to them $625,000, which was minus my operation's 15 percent and the $1,500 I took for each drop. Of the remaining $125,000, I paid out about $50,000 in expenses, to Gable, Whiteman, Sean, and Marc; for travel and hotels, and for the façade that was Balboa. I put about $75,000 in my pocket. A nice payday. But I wanted more.

Now the sting to end all stings was in danger of getting blown out of the water. They wanted a star, I'd give them a star.

"Not on my word," I said. "On the word of Nick Spero."

The Spero Family was a rival of the Civella Family. The head of the family, Carl Spero, had been killed when a bomb he was carrying accidentally exploded. Nick, I said, was a relative.

"Hey," Vern said sharply, "I don't want to be a figment of some screenwriter's imagination."

"Do you want to meet Spero or not?"

"All right," he said.

I called my old friend Marc. He had been kind of shaky back in Arizona but he proved to be solid and reliable during our stints as agents for the Kansas attorney general. He had grown up and would have loved to continue to be a cop. But after being charged with Don and I for the controversial motel bust, that career path was blocked. He became a plumbing contractor in Kansas City. We remained close, though. He was the only person left from those days who knew my past and whom I could trust.

Now it was showtime and I needed him back on stage. It wasn't that hard to convince him to put down the wrench and pipe putty for a few days to play a Mob kingpin in a real-life crime drama.

"Sounds like fun," he said. "Is everything cool with this?"

"As cool as an Eskimo's toilet," I said.

This time we brought Vern, Dick, and Dominic to St. Louis, closer to my home turf. We put them up at a downtown hotel, the Forest Park. They were sufficiently impressed that my reach was so great that I could fly them to the Midwest to meet more mobsters. They didn't know that it was also convenient.

It just so happened that in Chesterfield, Missouri, a St. Louis suburb, my father was opening a new Stanford & Sons restaurant— very upscale, lots of mahogany and green marble. I was certain that people associated with the Mafia would be at the premiere party. After all, the Mohawk Meat Company provided the meat to the restaurant. Before it was Mohawk, it was the B&C Meat Company. The "C" stood for Civella.

I didn't bring in our Butch Civella, of course, because the "made men" would know he wasn't the real one. For that same reason, I left Marc, our Nick Spero, at the hotel.

At the restaurant, I went to where Al Brandmeyer—the "B" in B&C—was sitting. He was seventy years old, with gray hair, but at six foot four and 280 pounds he still had the presence of someone you did not screw with. Years earlier, a Mob faction had stuffed Brandmeyer in a car trunk and then shot it up. Amazingly, as big as he was, the bullets only grazed him. They glanced off the tire in the trunk. Brandmeyer was a survivor.

"I need a favor," I asked him. He knew me only as Stan's son. "Just vouch for me."

"What are you talking about?"

"Just go along with what I say, please." I slipped him $1,000.

I told Vern who Brandmeyer was and then brought him over.

"Al, this is Vern. He came in from L.A. We're doing business together."

"Craig, he's a good boy," said the old man. "Knows what's what." He gave a big wink. Vern nodded.

We connected with our Nick Spero at the hotel. Marc was Jewish but he laid down an attitude that would have made Don Corleone proud. He was the same age as me but he seemed older. Maybe it was because he had become a family man and I was still playing around. Marc was a great actor. He should've gone to Hollywood with me.

"We cannot continue with you," Spero threatened Vern, "if you keep questioning our credibility and our methods and our people."

Vern wasn't backing off. "We started out and Craig tells us about dry cleaners, a gold mine, the film industry, construction, that you have businesses all over the country we can get into. That sounds good. But all we're into is this one little thing, this stupid record company." Dick spoke up. "We were promised diversification, that we would contribute to some of your businesses."

Spero threw up his hands. "It takes time."

"We're not happy with that," said Vern.

"We're not happy," Spero said, "that we see only $100,000 here and there."

Dominic chimed in: "That's not chicken shit."

"But it's not chicken salad either," said Spero. He stood up, walked to a window, and thought for a moment.

"Okay, I want everybody to be happy," he said. "That's what I'm here for. How about we get you into our offshore banking companies?" That was the next step in my scheme, a phony offshore banking operation.

Vern raised his eyebrows. He was hooked.

"I've read a lot about that," Dominic said. "The Caymans?"

"Too hot," Spero said, brushing him off. "Too many guys look-ing like us walking through the receiving line with Jonathan Winters Glad Bags of cash. I'm talking about an insurance company that runs a bank in Turks and Caicos."

"That's in the Caribbean," Dominic said authoritatively.

"No," Spero corrected him. "Actually, it's in the Atlantic."

Marc was a regular visitor to those islands as well as the Caymans. Not because of any offshore banking. He was an avid scuba diver and would take excursions down there every three months or so. He could describe the airports, the streets, and the banks to the smallest detail.

"This is already going?" asked Vern, hopefully.

Spero looked at me. "Craig, why don't you have Terry the Whale meet with our friends here and have him outline how it works?" Terry the Whale was in reality Gable's shyster lawyer. He too had agreed to help in our sting.

"And you," said Spero as he lightly jabbed a finger in Vern's chest, "will open the spigot so the money starts flowing again." Once a plumber, always a plumber.

Vern bit his lip. He was not used to having a finger jabbed in his chest.

In L.A., Vern called Farino and asked when the meeting with Terry the Whale would take place. But they would never talk to Terry because the lawyer had backed out. I guess you just can't trust a crooked lawyer to keep his word. Nevertheless, I kept his character alive. Farino told Vern, "It'll happen. There's no reason to talk to him yet."

"When will there be a reason?"

"Two or three weeks," said Farino. "I thought you were going to do another drop first?"

Soon after, Whiteman received a bag with $100,000 in twenty-dollar bills.

I called Vern to set up a meeting at Balboa.

"Is Terry the Whale going to be there?"

"No," I told him, "but Spero is coming in."

Vern was frustrated to the breaking point. At Balboa, with Dominic alongside, he got in Spero's face. Something had changed but I didn't know what.

"We're sick of this," Vern said to Marc, who was happy to come in for a Southern California vacation in return for a few hours of being in "Craig's movie." "Craig told us about his connects and we felt we'd sit with the people you say we're dealing with, the Civella type people, whatever you want to call them. But Craig doesn't bring us shit. He doesn't know anybody and we're not getting anything done."

"What are you talking about? I'm here," said Spero. "I don't even like L.A. and I fly all this way to be here."

"We don't see you making any decisions," said Vern. "Give us someone who doesn't have to pull a paper out of his pocket for the negotiating limits. We need someone who can make decisions. It sure as hell isn't Craig."

He was putting me down, just like my father. I felt my anger rising. I was on the edge of losing my grip on everything.

"You met Butch Civella!" I shouted. "Spero is right here. I haven't done anything?"

"You're a bullshitter," said Vern.

I was about to slug him but Spero remained calm.

"I don't think you know who you're dealing with," said Spero.

"Same here," said Vern coldly. "If you do something to us, any of this sting shit, we'll have the Colombians crawling up your asshole."

"Is that a threat?" I just about spit it at him.

"Dick's contacts go way back down there. You ever dealt with Colombians? They're out of their fuckin' minds. That's why we wanted to be involved with your people. A safety net. But now we don't feel like we're safe because we think Craig is writing a script and doesn't know any of these people he bullshitted that he knows."

Holy fuck! He was way too close to the truth. I had to dynamite those ideas of his right away.

I banged on the table, furious. "Hey motherfucker, if you're saying I lied, I'll kick your fuckin' ass!"

Vern was unruffled.

"We think these are just local people, maybe relatives," he said, "people who got a benediction from someone on high. We want to deal with the real horsepower." He snarled at me. "And Craig, don't pull that Khrushchev shit with me."

As a kid I learned the power of throwing the first punch. But if I did that now, the rest of the deal would be over. Of course, if Woodbeck were there, he wouldn't give a rat's ass. He would have grabbed Vern by the neck and slammed him up against the wall.

All I could do was repeat a few choice words.

"Go fuck yourself!" I stormed out.

"Wait here," Spero told Vern and Dominic. He found me downstairs in the lobby.

"What was that all about?" Marc asked.

I pulled myself together—eyes on the prize. "Go back up there," I told him, "and try to get the drops started again."

Spero returned to the office. "I'm sorry Craig got hot."

"Spero, personally I like Craig," said Vern. "But the fact remains that he has a certain history. He told us all the things he's done. The fact remains that he's writing a script right now! Dick said to me, 'Was that thing in St. Louis a script? Did he trot these people out to shake hands with us and say hello?' That's what we feel."

Spero was cool. He didn't even swallow hard.

"You don't trust me? You want to back out? Because that's why I returned to this room and told Craig to motherfuckin' wait downstairs. I came to see if you want to back out. Because the people I work with become very concerned about people who back out."

"That's why your people have been successful for a hundred years in this country," said Vern graciously.

"We hold our own," said Spero. "I don't know if you read about my family but my whole family was wiped out by the Civellas."

"What's your connection?" asked Vern. "Why didn't they do your ass?"

"I'm at the end of the family. The immediate boss is Willie the Rat, a Commasino. The Civellas are at the top. A lot are in jail, a lot are not. I can't talk about it; it bothers me. I'm lucky my life was spared. When they make a deal, it's a deal for life. I was a deal. I had to do some things. I feel fortunate."

If there were an Oscar for Best Performance in Front of Major Dope Dealers, Marc would have deserved one for his performance.

"Craig says he's gonna kick my ass. I'm not impressed by that."

"I understand," said Spero, the good cop to my bad cop. "I had no idea that the trust factor had fallen apart. I want to get our business rolling. I want this back on the road. What can I do for you?"

Vern leaned back in his chair and stroked his mustache.

"I told Farino that Dick wants a road map of where we're going and who we're going to see. Farino says, 'I got some names but I have to check to see if I can use them. I'll let you know Tuesday.' We call Tuesday and he says, 'You don't need to see anybody.'"

Spero nodded.

Vern continued. "I don't think he has the right answers to the fuckin' questions. I talked to Dick about this and we don't think Farino is a financier for the Teamsters."

Marc wondered if they knew he was not Nick Spero. If they did, he could be in serious trouble real soon.

"He might be one of the low-grade people and you pump him up," Vern said.

Marc's cover wasn't blown. He couldn't allow himself a sigh of relief but he sure wanted to.

Vern went on. "We expected some bullshit from you just like you expect some bullshit from us. We understood that and accepted it as long as it went along fine but I don't think it is."

Spero commiserated with him. "You have to understand there's a lot Farino and Craig are not told. There's a lot they cannot be told. But I can't be in L.A. on a daily basis. I will remove Farino from power. I know Craig flew off the handle but you're going to have to deal with Craig."

Vern was not pleased. "Well, we can decide on that later. We have other problems right now." He nodded towards Dominic.

"We asked for a list of the names and Social Security numbers of the salesmen who are supposed to be working for this record company," said Dominic. "We can't file our estimated taxes without knowing what profit we're claiming and we can't do that without the list."

"We have to look legit," added Vern. "We need to be audit-proof. If they want to look for…"

Spero picked it up. "They will go in the field and look up every name and Social Security number. I hear you and I want to get it cleaned up." He looked at Dominic the accountant. "We don't want 'knock, knock, my name is Bill Smith, Special Agent with the Internal Revenue Service.' Do you want to fool with those guys? I'll fool with anybody but not with the IRS."

Dominic smiled. "That's the truth."

"I'm not a subtle guy," said Vern. "If I was, I'd be a diplomat. We'd been looking around for the right people to do this business with us for almost two years and we're disappointed in you." He played his final card. "If we can find someone who can do what you've done for a lesser fee, we'd be crazy not to go for it."

Spero understood. "We'll take care of all of this."

He then tried to turn the conversation to a more positive note. "What do you think about this record deal? I'll tell you what I think: It's fantastic! Craig thought of that. I commend him highly, a brilliant idea. Hey, I'd buy one of those records."

But his effort didn't work.

"I wouldn't dispute that but it's the only idea we're working on," Vern complained. "We should be speaking with Civella again."

Spero hardened. He knew we weren't going to bring our Civella actor back for an encore. "Don't take offense," he said. "You stopped the dollars and the family is upset. He will not meet with you again."

Vern got up from his chair. "We're paying a high fee and getting steerage passage instead of sitting next to the captain."

"You want to meet someone else, maybe we can work something out," Spero offered, enticing him with every carrot he had. He just had to keep them in the game.

"No actors though, right?" asked Vern. Spero didn't even flinch as Vern suggested exactly what was going on. "Craig isn't going to do a casting call for a guy with fourteen scars on his face who meets us and says 'I'm Joe the Banana and I'm this and that,' right?"

Spero laughed and then smiled. "The only actor we have is Craig."

Vern laughed too, but then added, "Understand that we're sincere. We will not go on if we're not satisfied."

13

Getting Stung

A spokesman at Disney Studios said the studio is considering the movie for production. Glazer won't be playing the lead; those plans fell through. But there is another role he might play. "A cop," he said, with a rueful grin.

—*Los Angeles Times*, December 3, 1984

I WANTED TO measure Vern and the others for the sting. So during our meeting, Sean had been outside, sitting in a car and scanning the vicinity with binoculars. One of his men was across the street at a McDonald's also scoping out the area. I wanted to see if these were just a few guys I had to deal with or if Colombians really backed them up. Just like my first sting in Boston, I didn't want to go against more guys than I could handle.

After Vern and Dominic left, Sean came up to the office. He had spotted something suspicious.

Two cars. Each one had two men in the front seat, two men in the back. Circling the block.

"They're either hoods or Feds," Sean said. "Let me check out their tags." The next day he ran their license plates. The numbers were out of sync. In other words, they didn't exist.

Sean was worried. "I don't like this."

I didn't either. But whoever they were, I was sure they still wouldn't jam me up.

"If they're the big-time dealers they say they are and I get in trouble, I'll call the cops and help put them in jail. The cops will love me for that."

Sean wasn't so confident. "Yes, and one day you'll walk out of a movie theater and get blasted."

"Come on, what would the Colombians get out of that? There's no money in killing me."

"They would have five million reasons to kill you. These Colombians would cut your nuts off just to be macho." He paused. "And what if these guys are the cops?"

"You mean they might be tailing Vern?"

"Could be. Or maybe your dealers are cops too."

I was stinging cops who were stinging me? It didn't make any sense. "Why would cops give us hundreds of thousands of dollars?" I asked.

"Because they think you are who you say you are."

"But they came to me. That's how I got into trouble in Kansas when I was an agent. I gave the dealers the drugs. That was the whole problem."

"You might be right," Sean said, "but my advice to you is to get out now. You're going to get killed, ripped off, or arrested."

I let the money talk. "If I get these guys all in a room with several million dollars, will you help me?" He was quiet for a long moment.

"Me and a couple of mates come in with automatic weapons and take the money?" He shrugged. "I would be interested."

It's amazing how the fear factor drops off and logic and reason fly out the window when you tell someone, "If I can get you a share of five million dollars and not get you killed..." Go ahead, see what your friends would do, how far they would go, if you told them that.

The money was talking to me as well. I had lost Grandpa Bennie's investment in Video Village. I had been a fuckup. I wanted a big score, a big success. I was mad too, with myself and with Vern. He put me down and embarrassed me, just like Stan. He didn't think I was running things? Well, I would show him. I had reached the same crazy, dangerous, invincible-feeling point Woodbeck had before his murder.

"Fuck, I don't need any badge! All I have to say is, 'I'm Don Wood-dick! Freeze, motherfuckers!!!'"

But if I were going to get killed or arrested, I would go down swinging. I would have my revenge. As usual, I had an idea from the movies. In *Witness for the Prosecution*, Tyrone Power's character set up his alibi before he murdered a wealthy widow who had conveniently willed him her fortune the previous week. His wife, played by Marlene Dietrich, meanwhile pretended to hate her husband and so was called as a witness for the prosecution. She, of course, turned the tables on the prosecution and supported his alibi. He got off the hook.

Three days after the meeting at Balboa, I wrote a letter to my attorney, Richard Rosenblum, that would be my alibi. I sealed it, mailed it to him, and he placed it in a safe deposit box. The letter began…

Dear Richard,

   I am writing you this letter in the event of my death or arrest in connection with the following affair. I along with others who were helping both willingly and in some case(s) with my knowledge of this affair are about to break one of the biggest organized drug rings on the West Coast of America. As of today, June 26, 1984, I am close to putting all the relevent [sic] information together…

Whether they were the drug dealers they said they were, or if they were cops, as Sean thought they might be, then I would be a vigilante sting artist with a Get Out of Jail Free card.

My Marlene Dietrich was Rick De La Sota, the L.A. County assistant district attorney who was the prosecutor in Woodbeck's murder.

"Something is going down," I told him.

"Tell me more."

"I'm stinging the guys who killed Woodbeck."

"Don't do it," he said. "You're not a cop. Your immunity in the Woodbeck case will not cover you. Craig, you have your whole life ahead of you."

I was planning on it.

. . .

DAYS AND THEN weeks passed without hearing from Vern. The pressure I felt to make the big deal happen seemed to ease. Maybe I was better off. I hadn't won the jackpot but I had won a little. I actually felt somehow relieved. Maybe I wouldn't need the letter after all.

Then, two months after the contentious June 23 meeting, Vern called.

"Everyone on our side is pissed," he said. "There were too many questions and not many answers. We found other guys to do our business."

"So why are you calling me now?" I asked.

"Business is business. We have a hundred keys at the dock. Do you know anyone who could move twenty of them? If you find a buyer, there's $20,000 in it for you."

Meetings at New World about being promoted were going nowhere. I was without Gable because he had been fired when he couldn't account for money he was advanced. Peter Brown had moved out of our writing office and Low Oak was floundering. *Outlaws* had sparked some heat because of the trial but nobody was stepping up to the plate to make the movie. I could use the money.

I wasn't about to do a drug deal but I would have to use that as bait. I wanted to get back to the money laundering. They would need somebody to clean the cash from selling a hundred kilos. It didn't completely pan out before but maybe I could convince Vern to work with me again. Then I'd have another chance to sting him—and stinging Vern would feel especially good.

Even better, I was now certain he was not a cop. If he was, he would have busted me already for the money laundering and wouldn't be trying to set up a drug deal.

I needed someone to play the buyer and asked Hellman if he knew anybody with ready access to a lot of cash. He told me about Ivan Urlich, whom I had met at a party the week before. Ivan was about thirty-five years old, six foot five, with long hair and a beard. He wore a $2,000 watch and drove a sports car. He looked like Mick Fleetwood. He was also very charismatic. I cast him as a rock 'n' roll star from Australia; he was from New Zealand but nobody would know the difference. Ivan had just sailed a yacht from his home country to Hawaii to L.A., intending to upgrade the boat's guts before selling it. He had all the money he needed for the retrofit in cash. I suspected he was in the business of doing something more than simply transporting yachts.

"You flash some cash," I explained to him. "Tell them you're interested in buying the twenty kilos. If we feel comfortable, we set up an exchange for another day. When this is all done, I'll pay you $25,000 for the performance. Not bad, huh?"

"What if you rip me off? You are a sting artist."

"You can trust him," said Hellman. "I'll go with you." Hellman thought this would be a fun adventure.

Ivan put $50,000 in a gym bag and we went to an airport area hotel to meet Vern and Dick. Also there, for the first time, was George Venables, who said he was another American representative of the Colombians. About my age, 200 pounds and solidly built, he looked like a middle linebacker. They loved Ivan, who showed he was serious by flashing the cash and saying he could be a regular buyer. With the introductory meeting out of the way, we agreed to make the deal in a couple of days.

Vern, who was much friendlier than he had been at our last face-to-face, suggested I pick the location. I chose the Warehouse restaurant in Marina del Rey. We would meet the afternoon of August 31, 1984.

Sean was unavailable to back me up on such short notice. I called Marc but he had plans with his family and couldn't fly in. Ivan seemed pretty sharp but he was a lobster when it came to stings. I couldn't get a team together fast enough. A sting was out of the question, for the moment. I would have to stall on the coke deal and reel them in slowly on the money laundering.

Hellman came by my condo with Ivan and all of his money in the gym bag, exactly $271,915. We drove to the Warehouse in separate cars. I parked my Alfa Romeo and went to Ivan's rented Mustang convertible and told him: "I'll do the talking. When they ask you to go outside, look at the kilos, get a sample, and bring it back. But disagree with the price, say you don't like the way it looks, anything. Find a reason not to do the deal."

"Hey mate, what if it's excellent coke?"

"Then keep the sample. But do not do the buy. Because if you do, then that's a crime."

Ivan was all right with that. Besides, twenty keys would cost $400,000. He didn't have enough cash anyway.

Hellman was well-dressed as always—white shirt with a sweater wrapped around his neck, loafers but no socks. Ivan was the rocker with blue jeans and a cowboy shirt. I wore tennis shorts and a powder blue sweater with a t-shirt underneath. What I was not wearing was a weapon. There wasn't going be any need for a gun. This was to be the first of many meetings. The three of us walked in together. It was 4 p.m. and the place was jammed. I asked the bartender, "Is it always this busy?"

"It is Friday and it is happy hour," he said.

He looked a little familiar. "Do you remember me?" I asked.

"Sorry," he said. "Lots of people come through here."

I spotted Vern and Dick at a table and we sat down. Over his left shoulder I could see a swarthy, middle-aged man, clean-cut, wearing a sport coat, whom I'd seen somewhere before but couldn't place. Over his right shoulder there was an Asian woman sitting with a heavyset man. I had a flash of recognition that I had seen them both in the lobby at the airport hotel.

"I've been in here before and I've never seen it busy like this," I commented to Vern.

"Is that a problem? You picked the place," he reminded me. He took me by the arm and walked me to the bar.

"Listen, I didn't want your people to hear our business," he said, "but we've decided not to give you cash for being the middleman. Instead, we want to give you a key."

"Hey, I'll take a sample but I don't need a key. I'm not a seller." I wanted the cash, not the blow.

"You know people who use coke in Hollywood. What are you afraid of?"

"I'm just not a dealer."

"But don't you get high all the time?"

"No," I said, annoyed at his question. "You think I'm an addict?"

"Okay, okay," he said quickly in surrender, apparently not wanting me to get pissed at him. "We'll deliver the cash to you tomorrow."

Well, the deal wasn't going down so there would be no cash for that. But I hoped the meeting would set the stage for lots of cash going from Vern to me in the near future.

He went back to the table and I headed to the pay phone. I called Maria to tell her this might take longer than expected but to hang tight. She asked, "Everything okay?"

"Everything will be fine," I said. "I'll be home by six and we can go to Palm Springs for the weekend."

A half hour of chitchat with Vern, Dick, Hellman, and Ivan went by. I was getting restless. "So are we going to do this or not?" I said.

"We want Venables here too," answered Vern, who then went to the payphone. Jeez, they should've had everything ready. I downed a couple of mai tais and they improved my mood. I thought about what my next move would be with these shmucks.

A big blonde, drunk, seated behind me, banged into me with her chair. "You're a cutie," she slurred. I ignored her.

"Don't turn away from me." She eyed Hellman: "What's your name, babe?"

Venables came through the door and sidled up to our table. "Who wants to look at the stuff? Take me to your money and I'll show you the product. A car in the parking lot."

"No," Ivan said. "You first. I showed you I had money already."

"Is the cash in your car?" Venables asked.

Ivan nodded.

"Then let's go outside."

The two walked out, which is what I wished the drunk blonde would do. Then another drunk woman walked toward her and nearly fell into my lap. She distracted my attention. When I looked up, I suddenly saw a busboy, two waitresses, and someone who looked like the manager coming toward our table.

I stood up as I thought, "Fuck, this is a bust."

"Hey Craig, where you going?" said Vern. "Sit down."

"I'll be right back." I started to move away.

The drunken blonde pulled out a gun.

Everyone in the restaurant pulled out a gun.

I was glad I hadn't brought my own gun. I would have reached for it and I'd probably be dead already.

"DEA! You're under arrest! Don't move!"

"Let me see some ID," I yelled.

The drunken blonde, no longer drunk, showed me hers. It was the real deal.

"Are these guys with you?" I asked Vern.

"Glad you think this is funny because you're going to jail."

"What do you think you have me for?" On the outside, I was cool, calm, and collected. On the inside, I knew the shit had hit the fan.

"Conspiracy to distribute cocaine."

I was truly surprised. "What cocaine?"

Someone began to read me the Miranda warning but I interrupted.

"I waive my rights. I would like to make a statement. I am not a drug dealer. I set up this whole thing to put some bad guys behind bars. My attorney is holding a letter explaining everything."

I thought about my movie—and what a great scene the arrest was going to make. Everyone in the restaurant—the workers, the patrons—was a law enforcement officer. There were dozens of them. There were even agents in the palm trees outside the Warehouse.

I later discovered that when Venables walked Ivan to his vehicle, the "dealer" showed him a few fake bricks of coke and then cuffed him. Ivan never gave him the money. There was no exchange. Instead, the agents who surrounded him took his car keys and opened the trunk themselves. They raised the gym bag in the air like they had won the Super Bowl.

"Listen, Hellman is just an innocent bystander," I told Vern. "You should let him go."

"Can't do that."

"Vern, is that your real name?" I asked.

He nodded.

"What agency?"

"U.S. Customs." He was Vern Pitzker. Dick was Dick Madden, L.A. Sheriff's Department. Venables was Drug Enforcement Administration. Dominic was Dominic Rocha, Internal Revenue Service.

When Marc said he didn't want to fool with the IRS? He was talking right to the IRS. I don't know how Dominic kept from laughing. And Dick's bum ear he mentioned when we first got together? He just wanted me to speak directly into his microphone!

They were part of the multi-agency Pacific Task Force Against Organized Crime, the law enforcement group that would be seen in the film *Casino*. The Pacific Task Force was charged with investigating organized crime out of Las Vegas.

I had stung the people who were trying to sting the Mob.

Najarian, who introduced me to Vern and Dick, had been arrested for money laundering through video games and became a confidential informant. He paid his penance by connecting the Pacific Task Force to a player with the Mafia—uh, me.

When the article about Armantrout's trial for Woodbeck's murder appeared in the newspaper, they became suspicious. Then the FBI report on the surveillance of the St. Louis meeting revealed I had no real relationship to the Mob. Instead of mafiosi, they finally figured out they were dealing with a guy writing a movie about his life, a housepainter, a plumbing contractor, a music artist manager, and a cast of Hollywood sort-of actors.

Prior to the June 23 meeting, they broke into the Balboa office and placed video cameras and listening devices everywhere. Vern said, "I don't want to be a figment of this screenwriter's imagination." He meant it. When Vern told Spero he didn't want any actors playing mafiosi? He already knew that's what we had done. That meeting was their final attempt to salvage anything from an operation that had cost them nearly a million dollars of the taxpayer's money.

Vern and Dick were seriously pissed off. They were angry as hell with me for wasting their time and money, and for threatening any chance they had for career advancement. They were probably getting raked over the coals by their bosses. They needed something to show for it all. That's when they decided to give me to the DEA by offering the coke deal.

"I wasn't dealing and I wasn't buying," I told Venables as I was cuffed to the seat belt in the back of his vehicle before heading downtown.

"We'll be the judge of that," he said. "Can you tell us of any large drug operation?"

"No." Was he really so out of the loop that he didn't know that Vern and Dick were the supposed drug dealers?

"You just came on this case, didn't you?" Suddenly I realized that Venables and the DEA had been kept in the dark about what had happened before the phony coke deal. "Do you know I've supposedly been laundering money for Vern and the boys for a year?"

"What?" He was genuinely surprised.

"I pretended to launder money using actors posing as Mafia members. I'm a former law enforcement agent for the State of Kansas."

"You're not a cop now."

"I'm not a drug dealer either."

Venables seemed a little uneasy. He turned around in the passenger seat and looked me in the eye. "Craig, don't you get it? You became the target. And now you're going to go to prison for most of the rest of your life."

14

On Trial

"I have never seen a case like this," said Deputy Dist. Atty. Richard de la Sota.

—*Los Angeles Times*, December 3, 1984

LAW ENFORCEMENT LIKES to arrest its choice suspects on Friday or, even better, on a Friday before a Monday holiday. That way, the suspect isn't able to see a magistrate and try to get out on bond until the following Tuesday, when court is back in session. I was arrested on the Friday afternoon before Labor Day.

I was put in a cell at the DEA lockup downtown. Located inside a nondescript building and rarely mentioned in public or in the press, the temporary holding cell allows the agency time to interrogate and breakdown suspects before they have to go before a judge.

But I'll get out of this, I said to myself. I always had.

I told my story of the money laundering and the non–drug deal to the DEA agents who came in to talk to me. I even offered to help them in their work. "You could use someone like me," I boasted. "I'm better at this than anyone you've got. Look at what I did!"

I fantasized that maybe they would put me on some dangerous undercover mission. I could be the James Bond of the drug world. Man, the *Outlaws* movie would really be great then! But instead of being impressed that one guy had snookered a multi-agency government task force trying to bring down organized crime on the West Coast, they were offended. Nothing had changed since my undercover days in Kansas ten years earlier.

I called my father. He was upset and disappointed. He thought maybe I was finally going to succeed in Hollywood. Now I was going to be in the Kansas City newspapers again and Stan was going to have to wear it. "You're fucked," he told me.

I called Grandpa Bennie. He was on a plane to L.A. the next day.

After a few hours alone, I was transported to county jail with Ivan and Richard. We were put in a cell together.

Hellman was frantic. "What the hell did you get me into?"

"Am I going to get my money back?" Ivan asked. "Are they going to deport me?"

"Both of you shut up," I said, rightly assuming that the cell was bugged. "We've done nothing wrong. Here's what happened."

For the next two hours, I spun my tale of trying to sting a major drug ring that might somehow be connected to Woodbeck's death. Most importantly, I told them about the money laundering episodes that led up to the final day. I made myself out to be a vigilante hero, just like in *Outlaws*. That's what I wanted the Feds to hear. That's what I figured would save my neck and theirs. I wasn't scared. There was absolutely no way they were going to convict me and send me to prison. But I was embarrassed.

The King of Sting had been stung.

• • •

THE LOS ANGELES County Jail was a nasty place, filled with gang-bangers and street thugs. But Ivan, Richard, and I could at least sleep somewhat soundly at night because we were able to stay together in our own cell. They weren't as angry with me as you might think. They needed me. I had the story that could get them out. The next day, we were playing tic-tac-toe with M&Ms when I was taken from the cell. The DEA had considered my offer to help on future cases.

"That's quite a story," said an agent I had never spoken to before. "Unfortunately, because of what you've done in the past, any testimony you would give in any court would pretty much be thrown out. It'd be useless. You can't be trusted."

They were going to play hardball.

At about eleven that night, I was transported to the medium-security Federal Correctional Institution at Terminal Island. Though I had been in jail before, I had never been in prison. Big difference. Terminal Island was a dark and ominous place. My ankles were shackled and a chain connected them to another chain around my waist which was in turn connected to my handcuffs. From the moment I shuffled onto the bus, a guard kept a shotgun aimed at my midsection.

When we reached the prison, a sally port opened for the bus and we drove up to another gate. The gate behind us slammed shut. Keys attached to a chain were lowered from a guard tower and another guard unlocked the gate in front of us. The keys were then pulled back up to the tower. The gate opened and we entered the yard. The experience was overwhelming. I thought to myself, "This is prison, baby. Just like in the movies."

Terminal Island is where gangster Henry Hill, the main character in *Goodfellas*, served time. Another guest of the government had been Salvatore "Bill" Bonanno, the model for Michael Corleone in *The Godfather*. Dustin Hoffman often visited inmate Eddie Bunker to get the rights to his prison novel *No Beast So Fierce*, which became the film *Straight Time*. A former drug addict and bank robber, Bunker became Hollywood's leading authority on prison life, writing and directing the 2000 film *Animal Factory* and playing Mr. Blue in Quentin Tarantino's *Reservoir Dogs*. TI had also been home to Al Capone, Timothy Leary, G. Gordon Liddy, and Charles Manson twice, before the Sharon Tate murders. When I arrived, John DeLorean was a fellow resident.

Guards escorted me to the J2 holding unit. I met my cellmate, a six-foot-four, 280-pound black dude. He gave me the upper bunk. Thank God for small favors. But I kept my eyes open all night. The next morning I was glad to see that he held a Bible in his hand.

The bond hearing took place at the L.A. Federal Court Building. Because neither Richard nor Ivan was a U.S. citizen they were denied bond. I faced a maximum sentence of twenty-seven years. The government asked for a $2 million bond. At the hearing were my attorney Rosenblum, Maria, and, of course, Grandpa Bennie, who quickly stirred up the courtroom by talking so loud everyone could hear him.

"Goddamn you, son. I'm so ashamed of you. I found a bill at your apartment for a hamburger for twenty-four dollars. Why you ain't got nothing and you spend twenty-four dollars for a hamburger!"

"Hamburger Hamlet," I said. "It's the name of a restaurant."

"Why not eat at home?"

"Grandpa, I have a bigger problem right now."

"And get your hair cut, pardner. You look like a goddamn hippie!"

People were trying not to laugh.

"Sir, you're a relative?" asked the judge.

"He's my grandson," said Grandpa Bennie.

The judge seemed to smile.

Rosenblum objected to the high bond, pointing out that there were no drugs involved and that the whole affair had more to do with Hollywood than a crime. He held up the *Los Angeles Reader* front-page story. "They're doing a movie about him," he said.

He also emphasized that I was a former special agent in narcotics.

"Your honor, it would be very dangerous to send Mr. Glazer to prison. The press will no doubt write about him working undercover to bust drug dealers and organized crime. His life will be in danger. We request that you release him on his own recognizance."

The judge turned to Grandpa Bennie!

"Sir, how much can you post for your grandson?"

"$50,000. I got hard money. Right here in my pocket, your honor."

"Then that'll be the bond. I don't think Mr. Glazer is a flight risk."

After the paperwork was completed, I was released the next morning. The trial was set for the following February. I prayed I would never go back to TI.

Maria came to pick me up and hugged me, even though I was still in the clothes I was wearing when I was arrested. With her was Grandpa Bennie.

"Your grandpa is not going to be around forever to get you out," he warned. "Where's your goddamn father, the no-good son of a bitch?"

When a *Los Angeles Times* reporter asked Stan about me, he said I was a childish screwup. People I had known only a short time were far more generous. New World even let me keep my job. The reaction from Ken Dalton: "Jeez, this will make a great movie!"

Corman called me into his office: "Young man, you can stay, you're talented, but if the Feds come here, you're gone." They never came and so I continued to work there through my trial, which began in February 1985. With Dalton and another New World producer, Jeff Begun, I even formed a music publishing company.

Army Archerd came through again too, mentioning in his column that Low Oak had optioned Peter Brown's *Such Devoted Sisters—The Fabulous Gabors.* Brown would later cowrite *Oscar Dearest* about Joan Crawford, *Marilyn: The Last Take*, and *Howard Hughes: The Untold Story.*

I hired Brendan O'Neill as my federal attorney. O'Neill was a six-foot-two ex-college football player only a couple of years older than me, which may explain why whenever I went into his Santa Monica office it reeked of pot. He was a little inexperienced but he was young and aggressive and had worked under a tough former U.S. Attorney named William Keller.

It was going to be difficult to beat a conspiracy charge. Basically, if a third person hears two other people say they're planning to commit a crime and one of them takes a step toward actually doing it, then that's conspiracy—even if you never come close to going through with it. If you say, "Let's go buy a gram," then get in your car to pick it up but never do, you can still be convicted of conspiracy—a crime having a sentence of fifteen years. If that one step is a telephone call, it's an extra four years. You shouldn't even joke about something like that, just in case someone's listening.

At first, we thought we'd try the entrapment defense. After all, DeLorean had only recently been acquitted because of it. What that defense strategy said is that the government cannot induce someone who would not otherwise have committed a crime to go ahead and cross the line. But for the strategy to succeed you cannot be predisposed to commit the crime. Because of my past, the prosecution would probably say I was hardly an innocent citizen. They didn't trap me. They just took advantage of what I was all too willing to do.

So instead I decided to follow the script I had been writing my entire life: I was a good guy in a black hat—a vigilante trying to bust a drug ring. Yes, I broke the conspiracy law but the only people I took advantage of were people I thought were criminals. I had not bought or sold any drugs! Maybe I'd be convicted but they'd give me probation. How could they send me to prison?

Not only would I get off but my "not guilty" verdict would make a great ending to the *Outlaws* sequel they had just about written for me, a story about stinging the Pacific Task Force. To drive the point home even further that the only conspiracy was to distribute a movie, not cocaine, we gave Kazan's *Outlaws* script to the prosecution. After the jury was selected, we gave copies to them too.

When we heard that William Keller had been assigned as the judge in the case, I figured we had an advantage since O'Neill had worked for him. The distinguished-looking Keller reminded me of a younger John Forsythe from *Dynasty*. He had a reputation for being a stern, no-nonsense prosecutor. At the same time, he was only forty-nine years old and enjoyed surfing. I believe mine was his first case as a judge.

Leading the prosecution was assistant U.S. attorney Fred Friedman, who had joined the Criminal Division in Los Angeles after a stint at the U.S. Department of Justice as special assistant to then associate attorney general Rudy Giuliani, later the mayor of New York City. Ivan and I would be tried together. Hellman had agreed to cooperate with the government and pled guilty to one count of using a telephone in the commission of a crime.

Ivan's lawyer was Victor Sherman, one of those classic pit bull defense attorneys who would do anything to keep his client out of jail. Years later, in 1999, he would represent the lead defendant in the largest money-laundering case in U.S. history. He also became a national commentator during the O.J. Simpson murder trial, seen regularly on Court TV, MSNBC, and other media outlets.

The case the prosecution laid out on the first day was simple: This was about three days in August and three phone calls. Craig Glazer and Ivan Urlich agreed to buy kilos of cocaine. 'Nuff said. What else could there be? It probably seemed simple enough to the jurors as well. After all, in a federal case the defendant is not cloaked in a flag of innocence but a flag of guilt. The people selected as jurors have already served on other juries and expressed a willingness to be on a federal panel. They are primed to convict. Winning a federal case is an uphill battle.

But O'Neill and Sherman picked the prosecution apart. They laid out the entire money laundering scenario from the moment Najarian suggested the idea. They explained the money drops, Balboa Enterprises, the trips to Palm Springs, Vegas, and St. Louis. O'Neill put up a chart of my "Mob ties" and "gang." There were Farino, Civella, and the others. Under their aliases were their real names. Under that were their real occupations—plumbing contractor, music artist manager, actor, etc. There was no drug cartel, no Mafia connection.

O'Neill asked Vern: "Didn't you know they were acting?" Before he could answer, O'Neill said, "Of course you did." Then he played the undercover videotape taken at the Balboa office in which Vern accused us of being actors.

"Your bosses must have been disappointed in you," O'Neill continued. "Spending all that money, thinking you were getting these Mafia bigwigs and ending up with a bunch of actors. Wasted a lot of money, didn't you?"

Sherman went after them personally. "You took an oath when you joined Customs, didn't you?" he asked Vern.

"Yes."

"In Vegas, you met a young lady not yet twenty years old, and spent the night with her, didn't you?"

"She stayed in my room, yes."

"You're a married man. You took an oath when you got married, didn't you?"

"Yes."

"You're not good at keeping promises, are you?"

O'Neill asked Venables to explain sham cocaine. "So it's not cocaine at all, is it? You can't get high off this, can you?"

"No."

"Was there any actual dope?"

"No."

"In this transaction, who was the seller? Is he in this courtroom?"

"Yes."

"For the jury, can you please point him out?"

He pointed to Vern.

"And who was the buyer? The buyer of the cocaine that was not cocaine."

He pointed to Ivan.

I had been arrested in 1973 for selling drugs to dealers as part of my job as a special agent. So why weren't these agents arrested like I had been?

Sherman hammered Venables. "Did Mr. Urlich ever give you the bag with the money?"

"No. One of the agents retrieved it from the trunk of the suspect's car."

"So he never gave it to you?"

"That's correct."

"Oh, and how much did he have?"

"About $270,000."

"Hmmm, isn't that a little light for twenty kilos?"

"It was for ten kilos."

To make their numbers plausible, Vern claimed the deal was for only ten keys. Unfortunately, we couldn't dispute that or anything else about the arrest at the Warehouse. Though three audio or video tape recordings were made of the arrest, the government said it lost all three.

O'Neill went after Vern again. "This was a big case for you, wasn't it?"

"Yes."

"How long did it last?"

"More than a year."

"Were your task force superiors happy about the result?"

"We did our job."

"And you probably expected a promotion. What are you doing now at the Customs Service, following this big arrest?"

"I work at the airport."

"Doing what?"

"Security."

"You're a bag checker, aren't you? Not much of a promotion."

We beat up on the government agents for hours. There was no magic wand, no tricks, no "gotcha!" like on *Perry Mason*. Just a relentless pounding.

Hellman testified for the prosecution and admitted he sold small amounts of coke to people in the entertainment business. He said that, while he wasn't so sure about Ivan, he did believe that I was righteous in my motivation about stinging these drug dealers. His testimony didn't hurt my case at all and Fred Friedman was not happy. We were winning using the prosecution's own witnesses.

When it came time to present the defense case, O'Neill convinced me not to take the stand, because just like back in Kansas, it would open up my past to scrutiny. We did, however, subpoena Sheridan to talk about our sting of the Arabs at LAX and how we had helped the

LAPD. We wanted to establish that I had done a sting before where law enforcement "looked the other way," that I was a vigilante with a wink-and-a-nod from the government.

But judges in federal trials have great latitude. They can comment on the evidence or witnesses in ways judges at other levels are not permitted to. With Sheridan on the stand, Keller said: "I just don't believe this. I think you were out to rip somebody off and called the LAPD to cover your crime." Unfortunately, he was right.

Harold testified too, and he was brilliant. "I see Craig like I see Clint Eastwood in *Dirty Harry*," he said. "Eastwood chases the killer through Kezar Stadium and just about blows the guy's leg off. He shoots him because he knows there's a chance the killer is never going to prison for his crimes. So he punishes him right there. He shoots him, puts his foot on the wound, and tortures him. What he does is against the law and should put him in prison. But the audience knows that Harry is the good bad guy and the other guy is worse.

"Harry does what most people would want to do. Who does the audience root for? Dirty Harry. It's the same thing in *Death Wish*. The audience hopes Charles Bronson's character gets away. People root for Craig because they know he's not a bad guy."

Then O'Neill told the jury about the letter I had written in June, that had been sealed ever since. He called Rosenblum to the stand and handed it to him. Rosenblum dramatically opened the envelope. It was like being in a movie theater when you know the big moment is about to happen, the big revelation is about to be made, the big clue is about to be dropped on the audience. It was a scene right out of *To Kill a Mockingbird*. Only this time the audience was a jury that could decide the rest of my life.

Rosenblum read:

Dear Richard,

    I am writing you this letter in the event of my death or arrest in connection with the following affair. I along with others who were helping both willingly and in some case(s) with my knowledge of this affair are about to break one of the biggest organized drug rings on the West Coast of America. As of today, June 26, 1984, I am close to putting all the relevent [sic] information together.

If I am killed, the men who did it are the ones I am dealing with. Vern Pitzker, 6 feet 2 inches tall, balding, slim, clean cut, in his early or mid 30s. Dick Madden, stocky, grey and blonde hair, creased face, has a bad ear, says he is deaf in that ear from surfing, about 5 feet 9 inches tall, around 200 pounds, well built, says he is the boss, early 40s. Their accountant is a guy named Dominic, don't know his last name, short, balding, dark hair, late 30s, might be gay ... all say they live in the San Diego area ... might be true.

I believe they might be behind the murder of my partner Don Woodbeck. Don and I were sting artists who posed as cops and took down organized crime members like these guys in the '70s. Later I became a cop, Woodbeck worked with me. He was shot in the back in August of 1982.

At some point I will contact law enforcement to make the arrest at the end of the process. This could take months.

There is a movie being made about my life called *Outlaws*, by writer Nick Kazan. My agent is Harold Moskovitz of The Agency.

My mom and dad live in Kansas City. Stan and Rita Glazer, they are divorced and both living in Johnson County, Kansas. If I am killed or arrested please make sure they are contacted and given this letter.

I have been after men like these because my little brothers, Jeff and Jack, got hooked on drugs and it has ruined their lives and my family's. I have risked my life to do something about it. I am willing to die for what I believe in on this matter. If that happens I don't want my Mom not to know what really happened.

Make sure she is read this letter and my Grandfather, Bennie, too. Make sure they know I always loved them.

—Craig Norton Glazer

I could hear people sniffling with emotion. There wasn't a dry eye in the house. Ivan leaned over and said, "Wow, I think we're going to win."

Then Judge Keller blew us out of the water. He looked at me. "I bet you thought that was pretty clever, writing your Get Out of Jail Free card." He turned to the jury. "Well, I think people can see through that." I was stunned. What I had thought would be the clincher had been turned against me. Now I was just someone trying to cover his ass.

He was partly right. But what he didn't see was that I really wanted to be the good guy, and thought I might be killed before anyone would know how much.

We had one more card to play.

Our final witness was the head of the San Francisco DEA. Brian O'Neill, Brendan's brother, had been assistant U.S. Attorney, chief of special prosecutions, in Los Angeles for several years and was able to ask the DEA agent to review the case file. The agent agreed to testify that there was no drug deal, no conspiracy, and that law enforcement's actions were inappropriate. He thought that all I might be guilty of would be robbery, for taking the government's cash during the money laundering, but even that would be a state charge less onerous than a federal one.

I was euphoric. It would be very powerful to have someone like him take the stand and contradict his peers.

But he never did.

Keller denied admitting the expert testimony.

"You can get an opinion on the case from the DEA here," he said.

From the DEA agents who arrested me! An objective opinion from them certainly wasn't going to happen. Brendan exploded. "We will have this decision reversed by the Ninth Circuit." That was gutsy on his part. He knew Keller held a strong ambition to be senior judge. If Keller's decision was overturned on appeal, it might hurt his chances, and that in turn might damage O'Neill's future legal career.

There was a "good ole boys" network in federal trials regarding attorneys on both sides. Not only did the prosecuting attorneys want to be federal judges someday but so did the defense attorneys. None of them wanted to rock the boat when the captain—the judge—might someday have a say in whether they later became a judge. That's why few federal trials actually go to a jury. It's easier for everyone—well, except for the defendant—to just make a deal.

I was never offered a deal. The task force, Vern and his crew, wanted to string me up for embarrassing them.

In Keller's courtroom, it was the law according to Bill Keller. He was going to show just how tough he was with his first case on the bench. He would take his chances with an appeal. For his final argument, Friedman had his assistants carry in the bricks of sham coke and pile them onto the prosecution's table. It was the first time I had ever seen them. Then he piled Ivan's money onto the table, a huge stack of cash that he not so subtly let spill onto the floor. Friedman knew I was nothing in the world of drugs. Here he was prosecuting a guy for conspiring to distribute bricks of *fake* coke. Not too long afterward, he would prosecute an actual big fish, Max Mermelstein, one of the head operation chiefs for the Medellín cocaine cartel, believed to be responsible for 75 percent of the cocaine then shipped into the U.S. To avoid a heavy sentence, Mermelstein turned government witness and became the most important witness in the country against the drug kingpins.

Still, Friedman wanted to win. He made his point. "An innocent person would not have this money and try to buy what he thought were these drugs, would he?"

During a break, before our defense had their turn, I went into the restroom. Sherman came up to me. "You're not going to like my closing argument," he warned. "But I want you to know I think you're a pretty good guy."

I had no idea what he was up to. When I returned to the defense table, I looked at Ivan but he turned his eyes away. Sherman did what he thought he had to do to save his client.

"There is only one guilty person here," he said, "and it's this man." He pointed to me. "He is the mastermind criminal. He's having a movie made. Everyone else was just a pawn in his screenplay mind. My client is a boatbuilder. He was offered money to play a role. There is only one guilty person here." He pointed at me again.

O'Neill had foolishly agreed to let Sherman make the first closing argument. Following Sherman's diatribe, O'Neill did his best to paint a picture of what was a "revenge arrest." But with my fellow conspirator placing the blame squarely on me, my defense had been torpedoed. When Friedman had his turn again—in federal trials the prosecution gets the last word—he piled on.

"Glazer has a story for everything. You have his script. Even if we believe him, he had no right to take the law into his own hands. Who gave him the right to stick guns at people's heads, take their contraband, and arrest them? Who said he was the law?"

He looked in each juror's eyes. "We're the law. No. *You* are the law. If you set him free, you justify vigilantes everywhere."

My only hope was a hung jury. I felt that a couple of the women on the jury were sympathetic. At first we had Maria and Ivan's tall blonde girlfriend sit up front during the trial. When we saw that the women jurors might lean our way, we had them sit toward the back and not dress so conspicuously.

A day went by without a verdict and I grew a little more optimistic. On the morning of the second day, we heard the words, "The jury's in."

The court was packed. The jury foreman read the verdict.

"Guilty."

"Guilty."

"Guilty."

"Guilty."

All four counts.

All of the stings during the Arizona days, when we always got away, seemed so long ago. Being an undercover cop didn't work out the way I wanted either. Hollywood? The movie still wasn't made. I had lost, and the sense of failure was almost unbearable. I believed I could be a living legend. I thought I could pull it off. But while I had created the fantasy, I could not make it a reality. Now I was going to pay the price for failing—and it might be even worse as soon as someone in prison discovered that I had been an undercover cop just like the one who busted him.

Twice now I had been convicted for drug deals—and I never had drugs in my possession either time. I kept thinking something would happen to get me out of this nightmare. This was not in the script.

O'Neill immediately asked Keller for a bond on me while we appealed the case. We were going to ask for a reversal because of his denial of our expert testimony. Keller had other ideas.

"Bond is denied," he announced. "I think it's time he begins serving his sentence, whatever that might be, right now."

I gave my wallet to Grandpa Bennie and he gave me some money. I pulled off the ring on my hand, the one my grandfather Jack had given me when I was three years old, and gave it to Maria. Both she and Grandpa Bennie were crying.

I was handcuffed and two female marshals escorted me to the elevator. One of them saw how distressed I was and said, "You were expecting a trip to Jamaica?"

"Ma'am," I answered, "I've already been there."

15

Behind Bars

It is not a fragrant world but it is the world you live in.

—Raymond Chandler

WE WALKED THROUGH a tunnel and within a couple of minutes I was on a bus back to Terminal Island. After two weeks in the J2 cellblock, I was transferred into the general population, "the yard." But before the authorities did that, I had to sign a document acknowledging that, because I was a former law enforcement officer, they could not be responsible for my safety. You bet I was scared.

The only thing that saved me during those ninety long days at TI before I was sentenced was that two Israelis in the joint discovered I was Jewish and that I had stung Arabs funding the PLO. They protected me from the drug dealers who wanted to do me harm.

The pre-sentencing report recommended to the court that I serve two to three years in a prison camp. Everyone had heard about the so-called Watergate Camp at Boron in the California desert where Nixon henchmen Howard Hunt and Bob Haldeman had spent their sentences playing tennis and sunning themselves at the pool. That's where I would go.

With time served maybe it wouldn't be so long that I'd lose Maria. Maybe I wouldn't lose my Hollywood dream either. I held on to that fantasy of being famous as desperately and strongly as when I was a kid sitting in front of the TV watching Westerns. Sitting in a cell at TI, I had nothing else.

Stan and my mother, Rita, flew to L.A. for the sentencing. Grandpa Bennie was there too and so were Maria and Terri. Yep, Terri. I was shocked. After all I had done, my ex-fiancee was there to support me. Maybe I just never deserved her.

We presented a stack of positive letters—including one from long-time U.S. Senator Robert Dole of Kansas, who was majority leader and between bids for the Republican presidential nomination. He was a heavy-hitter and Stan had used his connections to somehow get him to ask the judge for leniency in my case. Since a fellow Republican, President Ronald Reagan, had appointed Keller, I crossed my fingers that Dole's letter would have a powerful effect on the judge.

"Does the defendant have anything to say before I pass sentence?" Keller asked. I hated being at someone else's mercy. I was always the one who took charge, threw the first punch. Now I was cuffed and chained. I was as helpless as I had ever been. My life, my future, was on the line. I imagined there was a movie camera filming the final words of the convicted. I stood.

"Your honor, I am not now nor have I ever been a drug dealer. I was a sting artist taking drugs and money from people I believed were the real drug dealers. But I know it wasn't right to take the law into my own hands. I realize what I did was wrong. I take full responsibility for that. To all of the young people who have heard about me and about this case, I want to tell them to not follow in my footsteps."

Then came the tough part, because it's the part I would have said even without an audience. "I would also like to apologize to my friends and, most of all, to my family." I tried not to look at Stan, my mom, and Grandpa Bennie because I knew I would break down if I did. I took a deep breath and continued.

"I hope the court will give me another chance to prove that I can make a positive difference in the world."

There was silence.

"Are we done?" Keller was not moved.

I sat down.

Keller asked Friedman what prison term he would recommend.

"Five years."

"That figures," Keller said in disgust. "I had to win your case from the bench. I think you are short of the mark."

He spoke directly to me. "This is a classic tale of a young man with a lot of talent who took the wrong path. You're intelligent. You sold a movie about your life. I've read all of these letters and they say some pretty nice things. Obviously a lot of people care about you and love you." Keller was—there is no other word for it—tender. But it was a fleeting moment.

"What a huge disappointment you must be to them, and to people such as Senator Dole. What a waste. But I don't have much sympathy. The jury found you guilty, regardless of your motivation or a movie story. The facts are the facts. You were deeply enmeshed in drug trafficking. You need a hard lesson, not another chance."

My heart fell through the floor. He addressed the courtroom.

"Narcotics is the greatest scourge in this country and toleration of conduct such as Glazer's would be tantamount to a temptation to others to engage in it."

Jeezus, he was going to give me the maximum twenty-seven years!

"However, I don't want to take his life away. He will still be relatively young when he gets out. Seven years plus five years' probation and a suspended sentence of an additional twelve years."

He slammed the gavel down hard.

A decade later, controversial, radical lawyer Stephen Yagman went so far as to accuse Keller of being anti-Semitic. Yagman also called him "ignorant, dishonest, ill-tempered, and a bully, and probably ... one of the worst judges in the United States." In retrospect, Keller probably would have hit me with a much stiffer sentence if not for the Dole letter.

O'Neill immediately asked for an appeal bond.

"Absolutely not," said Keller. He rose to leave but O'Neill called after him.

"We request that the court order him directly to a camp." O'Neill knew I wanted out of TI as fast as possible.

The judge walked back behind the podium. "Yes, you're right, I should put this in the record, counsel."

For one strange second I thought he'd say, "Just kidding. I just wanted to scare the crap out of you. Go home. You're free."

Instead, he said, "I recommend that Mr. Glazer spend seven years in a regular federal prison and not a camp." He made his feelings clear, though he would have no authority to send me anywhere in particular.

For the first time in my life, I couldn't bullshit my way out of a tough spot. For the first time in my life, all of the movies that might come to mind to inspire me had unhappy endings. Not even Burt Lancaster could escape Alcatraz.

Maria was upset but this time she didn't cry. Terri was hysterical, completely in tears. My mother shuddered as she wept. Tough ole Grandpa Bennie shook his head. Whatever Stan felt, he kept inside. When he came to TI to visit immediately afterward, he cracked jokes and entertained the inmates. I guess that was how he dealt with the situation. Like everyone else, he said, "Hang in there. It could've been worse." Not much consolation there.

I knew I wouldn't get a parole hearing for at least six months. An appeal would take at least a year and a half. I'd be eligible for mandatory release after four and a half years. That is, if an ex-undercover drug agent could survive that long.

. . .

TI WAS AN UGLY place. The dormitories of bunkbeds held some fifty men each. A metal locker with clothes, toothpaste, etc. sat in front of each pair of bunkbeds. Mostly, the guys in there worked the menial jobs available to us and tried to stay out of trouble. You did not want to get a "shot," a demerit that could send you to "the hole," solitary, and add to your time.

One way to stay clean was to put on a don't-fuck-with-me front. I was good at that. Not only did I pump iron at the weight pile, but I brought my leather workout belt to the handicraft shop and had an inmate carve a nickname on it I thought might help: STING.

Urlich and Hellman were also there. Ivan, convicted on a single count of conspiracy, was sentenced to seven years. He hung out with me and boasted that he was being useful by killing the rumor that I had been DEA. Meanwhile he spread the word that Hellman was a snitch for cooperating with the government. Because of that, Richard was the victim of constant threats from prisoners wanting to beat him up. He had received the maximum four years for his one telephone count even though he cooperated. The prosecutors were not pleased that he didn't nail me with his testimony. He got it coming and going.

I did have Ivan to thank for one thing. When Maria came to visit, he helped me get laid. It had been a few months since I was convicted and I was horny as, well, an inmate in a federal prison. She went to the visitors' restroom and I sneaked in with her. Ivan was supposed to kick the wall to warn me if the guards came by.

I lifted up her dress and she wasn't wearing underwear. We didn't have much time. I entered her but after only a few seconds I heard Ivan kick the wall. I had to pull out—and shoot my wad into a mop bucket. I zipped up my pants just as a guard walked in.

"You're never on time!" I yelled at Maria. She was surprised, not knowing what the hell I was talking about. "Dammit, can't you get anything right?"

"What are you doing here?" the guard asked me.

Maria finally picked up on my fake argument. "If you would give me the right time," she shot back, "then maybe I would!"

I told the guard I was sorry but that the argument with my girlfriend got heated and we had moved it into the restroom. He led us out.

Craig Norton Glazer, Inmate #80389-012, spent his thirty-first birthday at Terminal Island. A few people sent cards, including Kazan.

He was rewriting the script and tried to boost my spirits by confidently saying *Outlaws* would someday get made.

Maria had also said she would come that day. I waited for her in the visitors' room.

And waited. She never showed.

I shuffled back to my cell in what the convicts call the Walk of Shame. No matter what anyone from the outside tells you, you're in there alone. I found out later that Maria's previous visit was meant to say good-bye. Her lack of underwear was not a treat for me but for a new boyfriend in the car that brought her. I was gone, but for her the party had to go on.

Then one day before dawn, guards pulled me out of bed and put me on a van filled with hard-core prisoners. I was being transferred to the maximum security United States Penitentiary at Lompoc, 175 miles northwest of Los Angeles.

"How long?" asked a prisoner on the bus to Lompoc.

"Seven years," I said.

"So a little more than four years until mandatory release." He'd obviously been through this before. He could see the worry on my face: The Lompoc penitentiary had a reputation for being a very bad place. How could I survive?

"Just remember," he said, "winter, summer, winter, summer, winter, summer, winter, summer. Then you're out."

I hoped so.

•   •   •

THE LOMPOC PENITENTIARY was the sort of prison shown in movies—all concrete and steel, multiple tiers of cells, one or two inmates in each one. I had a cell to myself. The cell next to me was home to Richard Miller, the first FBI agent ever indicted for espionage, who was awaiting his second trial. He told me his story about being enticed with sex by a beautiful Russian spy. I felt sorry for the poor slob. But I thought it could be a helluva movie.

Lompoc also had Hollywood. That was the nickname of a big, muscular forty-year-old black trustee who had spent most of his life in prison. He was in charge of bringing inmates books, hot water for tea and coffee, and, most importantly, the portable cart with the telephone.

After I had been there three days, there was still no phone. As far as I knew, none of my friends or family even knew where I was, though the other inmates thought they knew *who* I was.

"Hey, Cell 25 has that DEA fuck! Gonna cut your balls off, DEA fuck!"

Great.

"Hey, Hollywood, what's the deal with the phone?" I asked.

"There are two kinds of people in here," he explained, "inmates and convicts. Inmates follow the rules. Convicts are mean motherfuckers. I'm a convict. You're an inmate. You're also an ex-cop. You're the bad guy. If you want the phone, you have to pay."

"But I don't belong in maximum security. Why am I even here?"

"You're asking the wrong man," said Hollywood in a voice surprisingly soft for such a hardass.

I sent numerous requests, called "cop-outs," to the prison administration asking to be transferred. No response.

Every waking moment for the next three weeks, I was afraid of being "saber stabbed," knifed by a short metal sword. Fear is a tremendous incentive for working out. Lifting weights made me bigger and stronger, and that meant something in prison. Also, since my conviction, I had no drugs or alcohol, and even stopped smoking. I was getting into the best shape of my life.

Finally, Hollywood said, "I can get you that phone. Stop by my cell."

When I did, he was leafing through a stack of gay porno magazines. I knew what he wanted. "That ain't for me," I said.

He looked me up and down. "Things could be better for you around here if it was."

"Sorry."

"Sure you're not interested?"

"Nope."

Hollywood didn't give me the phone but he didn't seem particularly pissed at me either.

In a prison like Lompoc, the lights are on twenty-four hours a day. They dim just a little at night but for the most part, it's hard to tell if it's noon or three in the morning. I couldn't sleep much anyway. When it was relatively quiet, you could still hear the muffled sounds of hundreds of men jacking off into their Kleenex.

A few hours after Hollywood's come-on, I was lying on my bed, head against the wall, my feet closest to the bars, reading Stephen King's *The Shining*. Maybe something that frightening would make my own nightmare not seem so awful. I was drifting off to semi-sleep when suddenly I felt a burning sensation. I jumped off the bed. Hollywood had thrown scalding hot water on me as he passed my cell. He thought my head was right there. The skin on my legs reddened but wasn't burned.

It was a message.

That night, Hollywood put a headlock on some Mexican kid, dropped him to the floor on his stomach, bent him back like an alligator wrestler does, and raped him. I figured I was going to be next. I snapped. I pulled the mattress from my bed, propped it up against the wall, and started beating on it like Ali on Frazier.

"I WILL FUCKIN' KILL YOU!" I screamed.

I went nuts. I didn't care if Hollywood had a weapon. If he came near me, I was going to hit him first with everything I had. I sent my own message: I was ready to fight for my life.

I never saw Hollywood again. Within a few hours I was on a prison bus filled mostly with Latinos headed to the medium-security Federal Correctional Institution at Safford, Arizona. I never knew why I had been sent to maximum security or why I was now being sent to medium security. Maybe someone had made a mistake. Maybe the government had thought I was dangerous. Maybe someone wanted to teach me a lesson. I didn't care. I was just glad to be out of that hellhole.

. . .

THERE WERE ADVANTAGES to being a Jewish inmate. Just like in school, I could take the extra religious holidays off. At Safford, as at TI, I also became a cook for the other Jewish prisoners. Since Safford was mainly Latino, there were only about twenty Jews, which made that chore pretty easy. The corned beef and gefilte fish was a nice break from Mexican food.

While I was there, I got a letter from Rabbi Margolies, who had thrown me out of the synagogue when I was fifteen years old. Now he was Dr. Margolies, rabbi emeritus at Beth Shalom. With a Ph.D. from Columbia, he had become a nationally known authority on ancient Jewish history. After seeing the stories about my conviction in the Kansas City newspapers, he found out from my parents where I was located.

"If you need help and are searching for God," he wrote, "just look at the end of your right arm and you will find him in your own right hand."

He meant that God was within me. Within each of us. Even me. That's a big concept and I'm not sure I understood it. But it was comforting. I had always run with a mainly Christian crowd. Shit, sometimes I was the one who acted anti-Semitic. But, for what it's worth, I never thought of myself as anything but Jewish.

Survival, however, knows no religion. Just to be on the safe side, I befriended the Aryan Brotherhood. I lied to Mike Amos, a six-foot-three, ripped, twenty-eight-year-old member of the AB, telling him my mother was Italian, which meant I wasn't really Jewish.

Since he had already spent several years in prison for being an accomplice in the murder of a federal agent, I also felt compelled to explain to him about my being a cop back in Kansas. Fortunately, he thought what I did was "cool." But a test of my loyalty soon arrived.

I was at the weight pile in the outdoor recreation area when a guy I knew only as T, a black bank robber, took my S-bar. Mike told me, "Go get it back. That nigger can't take that from you."

"Hey, I really don't care."

"You get it or it's your ass," he threatened.

I went over to him and said, "Look, T, how about you give me the bar." I just wanted to stay out of trouble.

"Don't talk to me," he said.

"Come on, man."

"If you want it, you'll have to take it."

I looked back at the AB guys. They were watching. I had no choice. I let fly with a punch that hit T square on the jaw. The next twenty shots were from him—on my face. He pummeled me until I landed in a cactus patch. The whole thing was over in two minutes.

Amos dragged me away and I quickly washed off the blood. If the guards saw evidence that I had been in a fight, I would be sent to the hole. The AB stood by and did nothing for the same reason. They weren't going to get into trouble for me.

But the next day they baited me anyway. "You're not gonna let a nigger beat you, are ya?" asked one of them.

"I'm not going to stab the guy and get a life sentence over nothing."

They looked at me like that was exactly what they wanted me to do.

I turned to Amos. "What's the punishment if I don't?"

"You can't hang out with us."

Well, they hadn't done me much good as it was. Fuck 'em. From that moment on, the AB never spoke to me in public. But privately Amos remained a friend.

In the TV room, I was watching *Miami Vice* when T came up to me.

"Did you learn anything?" he asked.

"Yeah, that you're a helluva fighter."

He smiled. It turned out that he had fought professionally. He was also from Kansas City, so we talked nostalgically about our hometown. "I can show you some shit to protect yourself," he offered. "With your big mouth you're going to need it."

• • •

WE COULD MAKE collect-only phone calls from a handful of pay phones in the yard. Because the Safford area was so small, with only a few operators, you would often get the same one.

"Are you Craig Glazer from Kansas City?" a woman operator asked after she had handled my calls a couple of times.

"Uh, yeah."

"Oh my God! I used to see you at Stanford & Sons. I was the red-head. Do you remember Jeannie? I thought you were cute."

The coincidence was amazing, even though I didn't remember her.

"My ex-husband was a police captain in Kansas City, Missouri. He really hated you." She said it like that was a recommendation in my favor.

A lot of women fantasize about having affairs with inmates. Maybe it's because they desire being completely, sexually overwhelmed— pretty likely with a man who hasn't fucked for a long time. Maybe it's because after such all-consuming sex, he's still in prison. Jeannie, a forty-ish, struggling-to-make-ends-meet, divorced single mom from Tucson, was one of those women.

I took a risk. If a prison official were listening on the line, I'd get a "shot." I asked her to come for a visit.

The guard in charge of the visitors' room agreed to give me a few minutes alone with busty Jeannie—and I fucked her in the visitors' restroom. There are scenes in movies like *Cool Hand Luke* where a prisoner does something so incredible that the other inmates stand up and applaud. Well, sorry, but those are just movies. Prisoners don't give a fuck about anyone except themselves. But when word got around about what I had done, I was the closest thing to a hero there was at the Federal Correctional Institution at Safford, Arizona.

But I still wasn't getting out anytime soon. Stan came to my parole hearing and gave an impassioned speech. The parole board didn't buy it. My next chance would be in twenty-four months.

. . .

I WAS STANDING in the shower when a pollo thought I had offended him. So he picked up the wooden bench we would sit on and hit me in the head with it. I was knocked loopy and started bleeding. Then he and a buddy of his slammed me against a wall. Thank God we were naked or otherwise they might have had knives and stabbed me.

By accident, Amos came by. He jumped in fully clothed and took care of those pollos with his heavy fists and heavy boots. Very Woodbeckian. I was still woozy so Amos had to wash the blood off my face as best he could. He stood me up and angled my head so the guards couldn't see that I had been hit. They assumed the two Mexicans had fought each other. The pollos were carried out on stretchers.

In a little over six months in prison, I had been beaten up twice and burned once. Any day I could be killed or raped. I had at least four more years behind bars ahead of me. I didn't see any light at the end of the tunnel.

I was assigned another lousy job on a brutally hot Arizona summer day—painting yellow stripes on the parking lot. It was 7 a.m. but already ninety-two degrees outside. After a while, I put down my paint bucket, sat on a can, and looked up.

The sky was beautiful—blue and soft and peaceful.

And suddenly I realized that I had gotten exactly what I deserved.

I was where I was because I deserved to be in prison. Given all that had happened, I was lucky. If I had been caught during one of the Arizona stings, I might be doing twenty years or life. A seven-year sentence was a small price to pay for my past.

What always got me through tough times was my anger at whomever I blamed for my problems. From when I was a kid, the guy I always blamed—the bad guy in the script of my life—was my father. For the Kansas arrest, I blamed Vern Miller, Margaret Jordan, the other special agents. For Don's death, I blamed Colombian drug dealers. For the Fed sting, it was Vern Pitzker. My desire to get back at them kept me going.

I saw no burning bush as I sat on that paint can. But a huge weight lifted off my shoulders. I was no longer angry. I told myself, "Shut the fuck up and quit bitching. This too shall pass."

As soon as I let go of my anger, good things started to happen. One morning, I saw on the daily sheet posted to announce new assignments a change in classification next to my name: I was now "1-OUT." I could hardly believe it. I was to be transferred from FCI, Federal Correctional Institution, to FPC, Federal Prison Camp. It was the happiest moment I ever experienced behind bars. I was going to the Watergate Camp.

I was given street clothes and a bus ticket for Boron, California, in the Mojave Desert, and sent on my way without a guard. I felt almost free. Jeannie even met me at a Tucson motel during a two-hour lay-over that was truly a layover.

The Boron camp was controversial for hosting the rich and famous. Supposedly it was more country club than prison. I wish it had been. While you could wear jeans and tennis shoes instead of prison clothes and boots, a new arrival's first job was the same as it was at most prisons—rearranging rocks on a landscaping crew. While there were recreational facilities, the tennis court was overgrown with weeds and the pool was the size of a postage stamp. True, there were no walls. But there might as well have been, because as long as I was #80389-012 the U.S. Government owned my ass.

With Boron only a couple hours from L.A., there were a few inmates connected to Hollywood. One of them was Seth Jaffe, who had been a bit player on TV series like *Cagney & Lacey* and *Remington Steele*. He was also a very funny writer and at the camp had written a couple of skits. We went to the warden, just like in those old Mickey Rooney movies, and said, "Hey, let's put on a show!" He allowed us to perform comedy skits in front of the camp's 700 inmates, including one we wrote called "The First Jew on the Moon."

While at Boron, I learned that my appeal had been denied two to one by a three-judge panel. Now my only chance for an early release was attaining "superior achievement." According to parole regulations, earning that could move my release date up by as much as six months. With that in mind, I joined the local Toastmasters Club, which encourages public speaking and leadership, and became an officer of that group. I also enrolled in Barstow Community College by mail, putting me on track to get an A.A. degree. Sure, Barstow wasn't Harvard but you take what you can get.

The best part of Watergate Camp was my job. After winning a prison typing contest—ninety-eight words per minute—I was allowed to work at nearby Edwards Air Force Base, Monday through Friday, in the Material Control section of the Civil Engineering Department.

I had my own desk and was given a WATS phone line. As always, I wanted more. I had money secretly wired to me and I paid my boss, a sergeant, $200 a month to give me the best jobs and free rein to do whatever I wanted.

My department was in charge of a huge warehouse stocked with uniforms. I picked out a sergeant's and a captain's uniform for myself and hid them in my office closet. When I wanted to go to the gym at the Officers' Club, I'd put on my captain's uniform, call for a Jeep, and have a driver come around to chauffeur me. I'd take the uniform off as quickly as I could to avoid any questioning eyes. But, frankly, military discipline on an enormous Air Force base like Edwards is pretty lax. I saluted and was saluted. No one asked who the hell I was.

In my sergeant's uniform at the NCO mess hall, I became friendly with a female Air Force sergeant whose husband was also a sergeant. It took a while but eventually she became suspicious. "You don't seem military."

I spoke carefully. "You know, they have inmates working here from Boron."

Her eyes widened. "You?"

"Would you turn me in if I was?"

She shook her head, and then said, "You know, my house is on the base." She was one of those women like Jeannie, but I never slept with her. I thought a nooner was too risky. Hell, everyone on the base carried a gun and this was not my turf. But we did make out. Unfortunately, another inmate working at Edwards saw us and snitched.

The next day I was at work when two guards from the camp arrived and ordered me to put my hands behind my back. They cuffed and shackled me, and said I was under arrest for "unauthorized contact" with Air Force personnel.

"How can you arrest me?" I said. "I'm already in prison! I mean, how much more arrested can I get?"

At the camp, the warden showed me a list of Air Force women on the base he said I had screwed. I wish I had, but I hadn't slept with any of them. Absent from his list, of course, was Carol, my former secretary at New World, whom I slept with whenever she would visit. What he revealed though was that I had been under surveillance. In fact, two Air Force women who had approached me the day before about a party were wearing wires. I had smelled something fishy and said "no thanks." I wasn't going to be stung again.

Nevertheless, I would be tried in a prison administrative court. They were determined to punish me for having sex with women! The trial would be held at TI. After a year at Boron, I was sent back to J2 on Terminal Island. Sonuvabitch!

Presiding over the hearing was a prison lieutenant, an ex-Marine. Fortunately, he had earlier been a guard at Boron and knew and liked me while I was there. "I'm going to believe you," he said.

I was found not guilty. But instead of being returned to Boron, I was reassigned to Lompoc. Not the penitentiary this time, but the prison camp outside the walls.

· · ·

My job at Lompoc Camp was a lot different than at Boron. I worked at the cattle farm that supplied both milk and meat to the prisons in the region. Driving cows into the milking pens twice a day, 5 a.m. and 3 p.m., wasn't too bad. Shoveling the cow shit was.

277

But other than that, Lompoc was much more of a country club than Boron. The tennis courts were lighted and you could play handball, baseball, bocce ball, or basketball. Just like Boron, the guards didn't carry weapons. Yet no one escaped. If you did and were caught, you might end up at the penitentiary next door—and no one wanted that.

Lompoc attracted the cream of the crop of white-collar criminals. One new inmate made a grand entrance by arriving in his black Rolls Royce. He was Tom Blackburn, the Texan responsible for re-branding MDMA as Ecstasy in the early '80s when the drug was legal. Thanks to him, Dallas college students could buy Ecstasy at certain bars by credit card. By the time the drug was banned in 1985, the DEA reported that 30,000 doses a month were being used in Texas alone. Blackburn became rich. Now he was in prison on a marijuana charge.

With some of his money, Blackburn invested in a proposed film documentary about boxing legends Muhammad Ali, Joe Frazier, George Foreman, Larry Holmes, and Ken Norton. "I understand you're in the movie business," he said to me. "If you help me in here, I'll help you when I get out."

"Yeah, right."

"Don't believe me?"

"Lots of guys in here tell stories." Hollywood bullshit was Hollywood bullshit, even in prison.

Back in Hollywood, Garnett's option on *Outlaws* was expiring. Harold said a fledgling producer named Chuck Roven, who had done *Heart Like a Wheel*, wanted to pick it up. Roven came to Lompoc to strike a deal. Garnett drove to the camp to try to talk me into staying with him. The project needed new blood. I decided to go with Roven, the husband of Dawn Steel, who had recently become the first woman to head a major film studio when she was named president at Columbia. For *Outlaws*, he hired Dan Jenkins, the sportswriter who authored the best-selling football novel *Semi-Tough*, to pen a new script.

I was writing too, on the typewriter at the camp library. The camera in my head was making notes on scenes and dialogue about a prison camp filled with rich people. I called it *Club Fed*. I didn't have to look far for material. One new inmate, Ivan Boesky, became the butt of jokes in the stand-up act I put together to perform for the prison. Boesky was the stock speculator who took home $200 million in the biggest Wall Street insider-trading scandal in history. He was also the model for Michael Douglas's Gordon Gekko character in *Wall Street*, which had just come out. Boesky coined the phrase "Greed is good."

"Hey guys, we no longer have to apply for a Rule 35, a request to the court for a reduction of sentence, because we now have Rule 22 thanks to Ivan Boesky," I told the crowd, who knew that Boesky had cooperated with the government. "What's Rule 22? That's when you give up twenty-two of your closest friends for a lighter sentence. Isn't that right, Ivan?" Everyone laughed except him.

"It's only a joke, Ivan. You have so much money, what the fuck do you care? Boesky is so rich that he wrote a check and the bank bounced."

No one liked him. An inmate once asked him for a cigarette and he took the half-smoked one in his mouth and gave it to him. The guy threw it on the ground.

"How about one out of the pack?"

"But those are new," Boesky said. "I need them." The $200 million man refused to give him a fresh cigarette.

"Man, you are one cheap fuck," said the inmate.

Club Fed, and the real thing, also had a woman. I was allowed to attend Toastmasters speech competitions in nearby Ventura, accompanied by a guard and also Nila, a cute, thirty-ish, American Indian–looking woman who was the warden's assistant. I would do "First Jew on the Moon," win in the Tall Tales category, and screw Nila in the restroom at Denny's.

Nila helped arrange my first full furlough from Lompoc—one week to go home to Kansas City. The prison authorities checked my plane ticket and where I was staying and gave me a 10 p.m. curfew for weekdays and a midnight curfew for the weekend.

I may be the only prison inmate in American history who used his furlough to make his professional comedy debut. I headlined, one night only, "The Craig Glazer Show" at Stanford & Sons, where Jeff and I had started to present stand-up comedy acts a few years earlier. Before I left, Jaffe warned me not to do so many prison bits because not everyone in the audience would be familiar with incarceration. But I had done the same forty-five-minute act in front of 700 inmates and I had killed.

Here, in the outside world, things were different. While I was doing my "The Parole Board" routine, I heard glasses clinking. Soon after, I heard nothing but silence. I bombed.

That was the only moment since my conviction where I almost wanted to go back to prison. Almost.

When I returned to Lompoc, a guard found me typing away on *Club Fed* in the library and gave me a "shot" for using equipment without permission, even though that had never before been an issue. My next scheduled furlough was revoked. That was too bad. I had intended to use the time to attend the cap-and-gown ceremony at my college graduation, and my mother was going to fly out for that.

• • •

WHEN MY NEXT parole hearing came up, I was turned down for the final time.

"What more do you want from me?" I pleaded. I had done everything I could to attain superior achievement—college, Toastmasters, created programs for the other inmates, and prepared for a life after prison with my writing and comedy.

I wrote to the U.S. Parole Commission and asked why they lied to prisoners saying they had a chance at early release if the truth was different. Why did they pretend to have a desire to rehabilitate inmates when they didn't reward those who did?

Ninety days later, I received a reply, a pink sheet of paper slipped under my pillow. They took four months off my mandatory release time. There probably have been others but I only heard about one other inmate whose time was cut for superior achievement—and he saved a guard's life during a prison fire.

On my last day, about forty-three months after I had been convicted, I walked to the weight pile, did twenty push-ups using two bars like a gymnast uses parallel bars, took off my "STING" belt, draped it over the bars, and left without looking back. On Thursday, October 27, 1988, at age thirty-five, I walked out of prison. I was given a check for $127 and a bus ticket to a downtown L.A. halfway house, where I would spend the next six months. My second day there, Harold picked me up.

"We have a pitch meeting on *Club Fed* at a bungalow at the Beverly Hills Hotel," he said. I smiled. When your life is based on fantasy, everything is possible.

Epilogue

It is a twist on an adage about art that Mr. Glazer's movie imitates a life imitating the movies.

—The Kansas City Star, May 17, 1981

BLACKBURN KEPT HIS word. After he was released, he pulled up to the halfway house in that black Rolls of his and we drove to the MGM lot in Culver City, where I met the director and the other producers of *Champions Forever*. Since they didn't know much about boxing, I became heavily involved in the editing and was given associate producer credit.

I was still in the halfway house when Sonny Landham showed up and took me to the Academy Awards. I'm guessing there haven't been many people who have been to the Oscars, brushed up against the biggest movie stars in the world, then taken off their tuxedo and slept that night in a rundown halfway house.

The *Champions Forever* premiere was set for Century City, with Ali and others as guests. My name was finally going to be on the big screen. This would be a shining moment in my life, all the brighter for having been in prison for the last four years. I invited Stan. He could see that his kid had done something worthwhile after all. But he couldn't seem to find the time to come.

Champions Forever became a critical and commercial hit. Then Blackburn instructed his attorney, Ed Masry, made famous in *Erin Brockovich*, to sell me all of the rights for only $10,000. He wasn't going to be around Hollywood anyway. The next day Blackburn went on the run from new charges, this time involving Ecstasy. He was captured in the mid-'90s, convicted, and sent to prison for a couple more years.

Outlaws went nowhere with Roven, who years later would take over the *Batman* movie franchise. *Outlaws* was then optioned by Universal, this time with Dan York as the studio executive. York commissioned a script from Robert Roy Pool, who would write *Armageddon* and *Outbreak*. When York wasn't happy with it, he suggested I write the script with him. We called it *The Killer, the Thief & the Liar*—J.D. was the killer, Woodbeck was the thief, and I was the liar.

About ten years earlier, Jeff and I had brought comics to Stanford & Sons for the first time. After I moved to Hollywood, Stan ran with the concept and by mid-decade had the restaurant in one location and the comedy club down the street. The club launched the careers of such major stars as Roseanne Barr, Louie Anderson, Sinbad, and Eddie Griffin, a former busboy at the restaurant. Robin Williams, Sam Kinison, Jerry Seinfeld, and Jeff Foxworthy performed on its stage. But Stan drove Stanford & Sons nearly into bankruptcy. So in 1990 he had the bank make a friendly foreclosure, with Grandpa Bennie buying the bar and restaurant business for my brother Jeff and I while he continued to operate the club.

I commuted between Kansas City and Hollywood. But nothing came of *Club Fed*, at least not with me. Other producers paid for the story idea and a really cheap flick came out in 1990. As for *The Killer, the Thief & the Liar*, Universal eventually said no. York told me what I couldn't say to myself: "Maybe you should go home."

I had come to Hollywood with dreams of being a star, being powerful, being famous, being rich. It was over. I was just a forty-something ex-con. I moved back to Kansas City in 1994.

The next year, no surprise, Stan was in money trouble again. Jeff and I made a deal with him where I would bring the comedy club back to the restaurant location and we would pay Stan a few thousand dollars a month until he got back on his feet.

We returned Stanford & Sons to its former glory as one of the most important comedy clubs in America. We opened with *Saturday Night Live* star Kevin Nealon and gave a stage to fresh new comics such as Larry the Cable Guy, Lewis Black, Dave Attell, Mike Epps, Lisa Lampanelli, and Katt Williams. Established comedians like Jimmie Walker, Tommy Chong, Bobby Slayton, and Damon Wayans became regulars.

Stan, my father, sued us. After a couple of years of hoping he would stand on his own, we had stopped sending him checks.

"Here's why they owe me: I'm their father," he later told *Smart Money* magazine. "I brought them into this world. End of argument. They are greedy little bastards as far as I'm concerned." He told a newspaper, "Obviously, in their case, greed outweighs love and family." Stan lost the lawsuit. He then tried to prevent us from using the name Stanford at a second club we opened in Overland Park. When that failed, he opened a comedy club nearby and called it Stanford Glazer's Comedy Club. He still insisted on competing with his sons, still insisted on wanting to be better than us. His club lasted only a year.

We stopped talking to each other.

In the meantime, my bad boy character grew more colorful than criminal, aided by opening a dance club at the restaurant venue. Stanford's became the hip-hop Studio 54 of the Midwest and attracted guests from Eminem and 50 Cent to Jewel. Because I led the turn-around of the Westport entertainment district, I was a frequent guest speaker, particularly on talk radio, on how to make Kansas City a better place to live and do business.

The year before the 2002 election for mayor, there was talk that I should run for the office. In Hearne Christopher's column in *The Kansas City Star*, I said that incumbent mayor Kay Barnes was "a very nice lady who means well. But what does she know of life? I've been in jail. I've been in a gunfight. I've hung out with movie stars. I've built a business up from the ashes. I've lived life."

Some people said, "You're out of your mind! You're an ex-con!" But I thought that's exactly why I should run: I was proof that the system did work, that an ex-con could make a positive contribution to his community.

I was a civic leader with a rock 'n' roll attitude, and became a regular on the number-one morning radio show in the Midwest, on 98.9 The Rock, hosted by wild 'n' crazy DJ Johnny Dare, a blond, Midwestern version of Howard Stern. Johnny turned Craig Glazer into a character called Guido, a Ferrari-driving, coke-snorting playboy.

The character wasn't far from the truth. I had started to do coke to stay awake—and I was addicted. I would buy eighty to a hundred dollars worth at a time but never kept even an ounce in my possession and never sold any, not even to friends. I didn't want anyone to think I might be a dealer.

But for those in power who were concerned that I might actually run for mayor, Guido sent up a red flag. In the summer of 2001, I received a letter from the FBI informing me that my phone was tapped. I figured I didn't have anything to worry about. Yes, I used coke, but the FBI wasn't wasting its time busting people for using.

What I did not realize was that while my past had been forgotten by some, it had not been forgiven by others. On the morning of September 11, 2001, I turned on the TV and was stunned to see the Twin Towers fall in New York City. My phone rang. It was a newspaper reporter with whom I regularly partied.

"Are you watching this?" I asked.

"We have a bigger problem," he said.

"How could there be a bigger problem?"

"The FBI is here at the office and they're asking about you."

Two "beeper dealers" had been nabbed and had given the FBI a list of people they sold to. Along with numerous celebrities, including sports stars, I was on their list. Yet I was the only high-profile person indicted. The Feds had no interest in any of the others. I was the target again.

I surrendered instead of being arrested. Any chance for a mayoral run was destroyed. The powers-that-be had achieved their goal. U.S. District Court Judge Nanette Laughrey was suspicious. At my preliminary hearing, she questioned the prosecutor.

"Did Mr. Glazer sell any coke?"

"No, your honor."

"He was a user?"

"Yes, your honor."

"Where are the other users on this list?" she asked.

"They had no priors, your honor. He did."

"So you arrested him because he had priors? Didn't he already pay for those crimes in the justice system?"

"Yes."

The judge was clearly frustrated trying to determine the point of the entire case.

"Mr. Glazer, what do you have to say?"

"Your honor, over the years I have embarrassed certain powerful people in the state of Kansas. And in 1984 I led an elaborate sting of a major drug ring on the West Coast. It turned out I stung the FBI, DEA, U.S. Customs, IRS, and Los Angeles Sheriff's Department." She looked surprised.

"They wanted revenge," I told her. "They still do. That's why I am here."

"I want to hear more about this, Mr. Glazer."

And so I told her some of the story of my life as the King of Sting.

After I finished, Laughrey asked if the prosecutor had any comment. He didn't say a word, just shook his head.

All of the charges were dropped except for one for conspiracy to distribute cocaine. My very savvy attorney, James Eisenbrandt, suggested that I plead guilty and avoid a trial.

"They are going to put on the stand a string of your nineteen-year-old girlfriends," he said. "They are going to ask them: Did Glazer pick you up in his Ferrari? Yes. Did you have sex? Yes. Did you do drugs? Yes. Did Glazer give you the drugs? Yes. Thank you. No further questions. Remember," he added, "nobody wins drug cases against the Feds."

Well, I certainly already knew that.

I pleaded guilty and, for the third time in my life, was convicted of a drug crime despite never having been arrested with any drugs. At the sentencing, Judge Laughrey praised me for all I had done for Kansas City and said, "I think we benefit in Kansas City by having you here in the community and making a contribution to it … There is no way I'm going to put you in prison."

I was given six months—three at a halfway house in Leavenworth and three under house confinement. I was already in substance abuse counseling. But I hadn't touched a drug since that September 11 phone call. I no longer had any desire to continue to destroy my life.

But a Glazer did run for mayor in 2002. With my encouragement, my seventy-year-old father took my place. We had spoken for the first time in two years when I learned about the FBI wiretap and asked him for a referral to a lawyer. Against incredible odds, with a ton of negative baggage, including his business failures and trying to unseat an incumbent, Stan received 42 percent of the vote.

He didn't win but he sure was entertaining.

• • •

THE BAD THINGS I've done I've paid for, and for the good things I've done, I've been rewarded.

Since 2003 I have been on the Board of Directors of Renaissance West, which operates drug and alcohol abuse clinics throughout Greater Kansas City. I speak regularly to students and others. I tell them my life story, my story of crime and punishment. There are those who say I've changed their lives. I don't think they're bullshitting me.

The biggest reward I received was Connie, whom I married in 2003. She was twenty-two years old; I was forty-nine. She knew about my past, about the women in my past, and married me anyway.

Grandpa Bennie, ninety-one years old, was at the wedding. A couple months later, I received a phone call saying he was in his car in the middle of the street and wasn't moving. I rushed there, put him in my car, and raced to the hospital. They placed him on a gurney and I held his hand. He could not speak but our eyes met and said, "I love you," and then, "good-bye." He died two days later.

Grandpa Bennie was more of a father to me than a grandfather. He was a little man with a big heart.

My mother died in the summer of 2007, right after we moved Stanford & Sons to the Legends entertainment district. It seems that tears and laughter have always been mixed in my family. My mother's last words to me were, "Yes, I had fun."

My marriage ended in early 2008. There were many reasons, but it was no coincidence that we broke up not long after Connie read the manuscript for this book. I'm not sure any woman could deal with someone who has had a life like mine. Sadly, there is nothing I can do to change the past.

Stan says the same thing. I realize you only get two parents in life, and he is my father. Did the apple fall far from the tree? Probably not too far, though sometimes I think not far enough.

· · ·

RIGHT AFTER THE *Entertainment Tonight* feature was broadcast following Don's death, Harold took a call at his office. It was from a ten-year-old girl named Marni—Don Woodbeck's daughter. He had never mentioned her to me.

Zana, Don's girlfriend back in Arizona when we were stinging dealers, the girlfriend he went to Colorado with, had given birth to his child. But, in the years that followed, she refused to tell Marni much about her father. Now the young girl had seen the *Entertainment Tonight* story and she wanted to know more.

She told me she had photos of Don and that she looked just like him.

"Is there anything good you can tell me about my father?" she asked. "All I heard was that he was a criminal. Is there anything about him that would make me proud?"

I hesitated a little and then said, "Your dad was the bravest, toughest man I ever met." I could hear the joy in her voice.

"He wasn't a bad guy?"

Once again, I could only explain life through a movie.

"Watch *Butch Cassidy and the Sundance Kid*," I told her. "He was the Sundance Kid."

My movie was never made. Maybe someday it will be. Maybe it no longer matters. Because all I ever wanted to do was tell my story—and now I have.

BUTCH

Y'know, when I was a kid, I always figured on being a hero when I grew up.

SUNDANCE

Too late now.

BUTCH

You didn't have to say that—what'd you have to say that for?
—*Butch Cassidy and the Sundance Kid*

Acknowledgments

WHEN THE TIME came to choose a coauthor, there was only one person who knew my story best—Sal Manna. As a journalist, he had also covered my story the longest, having interviewed Don Woodbeck, written a front-page story about his death, and reported on my getting stung. I could not imagine putting my story onto paper with anyone else.

Among the many others who deserve thanks and whose contributions and support are not mentioned in the text or are passed over too quickly are Connie Glazer, Dan York, Ron Hamady, Matt Blake, Ian Kleinert, Chris Nassif, Lewis Black, Steve Kramer, Jimmie Walker, Tommy and Shelby Chong, Michael Winslow, Pablo Francisco, Sonny Landham, Keith Pittell, John Trantham, Sandahl Bergman, Aaron Binder, Gina Ninci, Debbie Mandry, Ted McKnight, Bill Nigro, Johnny Dare, John Oldman, James Vowell, Roy Wenzl, Paul Wenske, Jeffrey Flanagan, Arthur Brisbane, Hearne Christopher Jr., Brian McTavish, Steve Penn, Tanna Guthrie, Max Floyd, Larry Moffit, Frankie Maas, Russ Johnson, and, of course, Mark Weinstein, Erin Kelley, and everybody at Skyhorse Publishing. To those we have unintentionally failed to mention, we offer our apologies.